INTERPRETING
ISAIAH

The Suffering and Glory
of the Messiah

INTERPRETING

ISAIAH

The Suffering and Glory of the Messiah

by

HERBERT M. WOLF

ZondervanPublishingHouse
Grand Rapids, Michigan

A Division of HarperCollins*Publishers*

INTERPRETING ISAIAH
Copyright © 1985 by The Zondervan Corporation
Grand Rapids, Michigan
Requests for information should be addressed to:
Zondervan Publishing House
Academic and Professional Books
Grand Rapids, Michigan 49530
Library of Congress Cataloging in Publication Data

Wolf, Herbert M.
    Interpreting Isaiah.

    Bibliography: p.
    Includes index.
    1. Bible. O.T. Isaiah—Criticism, interpretation, etc.   I. Title.

BS1515.2.W65   1985   224'.106   84–27105
ISBN   0–310–39061–3

Edited by John Hughes
Designed by Louise Bauer

Printed in the United States of America

98 99 / DH / 18 17 16 15 14 13 12

CONTENTS

PREFACE

The Book of Isaiah is filled with magnificent passages that describe the relationship between God and Israel and that introduce in amazing detail the person and work of Christ. Parts of Isaiah, however, are difficult to understand because of their poetic imagery. While teaching the Book of Isaiah to college students, I discovered that no text or commentary clearly explains its essentials without overwhelming the student with too many details. A commitment to sound exegesis, however, need not compel one to involve the readers in every aspect of the exegetical process. Keeping that in mind, in this book I will attempt to provide a thorough introduction to Isaiah that will enable the reader to understand its parts in the light of the whole.

The many quotations and allusions to Isaiah in the New Testament provide a vital clue to understanding this prophetic work. Indeed, one of the most fruitful challenges in the preparation of this book was the interpretation of those quotations and allusions, especially the ones that refer to the person and work of Christ.

Although this book is written from a premillennial perspective, its emphasis is not eschatology but exegesis. My main concern is to explain clearly the meaning of Isaiah's words and concepts. Only as we understand Isaiah's message to ancient Israel can we begin to fathom the meaning of his prophecies about the future of God's people in a world that will be judged and then marvelously renewed.

ACKNOWLEDGMENTS

I wish to thank the International Bible Society and the Committee on Bible Translation for assigning me to the committee that produced the first draft of the Book of Isaiah for the New International Version. During those many hours of intense work, the magnificence of Isaiah made a deep impression on me. I also remember with gratitude the late Edwin Palmer, executive secretary of the Committee on Bible Translation, who was a constant source of inspiration during those years.

I also wish to thank the Zondervan Publishing House for additional assignments on Isaiah in connection with NIV projects and for encouraging me to complete this book. I especially thank Dr. Stan Gundry for providing deadlines and for guiding the manuscript through the editorial process.

I also owe a debt of gratitude to Wheaton College and the Wheaton Alumni Association for a generous grant that allowed me to pursue this project. Thanks also to my students at Wheaton who have struggled with the Hebrew text of Isaiah and who have challenged and sharpened my thinking with their questions and observations.

I am grateful to Gary Madison for typing a large part of the manuscript and for his uncanny ability to decipher my handwriting.

Finally, I wish to thank my wife, Clara, who was unwavering in her patience while the book was in progress. Without her consistent encouragement, this book would not have been completed.

INTRODUCTION

The Book of Isaiah, one of the most important and best-loved books in the Bible, is sometimes called the Gospel of Isaiah because of the good news that characterizes its message. Indeed, no other Old Testament book contains as many references to the Messiah as does the Book of Isaiah. Its sixty-six chapters contain crucial passages that allude to Christ's incarnation, earthly ministry, and atoning death, as well as to His second coming and glorious world-wide rule. So important is Isaiah's prophecy that the New Testament alludes to it frequently and quotes directly from it no fewer than sixty-two times. Only the Book of Psalms is cited more often in the New Testament. Furthermore in Christ's preaching certain key verses from Isaiah played a prominent role.

Isaiah has also been called the Romans of the Old Testament because, like the Book of Romans, it sets forth God's case against sinners, unveils the wretchedness of the human heart, and reveals the way of salvation for Israel and the world. Under the hammer blows of Isaiah's message, God calls sinners to repentance and graciously promises forgiveness. It is no accident that in Romans Paul quoted Isaiah seventeen times—more than any other New Testament author. And, like Romans, Isaiah is a profoundly theological book that deals with a number of vital doctrines.

Because of the scope of his message and the magnificence of his poetry, Isaiah is the greatest of the major prophets. Most of the chapters of the Book of Isaiah are written in poetic forms that make full use of the possibilities inherent in Hebrew parallelism, and many scholars believe that chapters 40–66 contain the most beautiful poetry in the Bible. The power, imagery, and technique of Isaiah's writing are scarcely equalled any-where.

THE LIFE OF ISAIAH

Compared with what we know about Jeremiah, we know very little about Isaiah. His name means "the Lord [Yahweh] is salvation," a designation well suited to his overall message. He was the son of Amoz (not to be confused with Amos, the prophet), who, according to Jewish tradition, may have been related to the royal family. This may explain Isaiah's ready access to the kings of Judah, though it may also have been his prophetic office, not his family lineage, that gave him this access. If not of royal blood, it is likely that Isaiah came from a prominent family. He lived and ministered in Jerusalem most of his life.

On the basis of his vision in the temple, some believe that Isaiah may have belonged to the tribe of Levi. His portrayal as a singer in 5:1 might indicate that he was a Levitical singer, though no other evidence suggests that he served in that capacity. Jeremiah and Ezekiel were mem-bers of the priestly class, however, so the link between prophet and Levite is a possibility.

Most of our information about Isaiah's life comes from chapters 6–8 and chapters 36–39. When he received the spectacular vision in the temple, he expressed a willingness to serve that was an uncharacteristic response to a prophetic call. "Here I am. Send me!" he said (cf. Exod. 3:10–14; 4:1, 10, 13; Jer. 1:6–9). He learned at the same time that his ministry would not be a popular one, and this is illustrated by Ahaz's rejection of his advice (ch. 7). From chapters 7 and 8 it is clear that Isaiah was married and had two sons. If my view of 7:14 and 8:13 is correct, Isaiah's first wife died and he then married a prophetess. On the other hand, he may have had two wives. The two boys, Shear-Jashub and Maher-Shalal-Hash-Baz, were given symbolic names that illustrated the way God dealt with Israel. Hosea was another prophet whose children received names of national significance (cf. Hos. 1:6, 9).

The "disciples" mentioned in 8:16 may have had a relationship with Isaiah similar to the one that the "sons of the prophets" had with Samuel and Elisha, their teachers. Jeremiah's devoted follower, Baruch, was also a "disciple" of a prophet, assisting his master and helping to perpetuate his ministry.

Isaiah's most influential period came during the reign of Hezekiah. That godly monarch sought the intercession of the prophet and listened eagerly to the word of the Lord that he delivered (37:1–7, 21–35). During Hezekiah's illness, Isaiah facilitated his recovery by instructing the physicians to apply figs to the boil. By doing so, Isaiah functioned as a healer.

On two other occasions Isaiah was in direct contact with the leaders of the nation. Once he summoned Uriah the high priest as a witness to what may have been a legal transaction (8:2), and on another occasion he pronounced a curse on the high-ranking official Shebna, whose position Isaiah predicted would eventually be given to Eliakim (22:15–25—a prophecy shown fulfilled in 36:3). These examples illustrate Isaiah's authority among the leaders of his country. No individual or group enjoyed immunity from his searching, prophetic word.

Like Jeremiah and Ezekiel, Isaiah used graphic visual aids to communicate with Israel. Jeremiah wore yokes of wood and iron to symbolize the authority of Babylon, and Isaiah went about stripped and barefoot for three years to portray the upcoming exile of Egypt and Cush (20:1–6). The prophet's unorthodox attire left little doubt about the fate of those southern countries on which Judah had pinned her hopes.

Isaiah's behavior typified his frequent involvement in

the political affairs of Israel. He opposed the ill-fated alliance of Ahaz with Assyria, and later he repeatedly warned against relying on Egypt for relief from the Assyrians (30:2; 31:1). Interestingly, according to 2 Chronicles 26:22, Isaiah wrote a separate history of the reign of Uzziah.

Isaiah may have retired as a prophet shortly after the dramatic deliverance of Jerusalem in 701 B.C. According to the pseudepigraphical work *The Ascension of Isaiah*, during the rule of Manasseh Isaiah was killed by being sawed in two (cf. Heb. 11:37). Although the Scriptures are silent about his death, it would have been characteristic of Isaiah to have condemned the gross wickedness of Manasseh and consequently to have suffered at his hands.

Part I

INTRODUCTORY MATTERS

1

THE WORLD OF ISAIAH

The era in which Isaiah lived witnessed the rise and fall of kingdoms, as major military powers vied for control of Palestine. During his ministry, which spanned most of the second half of the eighth century B.C., Assyria emerged as the dominant world power. In 722 B.C. the mighty Assyrians captured the capital city of Samaria and brought about the full collapse of the northern kingdom of Israel. Thousands of Isaiah's countrymen were taken into exile, never to return to their beloved homeland.

The southern kingdom of Judah also staggered before the Assyrian juggernaut, and in 701 B.C. Judah nearly suffered the same fate as Israel. Judah had sided first with Assyria and then with Egypt during the stormy years between 734 and 701 B.C. By the close of the century, Hezekiah joined the coalition against Assyria, and the armies of Sennacherib advanced to punish the Judean king. But God miraculously intervened and crushed the invader's forces, granting Judah and Jerusalem a century-long reprieve. Yet before disaster struck his army, Sennacherib had devastated most of the cities of Judah and deported thousands of its citizens. In those traumatic times, Isaiah alternated between condemning and encouraging, as the moral and spiritual condition of the rulers and the people of Israel dictated.

But the historical scope of Isaiah's prophecies is far broader. He looked beyond the flowering of the Assyrian

Empire to the rise of the Chaldean kingdom of Babylon, and he portrayed the demise of Babylon before the onslaught of Cyrus's Median and Persian armies (chs. 41–48). Assyria fell in 612 B.C., and their Babylonian conquerors were defeated by Cyrus in 539 B.C. Thus Isaiah interacted prophetically with the three major empires between 750 and 539 B.C., outlining their impact on Israel and Judah and showing how they fit into the sovereign purposes of God.

A BRIEF PERIOD OF PROSPERITY IN ISRAEL

About 800 B.C., King Adadnirari III of Assyria weakened the power of Damascus, relieving the pressure the Syrians had exerted on Israel. This fact, combined with the decline of Assyria shortly after that, allowed Jeroboam II of Israel and Uzziah of Judah to enjoy a period of great prosperity from 790–750 B.C. Neighboring lands, such as Moab and Edom, once more came under Israelite or Judean control, and the combined territories of the two kings approximated the area ruled by King Solomon. The economic gains of both regions were considerable (2 Chron. 26:7ff.; 27:3ff.), but that did not prepare them for the ghastly invasions and sieges of the last half of the century. In Israel, more than in Judah, this prosperity was accompanied by an increase in idol worship, materialism, and oppression of the poor (Amos 4:1–4; 6:1ff.), though Isaiah 2:6–8 reveals that Judah was rapidly becoming like her northern relatives in these respects. Additionally, the rich were "buying out" the small farmers, creating a wider gulf between the wealthy and the poor (5:8–10).

THE GROWTH OF ASSYRIA'S POWER UNDER TIGLATH-PILESER III

During the reign of Tiglath-Pileser III (745–727 B.C.), Assyria began to reassert its authority over Syria and Palestine. In 740 B.C. this powerful monarch, also called Pul (1 Chron. 5:26), attacked the states of northern Syria, and by 738 B.C. he was receiving tribute payments from Damascus and Israel. A coalition against Assyria was formed by Hanun of Gaza, Rezin of Damascus, and Pekah of Israel. They hoped that Egypt would join them. But in 735 B.C. Tiglath-Pileser made a surprise attack in the west, winning the submission of these rulers. The Assyrians penetrated as far as the border of Egypt, where Hanun had fled for refuge. Later, after promising to be a dutiful vassal, this Philistine ruler was allowed to return to Gaza.

A year later Damascus attempted to organize another revolt against Assyria. Rezin and Pekah wanted the support of Judah in this venture, so they pressured Jotham (and later his son Ahaz) to help them (2 Kings 15:37). Their campaign against Judah is often called the Syro-Ephraimite War, and it likely came to a head in 734 B.C. According to Isaiah 7:1 and 2 Kings 16:5, Syria and Israel besieged Jerusalem in an attempt to overthrow Ahaz and to place "the son of Tabeel" on the throne (Isa. 7:6). "Tabeel" may be a personal name, but there is good evidence that it refers to a region located north of Ammon and Gilead.[1] The land of Tob, to the east of Gilead where Jephthah fled, may have been the same area (Judg. 11:3). Perhaps Jotham or Ahaz had married a princess from Tabeel, and her son was being groomed as the new king. The conspiracy may also have been aimed at the complete ouster of the Davidic dynasty.

When Ahaz learned about the forthcoming invasion, he was deeply alarmed. Apparently Ahaz had suffered heavy losses during a previous battle with these kings (cf. 2 Chron. 28:5), and he hoped to avoid another disaster. Isaiah was sent to calm Ahaz's fears and to assure the king that Rezin and Pekah would not prevail against him. Ahaz needed to trust the word of God and to abandon his plans to appeal to the king of Assyria for help. Otherwise Judah herself would eventually suffer at the hands of an Assyrian monarch (Isa. 7:17). This was the context in which Isaiah delivered his famous prophecy about the sign of Immanuel. God was with Judah and would protect her if Ahaz exercised faith. From 2 Kings 16:7-9 it is clear that Ahaz did request the assistance of Tiglath-Pileser, sending him silver and gold as payment, and the Assyrians eagerly returned to capture

---

[1] W. F. Albright, "The Son of Tabael," *Bulletin of the American Schools of Oriental Research*, 140 (1955): 34–35.

Damascus and to kill Rezin. Most of the cities of Israel were also captured and many of the people deported. Isaiah referred to this invasion in 9:1, mentioning the gloom that covered the regions of Zebulun, Naphtali, and Galilee. As a result of this campaign, the northern territory of Israel was annexed by Assyria. Galilee and Jezreel became the province of Megiddo. The coastal plain on the west was known as the province of Dor, and the region east of the Jordan was turned into the province of Gilead.

Out of appreciation for his "rescue," Ahaz journeyed to Damascus to meet with Tiglath-Pileser. There he was fascinated by a pagan altar and had Uriah, the priest, build one like it in Jerusalem. Subsequently, Ahaz began to worship the gods of Damascus and to plunge Judah into the idolatry that was so heinous to Isaiah (Isa. 2:20; cf. 2 Chron. 28:20–23).

The shattered remains of the northern kingdom came under the control of Hoshea, son of Elah, who assassinated the disgraced Pekah in 732 B.C. Tiglath-Pileser mentions Hoshea among his vassals[2] and mentions that Ahaz of Judah paid tribute to Assyria.

THE VICTORIES OF SHALMANESER V AND SARGON

After the death of Tiglath-Pileser III in 727 B.C., Shalmaneser V became king. Hoshea joined a revolt against him and was imprisoned by the Assyrians. Samaria itself was besieged and finally fell in 722/21 B.C. Both Shalmaneser and his successor, Sargon (Isa. 20:1), are credited with the capture of Samaria, but since Sargon probably did not ascend the throne until a few months after Samaria's fall, he may only have been a leading general at that time (a similar proleptic use of *king* in Isaiah 37:9 refers to Tirhakah, an Egyptian general who later became Pharaoh).

In 671 B.C. Esarhaddon of Assyria settled groups of foreigners in Samaria, while fighting against Tyre and Egypt

---

[2]Donald Wiseman, "A Fragmentary Inscription of Tiglathpileser III from Nimrud," *Iraq* 18 (1956): 126.

(cf. Ezra 4:2). This took place about sixty-five years after Isaiah had predicted that Ephraim would no longer be a people (7:8). The subsequent intermarriage of surviving Israelites with those who had been brought in by the Assyrians gave rise to the people known as Samaritans (cf. John 4:9).

Not long after Sargon became king, revolts broke out in Syria and in Palestine (720 B.C.). Yaubidi of Hamath and Hanun of Gaza led the uprising, but Hezekiah of Judah wisely withheld his support. Hamath (Isa. 36:19) was forced to become an Assyrian province, and king Hanun was taken captive to Assyria after he and his Egyptian allies lost the battle of Raphia. Arpad, in northern Syria (36:19), may also have been subdued during this same revolt.

In 715 B.C. the Ethiopian Shabako conquered Egypt, kindling new hope for freedom in Palestine. Perhaps, the Jews thought, with the help of the Pharaoh of this new dynasty (the twenty-fifth), they could cast off the Assyrian yoke. King Azuri of Ashdod led the uprising in 713 B.C., seeking the support of Edom, Moab, and Judah. By the time Sargon moved against Ashdod in 711 B.C., a man named Yaman had gained control of the city. He fled to Egypt, but Pharaoh promptly extradited him rather than engage Sargon in battle. It was on the occasion of Ashdod's defeat that Isaiah discouraged reliance on Egypt, predicting that the Egyptians and Ethiopians would be taken captive (20:1–6). Isaiah's actions indicate that Hezekiah and Judah had shown some sympathy to the revolt.

THE INVASION AND DEFEAT OF SENNACHERIB

The next opportunity for widespread rebellion came at the death of Sargon in 705 B.C. His successor, Sennacherib, had to deal with an uprising that reached from Babylon to Syria and Palestine. Once again Egypt promised to support the insurgents, and this time Hezekiah withheld the required tribute payment and wholeheartedly joined the alliance.

Sennacherib took swift and stern measures to handle the crisis. First, he succeeded in crushing the armies of Elam and Babylon that were led by Merodach-Baladan, who had once ruled Babylon from 721–710 B.C. All of Babylonia was restored to Assyrian control by 703 B.C. In 701 B.C. Sennacherib turned his attention westward, and many cities of Syria and Phoenicia quickly renewed their allegiance to him. Others—such as Sidon, Ashkelon, Ekron, and Jerusalem—continued to oppose him.

The events of Sennacherib's great campaign are recorded in Isaiah 36 and 37 and also in 2 Kings 18–20. Both passages place the war in the fourteenth year of Hezekiah's reign, but since Hezekiah began his rule in 727/26 B.C., and since the invasion undoubtedly occurred in 701 B.C., a serious chronological problem emerges. Some would solve the problem by shifting the start of Hezekiah's sole rule to 715 B.C., understanding 727–715 B.C. as part of a coregency with Ahaz. This theory would correlate nicely with God's promise to Hezekiah to add fifteen years to his life (Isa. 38:5), an event often dated in 703 B.C. Hezekiah's twenty-nine-year reign would then span the period of 715–687 B.C. Yet a close reading of 2 Kings 18:1–13 makes it extremely difficult to transfer the start of his rule from 727 to 715 B.C.

A better theory involves a textual correction of "fourteenth" to "twenty-fourth" as the original reading in 36:1. With a 727 or 726 B.C. inauguration, this would bring the date down to 703 or 702 B.C., when Sennacherib began his retaliatory measures. Although there is no manuscript evidence to support a different reading, the ancient method of writing numbers made scribal errors of this sort all too easy. For example, according to 2 Chronicles 36:9, Jehoiachin was eight years old when he became king, but the correct age is given as eighteen in 2 Kings 24:8.[3]

If Sennacherib had invaded during the twenty-fourth year of Hezekiah's reign, it would have been almost impossible for the events of Isaiah 38 and 39 to have occurred in 703 B.C. Hezekiah's illness is linked with the reign of Merodach-Baladan (721–710, 703 B.C.) in 39:1, for the erstwhile Babylonian king sent Hezekiah congratulations on his recovery. The embassy from Babylon is often interpreted as an attempt to gain

---

[3] E. J. Young, *The Book of Isaiah*, 3 vols. (Grand Rapids: Eerdmans, 1965–72), 2:540–42.

Hezekiah's support for the rebellion after 705 B.C., but it is questionable if the few months of Merodach-Baladan's second rule in 703 B.C. afforded enough time for the exchange of news and messengers reflected in chapter 39. Between 721 and 710 B.C., however, there was ample time for the diplomatic mission to have occurred.

If Hezekiah died in 697 B.C., his illness would have occurred fifteen years earlier in 712 B.C. At that time another Assyrian king, Sargon II, was in the process of conquering Ashdod, and Hezekiah may have feared that he would also attack Jerusalem. Thus the king referred to in 38:6 may be Sargon, not Sennacherib.

The invasion of 701 B.C. was extremely successful for Sennacherib. City after city capitulated as he moved down the coast. An Egyptian army was defeated at Eltekeh, and the city of Lachish, a fortress important for the defense of Jerusalem, was put under siege. At this point Hezekiah submitted to the Assyrians by paying three hundred talents of silver and thirty talents of gold (2 Kings 18:14), but after accepting them, Sennacherib demanded the surrender of Jerusalem itself. He sent his field commander to Jerusalem with a large army, but on the advice of Isaiah, the city kept its gates closed to the brash invaders. Lachish was destroyed soon afterwards, but while Sennacherib was dealing with the army of Tirhakah of Egypt, disaster struck. In one night the angel of the Lord killed the bulk of his forces—185,000 soldiers. According to Herodotus, field mice invaded the ranks of the Assyrians. Perhaps the Lord used a fast-moving bubonic plague to bring about the demise of the army. Stripped of his forces, Sennacherib had to abandon the campaign and return home.

The biblical record is supplemented by Sennacherib's own account of his achievements in his annals. He claimed to have conquered forty-six walled cities in Judah and to have captured 200,140 people. Hezekiah, he wrote, was shut up like a bird in a cage (cf. Isa. 1:8), and vast treasures were received from him as tribute.[4] Although such claims are doubtlessly exaggerated, the

---

[4]J. B. Pritchard, *Ancient Near Eastern Texts* (Princeton, N. J.: Princeton University Press, 1955), p. 288.

overall picture is accurate. The territory of Judah suffered terrible damage and never fully recovered from the devastation (cf. 8:8). Stephen Stohlmann has suggested that the figure of 200,140 represents the total population of the captured cities, all of whose inhabitants were registered for deportation. But in view of the crippling losses suffered by the Assyrians, it is an open question as to how many Judeans were actually deported.[5] Sennacherib himself was assassinated twenty years later by two of his sons, Adrammelech and Sharezer (37:38). Sennacherib's murder is also recorded in the "Babylonian Chronicle." Another son, Esarhaddon, succeeded him to the throne.

THE RISE OF THE CHALDEANS IN BABYLON

Throughout the Book of Isaiah there are extensive references to Babylon and the Chaldeans (chs. 13, 21, 46–48)—a fact that has raised questions about an eighth-century Isaianic authorship of the book. How, the skeptics reason, could an eighth-century prophet know that Jerusalem would eventually be captured by the armies of Babylon in 587 B.C. (39:6) and that Israel would be held captive in that far-off land (48:28)? And who could have predicted that the Medes—allies of Babylon in the seventh century B.C.—would be among the conquerors of Babylon in 539 B.C. (13:17)?

The position of the Chaldeans themselves was not a powerful one in 700 B.C. Referred to in Akkadian as the "Kaldu" (or "Kashdu") tribes, the Chaldeans are first mentioned in the Assyrian annals of the ninth century B.C. They are usually linked with the Aramean tribes, who frequently moved into Mesopotamia from the west, but that precise relationship is uncertain. According to Job 1:17, Chaldean bands were involved in a deadly raid against Job and his possessions, probably near Edom or northern Arabia. In Babylonia the Chaldeans occupied the marshland in the extreme south. Because of the terrain and their independent spirit, the Chaldeans proved difficult for the Assyrians to control, even during the height of their empire

[5] See *Scripture in Context,* ed. William W. Hallo, James C. Moyer, and Leo G. Perdue (Winona Lake, Ind.: Eisenbrauns, 1983), pp. 152–57.

(850–626 B.C.). They resisted paying taxes and turned to guerrilla warfare when the Assyrians invaded, and they often joined forces with Elamite and Aramean tribes to attack their northern overlords. During the reign of Tiglath-Pileser III, Ukinzer, the leader of the Amukkani tribe, seized the throne of Babylon, but by 729 B.C. the powerful Assyrian king had defeated the rebels and declared himself king of Babylon.

The tireless and resourceful Marduk-apal-iddina II of the Chaldean Bit Yakin tribe plagued the Assyrians throughout his reign. Better known as Merodach-Baladan (Isa. 39:1), he claimed the kingship of Babylonia in 721 B.C. when Sargon II was being crowned in Assyria. In the ensuing ten years, Sargon quelled rebellions in Syria and Palestine but could not depose the self-appointed king of Babylon until 710 B.C. Even then Merodach-Baladan did not give up. He seized power again in 703 B.C. and held it until Sennacherib drove him out a few months later. Esarhaddon (37:38) tried to conciliate the Chaldeans shortly after 681 B.C. so that important trade routes through the Persian Gulf would remain open.

With the rise of Nabopolassar in 626 B.C., Chaldean power steadily increased. Ably supported by the Medes, the Chaldeans captured Nineveh in 612 B.C., crushing the Assyrian Empire. Nabopolassar's brilliant son Nebuchadnezzar brought the Chaldean Empire to its zenith, demolishing Jerusalem and taking its residents captive.

Apart from divine revelation, it would have been impossible for Isaiah to have predicted the capture of Jerusalem by the Babylonians. The persistence and ingenuity of the Chaldeans in his own day, however, was a sign of their coming greatness. What the Assyrians came so close to accomplishing in 701 B.C. was achieved by the Chaldeans in 587 B.C.

THE ACCOMPLISHMENTS OF CYRUS THE PERSIAN

Even more remarkable than Isaiah's knowledge of the Chaldeans were his predictions about the Medes and Persians. The alliance between the Chaldeans and the Medes continued throughout the reign of Nebuchadnezzar, whose wife was a

Median princess. After his death in 562 B.C., however, the relationship between the two powers became strained. During the rule of Nabonidus (556–539 B.C.), the Medes cut off trading routes from the east, a policy that seriously hurt Babylon's economy.

Toward the end of the reign of Nabonidus and his coregent, Belshazzar, a dynamic Persian prince named Cyrus came to power. He had considerable influence among the Medes, and he led his armies in military conquest. Isaiah 41:1–5 foretells the amazing speed and effectiveness of his victories. After conquering the important kingdom of Lydia in Asia Minor, Cyrus attacked Assyria and Babylonia. Dissatisfaction with the economic and religious policies of Nabonidus paved the way for an easy takeover of Babylon in 539 B.C. Cyrus developed a reputation for treating conquered nations with unusual kindness, and many of the residents of Babylon viewed him more as a deliverer than an invader. Unlike the Assyrian and Babylonian conquerors, Cyrus made an effort to return captive peoples to their native lands. In the famous "Cyrus Cylinder" the king states that he sent images back to the sanctuaries in the holy cities and that he allowed various peoples to return home.[6] His restoration of the Jews to Jerusalem is a high point in Isaiah's message of comfort to Israel in 44:24–28 and 45:1–2,13.

[6]Pritchard, *Ancient Near Eastern Texts,* p. 316.

2

THE AUTHORSHIP OF ISAIAH

The question of authorship is one of the most controversial introductory issues regarding the Book of Isaiah. Scholars differ significantly in their opinions about the number of authors, the date Isaiah was written, and the place (or places) where the author (or authors) lived. Indeed, the Book of Isaiah ranks with the Pentateuch and the Book of Daniel as one of the main battlegrounds between liberal and conservative critics. Critical arguments revolve around theological, historical, and stylistic factors; and in the last category, even computers are being used.[1]

Most contemporary scholars believe that the Book of Isaiah was written by two or more authors who are referred to as Isaiah, Deutero-Isaiah, Trito-Isaiah, or the Isaianic School. But these scholars disagree about which verses should be attributed to which author. One of the most common theories regards chapters 40–55 as the product of the exilic Deutero-Isaiah (*ca.* 550 B.C.) and chapters 56–66 as the work of Trito-Isaiah (*ca.* 530 B.C.).[2] Because of the space left between chapters 33 and 34 in the major copy of the Dead Sea Scroll of Isaiah, a recent theory assigns chapters 34 and 35 to the corpus of 40–66.[3]

---

[1] Yehuda Radday, *The Unity of Isaiah in the Light of Statistical Linguistics,* Collection Massorah: Series 2 (Hildesheim: Gerstenberg, 1973).

[2] R. K. Harrison, *Introduction to the Old Testament* (Grand Rapids: Eerdmans, 1969), p. 766.

[3] Cf. John L. McKenzie, *Second Isaiah* (Garden City, N.Y.: Doubleday & Co., Inc., 1968), p. xx.

But other scholars argue for the unity of Isaiah. Books such as *The Indivisible Isaiah,* by Rachel Margalioth,[4] marshal an impressive array of stylistic arguments to show the unity of the different parts of Isaiah. Critics of this position assert that in some places Deutero-Isaiah copied the style of the first Isaiah or that some verses Deutero-Isaiah wrote were interpolated into early chapters of the Book of Isaiah.

DEVELOPMENT OF
THE MULTIPLE AUTHORSHIP THEORY

As early as the second century A.D., the Jewish writer Moses Ibn Gekatilla questioned the Isaianic authorship of chapters 40–66. His views were preserved and adopted by Ibn Ezra (1092–1167), a leading medieval Jewish scholar.

Modern criticism of the Book of Isaiah began with the German Johann Doederlein, who in 1789 argued for an exilic date for chapters 40 through 66. He believed that an eighth-century writer could not have predicted the fall of Jerusalem in 587 B.C., much less the rise of Cyrus the Great, who restored the exiles in 538 B.C.

Ernst Rosenmueller (1768–1835) of Leipzig raised doubts about chapters 13 and 14, which contain extensive references to Babylon. He argued that if Isaiah could not have written chapters 40 through 66, how could he be credited with some of the earlier chapters that contain similar material? Rosenmueller initiated the process of denying Isaianic authorship to much of chapters 1 through 39.

From 1892 to 1900 Bernard Duhm and K. Marti presented evidence that chapters 56–66 were written by Trito-Isaiah and should be separated from chapters 40–55. They argued that Trito-Isaiah wrote his material in Jerusalem around the time of Ezra (450 B.C.). Duhm argued that throughout Isaiah, there are insertions from writers who lived as late as the first century B.C. Duhm's theories convinced many other European scholars that at least three persons had authored Isaiah. Even the great

---

[4](New York: Yeshiva University Press, 1964).

conservative scholar Franz Delitzsch made room for a Deutero-Isaiah in the last edition of his commentary on Isaiah, though to the end of his life, he was never fully persuaded that anyone other than the eighth-century prophet had helped to author the book.

Recent studies have basically followed the nineteenth-century approach. For example, Claus Westermann argues that chapters 40–55 are a unit, with a clearly marked prologue in 40:1–11 and an epilogue in 55:6–11. The Servant Songs, he believes, were later insertions in the work of Deutero-Isaiah, and he argues that chapters 56–66 were written between 537 and 455 B.C., probably about 530 B.C. According to Westermann, Trito-Isaiah was the main author of chapters 56–66, though he expanded some material (such as chapters 59 and 63) that was composed soon after the fall of Jerusalem.[5]

Otto Kaiser is typical of those who distinguish several stages in the formation of the first 39 chapters of Isaiah. He attributes a few passages to Isaiah but argues that most of these chapters are the result of interpolations that continued into the third century B.C. For example, he says that 14:16 is dependent on 49:13 and that 2:2–5 and 4:2–6 were inserted by a postexilic redactor. Furthermore he denies the Isaianic authorship of many apocalyptic passages.[6]

R. K. Harrison, a conservative scholar, has developed a much more moderate view of multiple authorship. Following William Brownlee, Harrison understands the Book of Isaiah to be an anthology of the proclamations of the prophet compiled by his disciples (cf. 8:16). Harrison argues that Isaiah's disciples preserved his material in a two-part (or "bifid") form, chapters 1–33 and chapters 34–66. Harrison's theory is based in part on the break in the Dead Sea Scroll version of Isaiah that occurs after chapter 33. He believes that two scrolls were easier to handle than one long scroll and that they were used as a manual

---

[5] Claus Westermann, *Isaiah 40–66,* trans. David M. G. Stalker (London: SCM, 1969), p. 296.

[6] Otto Kaiser, *Isaiah 1–12,* trans. R. A. Wilson (London: SCM, 1972), p. 23.

of instruction. According to Harrison, the Book of Isaiah in its present form was completed about 630 B.C.[7]

Brownlee emphasized the balanced nature of the two halves of Isaiah. Its opening five chapters about ruin and restoration are paralleled by chapters 34 and 35, and the biographical sections in chapters 6–8 are paralleled by similar sections in chapters 36–39. Brownlee argued that the Book of Isaiah is the product of an Isaianic School and that it was edited into its present form by a writer in the third century B.C.[8]

ARGUMENTS FOR MULTIPLE AUTHORSHIP

The case for the multiple authorship of Isaiah depends heavily on the significance that one attaches to the change in perspective that occurs in chapters 40–66. In these chapters the prophet no longer predicted judgment or warned of captivity. He assumed that Jerusalem had fallen, that the temple had been destroyed, and that the people of Judah were in captivity. He mentioned no contemporary kings by name, not even Manasseh, the wicked son of Hezekiah, during whose reign Isaiah, the son of Amoz, would have written. Instead chapters 40–66 contain predictions about the return from captivity and the fall of Babylon. The prophet twice mentions by name a Persian king, Cyrus, whose reign did not begin until 150 years after the time of Isaiah (44:28; 45:1). If the prophet Isaiah wrote chapters 40–66, he seems to have abandoned his own historical perspective in favor of one that reflects the period close to 540 B.C.

Chapters 40–66 contain themes and theological ideas that are different from those in chapters 1–39. The Servant of the Lord is a prominent figure in chapters 40–66, and little is heard about the messianic king who is so important in chapters 1–39. Additionally the sufferings of the Servant seem inconsistent with the glorious rule of the Davidic Messiah (9:6–7; 11:1–9).

Isaiah 40–66 stresses the uniqueness of God and His superiority to the idols of other nations. These chapters also

---

[7] Harrison, *Introduction*, p. 785.

[8] William Brownlee, *The Meaning of the Qumran Scrolls for the Bible* (New York: Oxford University Press, 1964), p. 247.

emphasize the fact that Israel's God is a God of comfort and salvation, whereas Isaiah 1–39 emphasized His role as Judge.

Chapters 1–39 locate the remnant in Jerusalem (4:3; 37:4), but chapters 40–66 identify this group with the faithful exiles. Similarly the last half of the Book of Isaiah places a greater emphasis on the unity of the nation of Israel than did the preceding thirty-nine chapters. Chapters 40–66 indicate that all Israel will participate in the redemption from Babylon (43:1; 48:20), and in those chapters the distinction between the northern and southern kingdoms no longer pertains. Furthermore, chapters 40–66 portray the nation and the Servant as a missionary force that reaches out to Gentiles (49:6; 56:1–8).

The argument for multiple authorship is also based on stylistic and poetic factors. Although chapters 1–39 contain superb poetic passages, the most beautiful poetry occurs in chapters 40–66. There the author displayed remarkable dramatic ability, personifying cities and nature alike, and he deftly used exaggerated metaphor (40:15–16) and powerful imagery drawn from the sphere of human emotions. Passages that decry idolatry contain biting sarcasm (44:9–20). And the majesty, power, and depth of chapters 40, 53, and 55 awe the reader and captivate one's heart and mind.

The opening words of chapter 40, "Comfort, comfort my people," have often been used to illustrate the repetition that characterizes the style of Deutero-Isaiah. Double imperatives at the start of sentences are also found in 51:9 and 17, "Awake, awake," and in 52:11, "Depart, depart." Additional examples are found in 57:14 and in 62:10.

ARGUMENTS FOR THE UNITY OF ISAIAH

Admittedly some of the evidence in favor of multiple authorship is impressive. The most difficult argument to answer is the one based on the change in historical perspective that occurs in chapters 40–66. Is it reasonable to assume that in these chapters the prophet Isaiah would stop addressing his own generation? Perhaps so. In a sense Isaiah had already adopted such an ideal standpoint in 9:1–7 where he described the coming of the Messiah as though it had already occurred.

Perhaps John's experience in Revelation 4–21 would be analogous, for in those chapters the apostle "lived in the future" for an extended period of time.

In chapters 1–39 Isaiah had predicted the Babylonian Exile and the return of the captives (6:11–13; 39:6–7). The very name of his son Shear-Jashub meant "a remnant will return." So it is possible that during the reign of Manasseh, while Isaiah was in retirement, the prophet chose to address the generation that would have to endure the Exile. If so, Isaiah's harsh words about idolatry would have served to warn Israel against worshiping Babylonian idols. Since Isaiah's own generation had turned a deaf ear to his preaching, he may have given a message for their descendants to heed. Perhaps Isaiah intended that this strange procedure would catch the eye of his contemporaries as well. It is important to remember that Isaiah had witnessed the exile of the northern kingdom of Israel in 722 B.C. and that he had seen thousands of Judeans taken captive by Sennacherib. For Isaiah and many of his contemporaries, the exile of the northern kingdom was still a vivid memory.

Isaiah did not abandon his own generation entirely in chapters 40–66. His condemnation of idol worship was an important issue around 700 B.C. (2:8; 31:7), and the last half of Isaiah contains repeated references to worshiping in the gardens and to offering pagan sacrifices (cf. 65:2–4; 66:17). In fact, the idolatry and pagan worship denounced in 57:5–7 fits the mountainous terrain of Canaan far better than it does the flat, alluvial plains of Babylon. Furthermore almost all of the sins listed in chapters 57–59 were evils that Isaiah had preached against in chapters 1–39. For instance, the bloodshed and violence mentioned in 59:1–3 were similarly condemned in 1:15, and the theme of 43:22–24 is very close to that of 1:11–15.

If chapters 40–66 assume the Babylonian Exile as a backdrop, the reader is prepared for this by chapter 39. There Hezekiah's contacts with Merodach-Baladan of Babylon are explicitly stated to be a cause for the forthcoming exile (39:6–7), and this important episode in the life of the king of Judah leads into the extended section about the Babylonian captivity (chs. 40–66).

Some conservatives, notably J. Barton Payne, understand

the background of chapters 40–66 to be the withdrawal of Sennacherib in 701 B.C. and the tremendous consolation this brought to Jerusalem. If correct, such an interpretation would strengthen the theory that Isaiah wrote these chapters since he would have been addressing a contemporary situation.[9]

At the heart of the controversy over Isaianic authorship is the prophecy about Cyrus the Great. His rule and accomplishments are referred to repeatedly in chapters 41 to 48, and twice he is referred to by name. Liberal critics cannot accept the possibility that Isaiah knew about Cyrus more than a century before he was king. Yet the mention of King Josiah by a prophet from Judah during the reign of Jeroboam I (931–910 B.C.), three centuries before Josiah was born, establishes a precedent for such a prophecy (1 Kings 13:2). Furthermore Isaiah's contemporary, Micah, prophesied that Bethlehem would be the birthplace of the Messiah (Mic. 5:2). Thus if one believes that God can reveal information to His servants far in advance of the events, then the mention of Cyrus is not so incredible. As early as Isaiah 13:17, the prophet predicted that the Medes would conquer Babylon, and Cyrus was the leader of both the Medes and Persians. Significantly, chapter thirteen begins with a heading that attributes that oracle to Isaiah.

Differences between the subject matter and the theological ideas of chapters 1–39 and chapters 40–66 can partially be accounted for by the changed circumstances toward the end of Isaiah's ministry and by assuming that there was a lapse of time between the writing of those two sections. But correspondences between chapters 1–39 and 40–66 are really more striking than the differences. Even the Servant Songs in chapters 40–66 complement the passages on the Messiah in chapters 1–39 (cf. 11:1 and 53:2), and the reference to David in 55:3–5 preserves the link with earlier messianic thought in chapters 1–39. Furthermore the references to nations coming to Israel in 55:5 and in 66:20 match the famous verses about the nations streaming to Jerusalem in 2:1–4.

[9]J. Barton Payne, "The Eighth Century Israelitish Background of Isaiah 40–66," *Westminster Theological Journal* 29 (1967): 179–90; 30 (1968): 50–58, 185–203.

God's sovereignty and uniqueness are major themes in chapters 40–48, but the same emphases appear in Isaiah's word of encouragement to Hezekiah in 37:22–29. Passages of comfort and restoration are found in 27:13 and in all of chapter 35. An entire verse (35:10) is repeated in 51:11.[10] And the ideas and wording of chapters 40–66 closely resemble verses from Isaiah's contemporary, Micah (cf. Isa. 41:15–16 with Mic. 4:13; Isa. 49:23 with Mic. 7:17).

When one examines the verbal and stylistic relationships between Isaiah 1–39 and 40–66, the results are compelling. The similarities far outnumber the differences. The most impressive example of such continuity is Isaiah's distinctive title for God, "the Holy One of Israel." This title occurs twelve times in chapters 1–39 and another fourteen times in chapters 40–66. Elsewhere it is used only four times in the Old Testament. Since the doctrine of God's holiness was so important to Isaiah (cf. ch. 6), he used this title repeatedly, and it became an unmistakable sign of his authorship.

The famous Servant Song of 52:13–53:12 contains important links with earlier passages in chapters 1–39. In 1:5–6 the description of a battered, sin-sick nation is remarkably similar to 53:4–5. "Beaten" is the same word that is translated "smitten (of God)" in 53:4. "Injured" is rendered "infirmities" (53:4), and "welts" (ḥabbûrâ) is translated as "stripes" or "wounds" (53:5). These are the only two places where ḥabbûrâ occurs in Isaiah or in any of the prophets.

Isaiah 2:22 is a warning against putting too much reliance upon men:

> "Stop trusting in man,
>   who has but a breath in his nostrils.
> Of what account is he?"

The word translated "Stop trusting" (literally, "cease"— ḥidlû) occurs in the phrase "*rejected* by men" in 53:3. "Of what account" also occurs in 53:3 where it is rendered "we *esteemed*

[10]Gleason L. Archer, Jr., *A Survey of Old Testament Introduction*, rev. ed. (Chicago: Moody Press, 1974), p. 345.

him not." In no other Old Testament passages do these two words occur together in the same context.

The verbs "to be high and lifted up" (*rûm* and *nāśā'*) are used as a combination several times in Isaiah. In 2:12 God threatens judgment against "proud" and "exalted" men. In 6:1 the Lord is "seated on a throne, high and exalted," and in 52:13 the Lord's Servant is "raised and lifted up." The correspondence suggests that the Servant will be given an eminent position following His suffering, and it suggests that the same author wrote each of the passages.

Chapter 40 is another passage that is closely associated with concepts that occur in Isaiah 1–39. Verse 8 of chapter 40, with its promise that "the word of our God stands forever," reflects the language of 7:7 and 8:10, where the Lord assured Ahaz that the plans formed by arrogant nations against the people of God would not come to fruition. The ideas and proposals of these nations would fall by the wayside, but the purposes of God are never thwarted.

The end of chapter 40 contains the famous verses about gaining new strength by waiting on the Lord. Verse 30 describes the exhausted men as "weary" and as those who "stumble." The same two terms are used in 5:27 to portray an Assyrian army that was empowered by the Lord.

Rachel Margalioth has assembled a large number of additional examples of this sort. One significant area she has investigated is the way that Isaiah used the same words in passages about judgment and in passages about comfort. The land that will become desolate and forsaken will one day no longer be called forsaken and desolate (6:11–12; 62:4). God will "break down the wall" around Israel (5:5), but someday Israel will be able to "wall up the break" (58:12).[11]

These examples strongly suggest that the Book of Isaiah was written by a single author. To escape this conclusion, one must argue that someone who lived after Isaiah was so heavily influenced by him that he consciously copied Isaiah's style. One could also argue that the phraseology of later "Isaiahs" was

---

[11]R. Margalioth, *The Indivisible Isaiah* (New York: Yeshiva University Press, 1964), p. 140.

interpolated into earlier chapters, but such a judgment is hopelessly subjective.[12]

THE IDENTITY OF DEUTERO-ISAIAH

A serious problem facing proponents of a multiple authorship theory is how a writer (or writers) who produced such magnificent poetry and profound theology could have vanished without leaving the mark of his own personality on his writings. J. A. Alexander, a leading Isaianic scholar of the last century, noted that this would be unparalleled in the history of literature.[13] And why would Deutero-Isaiah's writing be attached to the inferior work of a Palestinian prophet?

With the possible exception of Malachi, the names of all the other writing prophets are preserved in their books. Even the name of Obadiah, who wrote a mere twenty-one verses, has not been lost to posterity. Prophets such as Ezekiel or Daniel, who would have been contemporaries of an exilic Deutero-Isaiah, appear to have been totally unaware of the existence of such a person. Furthermore the ideas and theology of exilic writers like Daniel and Ezekiel are not very similar to the ideas and theology of Deutero-Isaiah.

Postexilic Judaism seemed equally oblivious to the existence of a Deutero-Isaiah. In Ecclesiasticus (49:17–25), written about 200 B.C., Ben Sira mentioned that Isaiah comforted those in Zion who mourned. Nothing in Ben Sira's words refers to anyone other than the eighth-century prophet.

Although I deny the existence of a Deutero- (or a Trito-) Isaiah, I admit that there are significant differences between chapters 1–39 and chapters 40–66. Thus if one were to refer to "First and Second Isaiah" in the same sense as "First and Second Timothy" or "First and Second Peter," this would not be objectionable. Chapters 40–66 are a "new letter," perhaps

[12] In a recent book, Avraham Gileadi presents additional arguments for the unity of Isaiah on the basis of its literary structure. See *The Apocalyptic Book of Isaiah* (Provo, Utah: Hebraeus Press, 1982), pp. 171–80.

[13] Joseph A. Alexander, *Commentary on the Prophecies of Isaiah,* 2 vols. (1875; reprint, Grand Rapids: Zondervan, 1953), 1:66.

written many years after chapters 1–39, but the same prophet was responsible for both sections!

This conclusion agrees with the verdict of the New Testament, which regards Isaiah as the author of the entire book. Matthew 12:17 and 18 cites Isaiah 42:1 as "what was spoken through the prophet Isaiah." Both Matthew (3:3) and Luke (3:4) quote Isaiah 40:3 as the words of Isaiah, and Paul's citations from 53:1 (Rom. 10:16) and 65:1 (Rom. 10:20) are in a similar vein. In John 12:38–41 quotations from Isaiah 6 and 53 are attributed by John to Isaiah, the eighth-century prophet.

THE DEAD SEA SCROLLS

As I have already pointed out, the copies of Isaiah found among the Dead Sea Scrolls have had an important bearing on questions of authorship. Isaiah was one of the favorite books of the Qumran community, and two main copies of Isaiah were discovered there. The Saint Mark's Isaiah Scroll (1Q Isaᵃ) contains the entire Book of Isaiah and preserves many readings that differ from the traditional, or Masoretic, text. The Hebrew University Scroll (1Q Isaᵇ) contains significant portions of Isaiah, especially from chapter 38 to the end of the book. Its wording is extremely close to that of the Masoretic text. Several other fragments of Isaiah were found in cave four.

The Qumran manuscripts were clearly copies, not the original autographs. According to Millar Burrows, the Book of Isaiah must have been completed several centuries earlier.[14] Since the Saint Mark's Scroll is dated around 150 B.C., it is very difficult to support arguments that important editorial work on Isaiah occurred in the second and third centuries B.C. Yet, as I indicated above, a number of scholars have come dangerously close to saying just that. The existence of the Isaiah scrolls from Qumran completely rules out Duhm's theory that Isaiah contains first-century insertions.

The Saint Mark's Scroll has a space of three lines between chapters 33 and 34 but no break between chapters 39 and 40.

---

[14] Millar Burrows, *The Dead Sea Scrolls* (New York: Viking, 1955), p. 109.

According to Masoretic counting, the midpoint of Isaiah is 33:20. Therefore the space at the end of chapter 33 may reflect a custom of copying the book in two scrolls to facilitate handling.[15] On the basis of this Masoretic dividing point, however, several scholars now regard chapters 34 and 35, or chapters 34–39, as part of Deutero-Isaiah, as I have indicated earlier in this chapter.

Recent English translations of Isaiah have adopted a number of readings from the copies of Isaiah found among the Dead Sea Scrolls. Some of those readings agree with the Septuagint and other ancient versions. In 14:4 "fury" is preferable to the unknown Masoretic word, and "the lookout" in 21:8 makes much more sense than "a lion." Other improvements are "witnesses" in place of "cities" in 33:8 and "fierce" instead of "righteous" in 49:24. Except for 33:8, the other changes are also supported by at least one other ancient version. In 53:11 the two major Dead Sea Scrolls agree with the Septuagint in inserting "light" after "see," so the verse could be translated, "After the suffering of his soul, he will see the light (of life) and be satisfied." It should be noted, however, that throughout the Saint Mark's Scroll there are a large number of scribal errors and inferior readings. Great caution must be exercised when modifying the Masoretic text of Isaiah in the light of the textual evidence from Qumran.

---

[15] Harrison, *Introduction*, p. 787.

3

THE STRUCTURE OF ISAIAH

THE IMPORTANCE OF CHAPTERS 36–39

The key to understanding the structure of the Book of Isaiah is to understand the four chapters that constitute the historical interlude, chapters 36–39. These chapters provide the hinge, or bridge, that joins chapters 1–35 and chapters 40–66. Chapters 36 and 37 bring to a climax the material that deals with the Assyrian threat. Isaiah had predicted the collapse of the Assyrians, a nation that God had used as a tool to punish His people Israel (10:32–34; 14:25). When Isaiah wrote the first thirty-five chapters of his prophecy, Assyria was the leading world power.

Chapters 38 and 39 form an introduction to chapters 40–66 and form a bridge between Isaiah's treatment of the Assyrians in chapters 1–35 and his treatment of the Babylonians in chapters 40–66. King Hezekiah's pride in showing off the treasures of Jerusalem became the occasion for Isaiah to announce the coming Babylonian captivity. Just as his earlier predictions regarding Assyria were remarkably fulfilled in chapters 36–37, so his prophecies about Babylon were sure to come true. The portent of coming judgment (chs. 40–66) was to bring hope to the generation that would be taken captive; in those chapters they would read about God's promise of a future restoration. And the fulfillment of Isaiah's prophecies in chapters 36–37 also

ASSYRIAN BACKDROP		HISTORICAL INTERLUDE		BABYLONIAN BACKDROP
1 — 35	36	Assyria defeated / Babylonian captivity predicted (37 38 39)	40	66
POETRY		PROSE		POETRY
A		B		A
Ahaz		Hezekiah		Cyrus

guaranteed the fulfillment of God's promises in chapters 40–66 to restore Israel.

The pivotal function of chapters 36–39 is displayed in their odd chronological arrangement. Most interpreters agree that the events in chapters 38 and 39 precede those in chapters 36 and 37. This order is difficult to account for unless it reveals Isaiah's intention to help the reader move from the section of his prophecy that deals with the Assyrians (chs. 1–35) to the section that deals with the Babylonians (chs. 40–66).

The central location of the historical interlude gives Isaiah an A B A structure (as illustrated on the opposite page). Section B (chs. 36–39), which is basically a historical section written in prose, is bracketed on either side (chs. 1–35 and 40–66) by sections that are mainly poetic. The Book of Job is similarly arranged. Its large middle poetic section is bracketed by a prose prologue and epilogue. The Book of Daniel shifts from Hebrew to Aramaic (2:4) and then back to Hebrew (8:1) to form a different kind of A B A structure. Outside of the Bible the prose section of the Hammurabi Law Code is sandwiched between a poetic prologue and a poetic epilogue.[1]

THE STRUCTURE OF CHAPTERS 1–35

Within the large poetic sections of Isaiah, there are helpful structural clues. Early in the book there are three distinctive headings that refer to Isaiah by name. Each one is different, but all three contain some form of the word ḥāzâ, "to see." The first and longest, in 1:1, is the title to the entire book, "The vision [of] Isaiah son of Amoz." "Vision" can refer to specific visions (29:7) or it may mean revelation in general (1 Sam. 3:1). Other prophetic books are usually introduced with a reference to the "word" of the Lord, but Obadiah 1:1 uses the same term for vision (ḥāzôn). The rest of Isaiah 1:1 indicates a historical setting that covers the years from 740 to 697 B.C.

The second heading (2:1) introduces the prophet's opening message to the people. This message extends through chapter 4.

---

[1] Cyrus H. Gordon, *The Ancient Near East,* 3d ed. rev. (New York: W. W. Norton & Co., 1965), p. 83.

Isaiah 2:1 says, "This is what Isaiah . . . saw concerning Judah and Jerusalem." Here the verb "saw" is used, rather than the noun and verb together. As in 1:1 the order "Judah and Jerusalem" is preserved. Outside of the headings, *Jerusalem* often appears before *Judah* (cf. 3:1; 5:3; etc.). The main sphere of the prophet's activity was in the capital of the southern kingdom.

The last heading that contains Isaiah's name is found in 13:1: "An oracle concerning Babylon that Isaiah son of Amoz saw." This verse introduces the section (which continues through chapter 23) on prophecies against the nations. As I noted in chapter 2, the specific mention of Isaiah in 13:1 is important because the entire chapter is often said to have been written by someone else.

A break in the outline should probably be placed after chapter 6. Chapters 6 and 7 begin with important dating formulae that indicate a historical gap of about six years between the two chapters. The vision of chapter 6 portrays the call of Isaiah and forms a fitting conclusion to the first five chapters. In his opening messages, Isaiah exposed the sinful attitudes and actions of the nation of Israel, particularly its disregard for the holiness of God. In mocking tones they had challenged God to take action: "Let the plan of the Holy One of Israel come, so we may know it" (5:19). In the sixth chapter Isaiah describes his own encounter with the Holy God whose awesome majesty requires repentance and respect. Although God's call to Isaiah preceded his preaching ministry, the prophet delayed his presentation of this experience to heighten its impact on the people of Israel. They needed to see a revelation of God's holiness against the backdrop of their sinfulness.

Chapters 7–12 are another natural unit. They emphasize the birth and ministry of the Messiah. A poem of thanksgiving concludes this section in which Isaiah's own children play a significant role. His son Maher-Shalal-Hash-Baz bears a name that includes the same terms for "hurry" and "hasten" that are used in the strategic passage in 5:19. This young son symbolized God's promise that He would bring quick judgment on Judah's enemies (8:4). This judgment would be followed by the divine punishment of Israel. The name of Isaiah's older son, Shear-

Jashub, means "a remnant will return." The importance of this name is evident in 10:21–22 where Isaiah warned that destruction and exile were coming on Israel. Along with the warning there is the promise that a minority of true believers would be faithful to God. The return of the exiled remnant to Israel is a major theme of chapters 40–66.

The oracles concerning the nations are found in chapters 13–23. Most of the prophetic books contain sections that refer to foreign powers (cf. Jer. 46–51; Ezek. 25–32). Eight times in Isaiah 13–23 *oracle* is used to introduce an announcement of judgment, but only the oracle against the Philistines is dated (14:28). In the case of Assyria in 14:24 and of Cush (Ethiopia) in 18:1, *oracle* is omitted.

In chapters 13 and 14 Isaiah denounced the world powers. The nation of Babylon would bear the brunt of God's judgments, though Assyria is also mentioned (14:25). From 14:28 through 17:14, countries located close to Israel's borders are named—nations such as Philistia, Moab, and Damascus—Judah's perennial enemies. Chapter 17 links Israel with Damascus because Damascus attacked Judah during the Syro-Ephraimite war. In chapters 18 and 19 the southern nations of Ethiopia and Egypt are discussed.

Interestingly, chapter 21 contains another oracle against Babylon (vv. 1–10) and then focuses on Edom and Arabia (vv. 11–17). Like Amos, Isaiah placed Judah among the "foreign" nations (22:1–25; cf. Amos 2:4–8). Finally, chapter 23 describes God's judgment against the commercial center of Tyre, one of the last kingdoms to suffer punishment.

The longer prophecies against Babylon (chs. 13–14) and Moab (chs. 15–16) conclude with epilogues (14:24–27; 16:13–14). The historical interlude in 20:1–6 probably functions as an epilogue to chapters 18 and 19. In 20:1–6 Isaiah described how he walked around naked to symbolize the shameful captivity in store for Egypt and Ethiopia. In 22:15–25 Isaiah prophesied the downfall of an individual, Shebna, a Judean official. On two occasions, 14:1–2 and 19:23–25, the prophet gave messages that promised blessing and restoration for Israel and, unexpectedly, for Egypt and Assyria. The return of just rule to Zion is portrayed in 16:5.

Chapters 24–27 are often called the "Apocalypse of Isaiah." They describe the opposition of the nations of the world to God, an opposition that results in an eschatological conflict in which the wicked are defeated and God's rule is established on Mount Zion. Calvin and Delitzsch regarded these chapters as the summary of the previous prophecies against the nations, as the grand finale to chapters 13–23.[2] In these chapters the enemies of God are seen as one entity that is symbolized by the name *Moab* (25:10).

In chapters 24–27, several references to a "city in ruins" (24:12) or to a "fortified city" (25:2; 27:10; cf. 26:5) bear the earmarks of a world city, a Babylon that opposes God. Triumphantly arrayed against such a city is the city of God (26:1). As they celebrate the overthrow of this wicked city (25:1–5) and the restoration of Israel (26:1–19), the righteous are described as erupting into psalms of praise. In 27:2–6 the Song of the Vineyard portrays the fruitfulness of Israel—a sharp contrast to the vineyard song in 5:1–7 that depicted the destruction of the nation. The final two verses in chapter 27 describe the glorious return of the exiles in terms similar to those used in 2:1–4 and in 19:23–25.

In chapters 28–33, Isaiah again concentrated on Judah and Israel. This section is characterized by the word *woe*, which begins every chapter except 32 (cf. 29:15). The content of these chapters shifts back and forth between judgment and blessing, and each chapter contains passages of encouragement (28:5–6, 16; 29:5–8, 17–24; 30:18–33; 31:4–9; 32:1–8, 15–20; 33:1–24). The interchange between doom and hope is remarkably regular.

The chapters in this unit (chs. 28–33) seem to be arranged in pairs. Chapters 28 and 29 foretell the coming judgment on the capital cities of the northern and southern kingdoms respectively—Samaria and Jerusalem. Chapters 30 and 31 deal with Judah's reliance on Egypt for military assistance. Chapter 30 is the longer of the two and includes a short oracle "concerning the animals of the Negev" (30:6–7). Chapter 31

---

[2] Franz Delitzsch, *Biblical Commentary on the Prophecies of Isaiah,* trans. James Martin, 3d ed., 2 vols. (1877; reprint, Grand Rapids: Eerdmans, 1967), 1:423.

concludes the topic of judgment in a more propositional and summary form.

In chapters 32 and 33 Isaiah brought this section (chs. 28–33) to a climax by emphasizing the righteous rule of the messianic king. For the first time, *woe* is not applied to Israel (33:1). The doomed "destroyer" is probably Sennacherib, whose destruction in 701 B.C. offered hope that God would someday bring unending peace to Jerusalem.

The relationship between chapters 28–33 and chapters 34–35 corresponds to the one between chapters 13–23 and chapters 24–27. In each case an apocalyptic section provides a dramatic conclusion to the preceding chapters. World-wide judgment will usher in a time of unparalleled joy and blessing. In chapters 24–27 the nation of Moab symbolized evil (25:10), and in 34:5–6 Edom fulfills the same role. In 24:4 the earth "dries up" and "withers," and in 34:4 the starry host withers away. On the positive side, 25:8 speaks of the elimination of death and tears, whereas 35:10 says that "sorrow and sighing will flee away." Both chapters 24–27 and chapters 34 and 35 end with descriptions of the return to Jerusalem (27:12–13; 35:10).

The strategic nature of the historical interlude (chs. 36–39) has already been discussed at the start of this chapter. Its integral relationship with earlier material in Isaiah may be seen by comparing 7:3 with 36:2. At the same aqueduct of the upper pool where Ahaz stood firm in his resolve to make an alliance with Assyria, the Assyrian commanding general demanded the surrender of the whole kingdom of Judah. Isaiah had warned that the alliance would prove to be disastrous (7:17).

Another interesting parallel between this historical section (chs. 36–39) and previous chapters is the use of the sign in 37:30. Isaiah had promised Hezekiah that within three years agriculture in Judah would return to normal. A similar three-year period was portrayed in chapter 20 where Isaiah predicted the captivity of Egypt by walking stripped and barefoot (v. 3). And it is also likely that about three years elapsed between the birth of Isaiah's son Maher-Shalal-Hash-Baz and the time the boy could talk. God had promised that before he could speak, Israel would find relief from her enemies (8:4). Verse 18 of chapter 8 says that Isaiah's children were "signs" in Israel. Though the form and purpose of these three signs were quite different, the correlation between them is nonetheless remarkable.

Chapters 36–39 provide the final biographical data about Isaiah. Combined with chapters 6–8 and with chapter 20, they afford a brief but significant glimpse of the life of the great prophet.

THE STRUCTURE OF CHAPTERS 40–66

The last twenty-seven chapters of the book are the most difficult to outline. They do not fall into clearly marked divisions, and the themes are interrelated in an intricate progression. The first eleven verses of chapter 40 can properly be called the prologue to the rest of the book. They provide a synopsis of the major themes: comfort and good news for Jerusalem and the coming of the Lord.

A convenient refrain at the end of chapters 48 and 57 may provide the best structural clue for dividing these chapters: "There is no peace . . . for the wicked." In 48:22 this refrain is somewhat isolated from the context, but in 57:21 it is closely related to the previous two verses. Perhaps the detailed description of the eternal fate of the wicked in the last verse of Isaiah is to be regarded as an expansion of the same refrain.

The resulting nine-chapter segments in 40–66 exhibit distinct characteristics. Chapters 40–48 emphasize the deliverance from Babylon and the doctrine of God. Chapters 49–57 could be titled "Salvation Through the Servant," with a corresponding emphasis on the doctrine of soteriology. The final chapters (chs. 58–66) focus on the theme of "Salvation in the Last Days," or eschatology. But these are not mutually exclusive categories by any means.

Chapters 40–48 extend comfort to Jerusalem by promising that God will prepare the way for the exiles to return from Babylon (40:3–4). Roads would be cleared of stones, and hilly terrain would be leveled. The same theme and terminology occurs in two other places as well (57:14; 62:10–11; cf. 49:11). In 40:3 and in 62:10 the roadway is linked with the coming of the Messiah, just as the return from Babylon, the first coming of Christ, and His triumphal second coming are united in these contexts.

The progression of the argument in chapters 40–48 makes use of a number of legal terms. To prove His power and His love, God is portrayed as one who conducts a legal case against the nations and their idols (41:1; 43:9) and against Israel and her unbelief (43:26). Israel is called to witness that God has rescued her in the past and that His former predictions came true (43:10, 12; 44:8). The nations are challenged to meet the Lord in court (41:1) and to present their witnesses (43:9).

God's superiority over the idols and soothsayers is proved by His ability to predict the rise of Cyrus, whom He would use to restore His exiles. From 41:2 through 48:14 there are several references to this Persian king who would carry out God's purposes (41:2, 25; 45:13). And in 44:28 and in 45:1 the name *Cyrus* actually appears.

The uniqueness of Israel's God is underscored repeatedly as the lawsuit develops. Eight times Isaiah asserted that the only true God is Yahweh (43:11; 45:5, 6, 14, 18, 21, 22; 46:9). To drive the point home, no two of these statements are exactly alike. In 47:10 Babylon (and her idolatry) claims: "There is none besides me." But the capture of Babylon by Cyrus would reveal the folly of this boast.

Another refrain that emphasizes God's work as creator and sustainer of the world is "I am the first and the last." In slightly varied forms this line occurs in 41:4; 44:6; and in 48:12. Its meaning is close to that of the phrase "I am the Alpha and the Omega" of Revelation 1:8.

Chapters 40–48 also introduce the important theme of the Servant. In 41:8–9 and in 42:19 the Servant is equated with the nation of Israel. The first seven verses of chapter 42 comprise the first Servant Song and present aspects of the ministry of the Messiah.

The last three Servant Songs are reserved for the central section, chapters 49–57. Here Isaiah developed the theme of salvation in its world-wide dimensions. This concept is inherent in the expression "a light for the Gentiles" (42:6), but it is more explicit in the second Servant Song where the Servant is "a light for the Gentiles" that He "may bring my salvation to the ends of the earth" (49:6; cf. 52:10). God's method of providing salvation through the suffering of Christ is seen in the third and fourth Servant Songs (50:4–9; 52:13–53:12).

In chapter 55 an invitation is extended to the whole world to avail itself of this salvation. The following chapter promises that foreigners and eunuchs—who were often excluded from Israel's worship—would have free access to God's house of prayer on Mount Zion (56:4–7). Gentile believers may also be included as 57:13 indicates: "But the man who makes me his refuge will inherit the land and possess my holy mountain."

The salvation of Gentiles would not be at the expense of Israel, whose return to the land and full restoration to Zion remain in view in this section (52:7; 54:1–17). The emphasis on Gentile conversion was a warning to Jewish idolaters and Sabbath-breakers that their nationality did not guarantee their salvation (56:9–12; 57:1–13). Israel per se was no longer God's servant, but true believers among both Jews (54:17) and Gentiles (56:6) would be His servants.

Chapters 49–57 do not continue to use the legal terminology that was prominent in chapters 40–48, though an outstanding example of the perversion of justice is given in 53:7–9. Throughout Isaiah, God spoke through the prophet to condemn injustice in court and the exploitation of the weak (1:17; 10:2). But when His own Son was arrested, His trial was a farce. A righteous man was sentenced to die.

As the Book of Isaiah moves toward a climax, the last nine chapters develop many of the earlier themes. References to the return from Babylon fade into the background, and greater emphasis is placed on the Second Coming, the millennial rule, and the new heavens and new earth. Chapter 60 gives classic expression to the justice and prosperity that will characterize Christ's millennial rule. In this chapter the "holy mountain" of Jerusalem, not mentioned since 57:13, becomes the focal point of world government and worship (65:11, 25; 66:20)—a condition predicted in 2:2–4.

Eschatology includes the judgment of the wicked, and 63:1–6 describes the judgment of Edom in terms similar to the apocalyptic material in chapter 34. The wrath and retribution of the wicked are also discussed in 59:18 and in 66:14–18.

So distinct are the portrayals of salvation and judgment in chapters 58–66 that this section is sometimes called "The Book of Light and Darkness." Those who follow the evil ways of oppression and greed will find themselves in deep darkness, but those who turn to the Lord and pursue justice will be bathed in light (58:8, 10; 59:9; 60:1). And God Himself will be an "everlasting light" in the new age of righteousness and prosperity (60:19).

As the Book of Isaiah comes to a close, we read an agonizing lament (63:7–64:12), an appeal for God to take action on behalf of His suffering people. Isaiah had made so many glorious promises of future blessing that the hearts of the people longed to see some of them fulfilled. God's answer to the plea of His people is given in chapters 65 and 66. There would be joy and plenty in store for the godly, but the rebellious could only anticipate judgment. Chapter 66 in particular emphasizes the contrasting futures of the righteous and the wicked—unending peace or eternal punishment.

Eight times in chapters 65 and 66 Isaiah mentioned the "servants" of God (65:8, 9, 13, 14, 15; 66:14). The emphasis of the plural form *servants* reflects the same usage in 54:17 and 56:6. Only believing individuals within Israel (and the nations) may hope to enjoy God's blessing. *Servant* in the singular does not occur after 53:11.

Several key expressions in chapters 40–66 appear as double imperatives at the start of a verse. The first is "Comfort, comfort" (40:1), which states what may be the main theme of the entire section. From 51:9 through 52:11 four such pairs are used. The first three (51:9, 17; 52:1) are all translated "Awake, awake" (although 51:17 uses a reflexive stem from the same root). God is called on to intervene on behalf of Israel, and then Jerusalem is told to "awake." A repentant Israel would find a responsive God. God's answer was "Depart, Depart" because Israel would soon be freed from Babylon (52:11).

In 57:14 the return to Jerusalem is again considered. Isaiah said, "Build up, build up, prepare the road!" The final example continues in the same vein: "Pass through, pass through the gates! . . . Build up, build up the highway!" (62:10). This is the only verse in Isaiah that contains two pairs of double imperatives.

The last verse in Isaiah (66:24) supplies a sobering complement to its very first words (1:2). Isaiah began his prophecy by lamenting the rebellion of Israel, and he referred to their stubbornness time and again (e.g. 30:1; 48:8). Now at the end of the book, the prophet used the same term found in 1:2 (*pāša'*) to describe the terrible fate of those who persist in rebellion.

4

THE POETRY OF ISAIAH

Scholars have long marveled at the literary beauty and at the depth and power of Isaiah's poetry. Most of the Book of Isaiah was written in parallelism, the primary form of Hebrew poetry. Isaiah employed a wide variety of poetic devices in individual verses, building the verses into hymns of praise (cf. 12:1–6; 38:10–20) and national lament (63:7–64:12), into oracles (13:1–23:18), a taunt-song (14:4–21), satire (44:9–20), and even wisdom poems (28:23–29). The Song of the Vineyard in 5:1–7 (cf. 27:2–6) is a terse, evocative, poetic masterpiece with a devastating application.

Every Hebrew teacher looks forward to the day when he can take his students through the Hebrew text of Isaiah and introduce them to its intricacies and complexities. Students who can survive the rigors of Hebrew grammar and syntax long enough to reach Isaiah will be amply rewarded. They will be stretched and challenged, but the richness of the book will more than repay the effort expended to appreciate its beauty and technique. And so in this chapter I will briefly summarize the different poetic devices and symbols that Isaiah used.

POETIC DEVICES

Alliteration

The opening line of the prophecy, which sets the poetic tone for the entire book, contains two examples of alliteration.

"Hear, O heavens!" reflects the Hebrew alliteration nicely (*šim' û šāmayim*), and "Listen, O earth!" stresses roots that begin with aleph (*wᵉha'ᵃzînî 'ereṣ*). The oft-mentioned "briers and thorns" (5:6; 7:23; 9:18 etc.) appears in Hebrew as *šāmîr wāšāyit*. Another negative pair, "ruin and destruction," also begins with the letter shin: *šōdwᵉšeber* (51:19; 60:18). In Isaiah 35:10 (=51:11) the English translation contains an alliterated pair in the famous line "and sorrow and sighing will flee away." In Hebrew it is the previous pair, "gladness and joy," that begins with the same letter: *śāśōn wᵉśimḥâ*. A double example of alliteration occurs in Isaiah 14:22. There the Lord announces that He "will cut off from Babylon her name and survivors" (*šēm* and *šᵉ'ār*), "her offspring and descendants" (*nîn* and *neked*)."

Assonance

Although Hebrew poetry does not have lines that rhyme at the end, sometimes within a given verse certain words have the same sound (or sounds). When this involves the initial sound of the word, this phenomenon is similar to alliteration. In 1:4 the line "Ah, sinful nation" begins with the two words *hôy gôy* followed by the word "sinful" with another "o" vowel, *ḥōṭē'*. Verse 23 starts with two virtually indistinguishable "s" sounds, *śārayik sôrᵉrîm*, successfully translated as "Your rulers are rebels." Isaiah 24:17 manages to repeat an entire syllable three times in succession—*paḥad, paḥat*, and *paḥ* ("Terror and pit and snare await you"). Alliteration is again combined with assonance in the trio of words describing the Day of the Lord (22:5). The Lord has in store "a day of tumult and trampling and terror" (*mᵉhûmâ, mᵉbûsâ, mᵉbûkâ*). The vowels in all three words are identical.

Two different verses make use of varied forms of the same Hebrew verbs *bāgad* ("betray") and *šādad* ("destroy, loot"; 21:2 and 33:1). In 33:1 four similar sounding forms of each verb occur in an alternating pattern. The word translated "crown of beauty," *pᵉ'ēr*, (61:3) has the same three consonants and almost the same vowels as the nearby word "ashes," *'ēper*. The basic difference is the order of the first two consonants. The two words sound very similar.

Occasionally, assonance will merge with onomatapoeia, where the sound of a word helps to convey its meaning. In 17:12 Isaiah compared the raging of the nations to the roaring of the sea, using the words *hᵃmôn* and *šᵉʾôn* and a great many "m" and "n" sounds. One can almost hear the churning waters as the verse is read out loud.[1] Another powerful combination is the "overwhelming scourge" or "whip" mentioned in 28:15 and 18. The opening syllables are identical in Hebrew: *šôṭ šôṭēp̄*.

Wordplay

Isaiah was a master of wordplay, or paronomasia. The application of the famous Song of the Vineyard (5:7) employs a set of words that drives home the point. Judah was guilty of injustice, even murder, though the nation pretended to be God-fearing. This hypocrisy is highlighted when the Lord said that Judah's "justice" (*mišpāṭ*) turned out to be "bloodshed" (*mišpāḥ*), a word with only one different letter. The Lord expected "righteousness" (*ṣᵉḏāqâ*) but heard only "cries of distress" (*ṣᵉʿāqâ*). In English one might say, "God looked for 'right' but instead found 'riot.'"

Less spectacular is the play on the name of Jeremiah's home town, Anathoth, in 10:30. This town was located just north of Jerusalem and was in the path of the Assyrian armies. The people's plight led the prophet to exclaim, "Poor Anathoth!" (*ʿᵃniyyâ ʿᵃnāṯôṯ*). Another pair of words beginning with the same two consonants is "destruction from the Almighty" (*šôḏ miššadday*). The name "Almighty" is sometimes anglicized in the phrase "God Almighty" (Heb. El-Shaddai; cf. Gen. 17:1). The destruction sent by the Lord Almighty on the Day of Judgment will be mighty indeed.

Another example also found in a context of doom is the lament over the collapse of Moab. In 15:9 Isaiah stated that "Dimon's waters are full of blood." The words "Dimon"

---

[1] E. J. Young, *The Book of Isaiah*, 3 vols. (Grand Rapids: Eerdmans, 1965–72), 1:472–73.

(*dîmôn*) and "blood" (*dām*) contain two identical consonants, indicating that the city of "Dimon" will mean something like "Blood City." Since there is no city named "Dimon" in Moab, it is likely that the well-known city of "Dibon" (15:2) stands behind the wordplay.

Judgment on Edom is expressed in "an oracle concerning Dumah" (21:11). Here again Isaiah apparently played with the similarity in sound between "Edom" ('*edôm*) and "Dumah" (*dûmâ*). "Dumah" means "silence" or "stillness," a sober warning that Edom would lie desolate after enemy armies had conquered her.

Hyperbole

Since poets sometimes express themselves in exaggerated fashion for effect, one must be careful not to interpret them too literally. For example, the lament over the vines of Moab mourns the trampling of the shoots that once "went as far as the sea" (16:8). In a similar fashion the psalmist defined the northern border of Israel by saying that it sent "its shoots as far as the River," the mighty Euphrates (Ps. 80:11). Hyperbole is also evident in Isaiah 37:25 where the King of Assyria boasts that he "dried up all the streams of Egypt" with the soles of his feet. This is a poetic way of stating that he was able to cross those streams. If the king of Babylon is the speaker in 14:13–14, we would again interpret the assertions as hyperbole, but this is complicated by other possible identifications of the speaker.

An eschatological context underlies the interpretation of Isaiah 30:26 and its description of a sun that is seven times brighter and a moon that shines like the sun. Such brilliance may be a figurative description of the glory of God. Similarly the splendor of the New Jerusalem is depicted in terms of a vast number of precious stones. The foundations of Jerusalem will be made of sapphires, the battlements of rubies, and the gates of sparkling jewels. Even the walls will be made of precious stones (Isa. 54:11–12).

Chiasmus

Chiasmus is a technique in which the poet reverses the order of a series of nouns or the arrangement of the parts of a sentence. Perhaps the clearest example is Isaiah 6:10, where in three successive lines the prophet refers to the heart, the ears, and the eyes. Then in the next three lines he reverses the order and mentions the eyes, the ears, and the heart. This "mirror image" is diagrammed as *a b c ć b́ á*. Sometimes the grammatical structure will be changed to achieve a certain effect. In 1:18 the Hebrew order is reflected in the following translation: "Though your sins are like scarlet, like snow they shall be white; though they are red like crimson, like wool they shall be." The prepositional phrases in the middle of each distich present an *a b b́ á* arrangement. In 40:12 each element of a clause is reversed in the succeeding clause: "Who has measured in the hollow of his hand the waters, or the heavens in the breadth of his hand has marked off?" The verb is first in one clause and last in the second. The noun for "waters" is placed right next to "heavens." The total arrangement gives an *a b c ć b́ á* pattern. An added feature is the assonance between "waters," *mayim*, and "heavens," *šāmayim*.

A more extended chiasmus occurs in 16:7–11, toward the end of Isaiah's lament over Moab. As he grieved over the devastation of the land, Isaiah mentioned four cities, repeating their names in reverse order. Kir Hareseth, Heshbon, Sibmah, and Jazer are cited in verses 7 and 8. Verse 9 refers to Jazer, Sibmah, and Heshbon followed by Kir Hareseth in verse 11.

Inclusio

A variation of chiasmus is the technique of beginning and ending a particular unit in the same way. The intervening material is included in the "envelope" between the two points. In 66:4 the first and last verbs are forms of the verb "choose." The people chose what displeased God, so He chose "harsh treatment" for them. Similarly the verb "ruined" provides the starting and stopping points in 6:11 (cf. *šᵉmāmâ* in 1:7). Isaiah 53:6 begins and ends with the word *kullānû*, "all of us." "All of us" have gone astray, but in His mercy the Lord laid on Christ the sin of "all of us."

In a way the entire Book of Isaiah is included between two verses that describe rebellion. Chapter one begins with the statement that Israel rebelled against God (v. 2), and the last verse of the book uses the same verb, *pāša'*, as it portrays the horrible fate of all who rebel against God.

Personification

The most famous poetic feature in Isaiah is personification, a device by which the sun, the desert, cities, and countries all behave as if they were people.[2] Isaiah was especially fascinated by trees and mountains, and frequently he personified them. It was the pine trees and cedars of Lebanon that exulted when Babylon was destroyed (14:8), but Lebanon was ashamed and withered when Assyria ravaged the land (33:9). The mountains and the trees will burst into song when the Lord redeems His people (44:23; 49:13), and "all the trees of the field will clap their hands" (55:12). The desert and parched land rejoice (35:1), and "the desert and its towns raise their voices" over God's victory (42:11). Heaven and earth are called on as witnesses (1:2), and "the earth reels like a drunkard" when the Lord unleashes His judgment (24:20). The sun and the moon are ashamed (24:23), and the grave "opens its mouth" to swallow sinners (5:14). In 14:12 the King of Babylon is the "morning star" that has been "cast down to the earth."

Cities and countries are sometimes depicted as daughters or widows. The "Daughter of Zion" is the city of Jerusalem (1:8) and "Virgin Daughter" represents a city whose walls had not been breached (cf. 37:22; 23:12; 47:1). A city that had been destroyed was spoken of as a widow (47:8; 54:4) or barren woman (49:21; 54:1). Zion is the barren woman who bursts into song as the people of Judah return home (54:1). Early in Isaiah the gates of Zion lament and mourn in anticipation of Jerusalem's destruction (3:26). The ships of Tarshish are also

[2] Cf. Sheldon Blank, *Prophetic Faith in Isaiah* (New York: Harper & Row, 1958), pp. 75, 82.

called on to wail when the great commercial center of Tyre is destroyed (23:14).

Abstract qualities are personified in 59:14–15. Isaiah lamented that "justice is driven back" and "truth has stumbled in the streets" of Jerusalem. We might also compare the reference to Israel as the deaf and blind Servant of God (42:18–19). In 41:8 the Servant of the Lord clearly refers to the nation.

A final example is the personification of the arm of the Lord in 51:9. Since the arm of the Lord had dried up the Red Sea and ransomed Israel from Egypt (cf. 50:2), Isaiah called on that same mighty arm to "awake" and to swing into action. In subsequent paragraphs Jerusalem (or Zion) is also urged to awake and clothe herself with strength (51:17; 52:1).

THE USE OF SYMBOLISM

To effectively communicate his message, Isaiah drew on many facets of nature and human life. His similes and metaphors are based on a wide range of subjects, including items as mundane as chaff and as spectacular as the cedars of Lebanon. The variety and scope of his imagery helps to drive his message firmly into the hearts and minds of his readers. Certain symbols appear again and again, though their meaning is not always the same. A river may symbolize both peace and destruction, and grass can represent either luxuriant growth or frailty. The vineyard and its grapes are flexible symbols throughout Isaiah. They are used in positive and negative ways. Isaiah was a keen observer of nature and human behavior, a fact that contributes to the beauty and forcefulness of his prophecy.

Mountains and Trees

As I noted in the study of personification, mountains and trees were favorite subjects of Isaiah. The forests of Lebanon are a symbol for the armies of Assyria (10:18, 34; cf. 29:17), and the lofty cedars of Lebanon can represent proud rulers (cf. 2:13). The mountains stand for the nations (2:14; 41:15) and for the land of Judah (65:9). The oaks of Bashan represent exalted rulers (2:13), and "oaks of righteousness" are individuals in Judah with solid faith and stability (61:3). By way of contrast, the idolater was compared to "an oak with fading leaves" (1:30).

Poplar trees symbolize those who are blessed by the Lord (44:4), and a restored and fertile land will possess the pine and myrtle tree, the fir and the cypress (41:19; 55:13). In the new heavens and new earth, men will enjoy life-spans as long as "the days of a tree" (65:22).

Isaiah also utilized terms like *shoot* and *branch* to refer to the coming Messiah. The Messiah was to be a shoot from the stump of Jesse (11:1), "a tender shoot" (53:2), "a Branch" who would bear fruit and be beautiful (4:2; 11:1). Another important term is the "Root of Jesse," a title applied to Christ in Revelation 5:5 and 22:16 (cf. Isa. 11:10). In 14:29 *root* refers to offspring. The palm branch is a symbol for the elders and other leaders of Israel (9:14) and of Egypt (19:15).

Plants and Grass

Plants and grass also represent people and nations, usually drawing attention to their weakness. For example, the two verses that mention the palm branch contrast it to the reed, a symbol for less significant leaders (cf. 9:14–15). Egypt's lack of dependability as an ally is compared to leaning on a "splintered reed of a staff" in 36:6. A bruised reed is a symbol of weakness and humility in 42:3 (cf. 58:5).

Grass represents that which is transitory and quickly fades. Men are mortal; they are here today and gone tomorrow. They lose their bloom as rapidly as do flowers (37:27; 40:6–8; 51:12). Two passages, however, speak of grass in a positive way. Those on whom God will pour out His Spirit "will spring up like grass in a meadow"—well watered and fruitful (44:3–4; cf. 35:7).

A closely related symbol is that of chaff or stubble. Enemy armies—probably the forces of Assyria—are referred to as those who are "driven before the wind like chaff on the hills" (17:13; cf. 29:5). Rulers of nations take office, but the Lord sometimes sends a whirlwind to sweep them away like chaff (40:24). God raised up King Cyrus to scatter rulers like windblown chaff (41:2), and even Israel will one day thresh the nations and reduce them to chaff (41:15). Isaiah also promised that Babylon's astrologers and stargazers and all of their useless counsel would eventually burn like stubble.

Briers and thorns are sometimes used literally (cf. 7:23–25) and sometimes symbolically. In 9:18 the wickedness of Israel is compared to a great fire that consumes the land with its briers and thorns. The very next chapter describes the fire of God that destroys the Assyrian army, referred to under the symbolism of forests, thorns, and briers (10:17–18). When the Lord restores Israel and makes it a fruitful vineyard, there will be no briers and thorns—no evil and no enemies—to harm the vineyard (27:2–5).

Water and Storms

In a part of the world where water is relatively scarce, it is easy to explain Isaiah's many references to streams, wells, and rivers. It is not always easy, however, to know whether a given reference is literal or figurative. Often the physical and the spiritual are intertwined, as in the phrase that says, "You will draw water from the wells of salvation" (12:3). God saved Israel from the enemy, and He also provided water for them in the desert. The "streams of water in the desert" signify that God will meet physical needs as well as spiritual ones (cf. 32:2; 35:6–7). In 44:3 the pouring of water on thirsty ground is compared to the pouring out of the Spirit of God amidst great blessing (cf. 32:15). So abundant will be God's provision that the streams will flow even on mountains and hills (30:25; 41:18). And in 58:11 the faithful are given constant strength, "like a spring whose waters never fail."

Isaiah 8:6 mentions "the gently flowing waters of Shiloah" that were rejected by Judah. These waters probably refer to the Gihon Spring, the main source of water for Jerusalem, a symbol of the Lord's sustaining strength. Because the nation had rejected the gentle waters, the Lord would send against her the mighty flood waters of the Euphrates River. He would send the king of Assyria and his army (8:7). In 28:17–19 overflowing waters also represent enemy armies. Yet in two other passages, 48:18 and 66:12, a river is symbolic of peace and prosperity.

Floods and storms are normally related to the judgment of God. The Lord was to come against Israel "like a hailstorm . . . like a driving rain and a flooding downpour" (28:2). Rain, hail, and a thunderstorm would likewise overwhelm Assyria when the Lord turned His hand against the armies of the north (30:30; cf. 32:19). Jerusalem was soon to be laid in ruins by Babylon, but the storms would end and she would be comforted and rebuilt (54:11). The Lord "will come like a pent-up flood" to drive back the enemy and to redeem His people (59:18–19).

Light and Darkness

The contrasting symbols of light and darkness occur repeatedly in Isaiah. Light is associated with joy, healing, and salvation, and darkness is linked with gloom, distress, and judgment. In 2:5 Israel is urged to "walk in the light of the Lord," and by 60:19–20 the Lord is described as the everlasting light for His people. Light is connected with the person of the Messiah (9:2; cf. v. 6), and the Servant of the Lord is called "a light for the Gentiles" (42:6; 49:6). According to 49:6, this light will bring salvation to the ends of the earth. Light is parallel to healing in 58:8, a passage that speaks of God's provision and blessing for those who help the poor and oppressed (cf. 58:10–11). The "light of life" (53:11) may be a reference to the resurrection of Christ. In 14:12 the fallen king of Babylon is called the "morning star."

Darkness is a consequence of sin and is linked with the threatening clouds of enemy invasion. The Assyrian onslaught against Israel and Judah in the latter half of the eighth century B.C. is vividly portrayed as a day of distress, darkness, and despair (5:30; 8:22). Israel failed to respond to the word of God and was cut off from the light of dawn (8:19–20). Unable to carry out justice, Israel was plunged into the darkness of bondage and helplessness. According to 60:2, the earth will be covered with the darkness of sin and oppression, but God's glorious light will shine on Zion.

Darkness acquires a good connotation when it refers to the shadow of God's hand. The Lord "covers" or "hides" His own in the protection of His hand (49:2; 51:16), and He will again provide a cloud and canopy to shield Jerusalem from the heat of the day (4:5–6). But if Judah looked to Egypt's shade for protection, the Pharaoh would disappoint her (30:2–3).

Fire

Fire stands for both purification and judgment. The former is twice represented by the process of refining (*ṣārap*) away impurities in a furnace (1:25; 48:10). "The furnace of affliction" (48:10) may refer to the Babylonian captivity. Jerusalem would be cleansed by "a spirit of fire" (4:4), but not before it became a veritable altar-hearth, or "Ariel" (29:1–2). Cleansing does involve judgment, and we are told that God's "anger burns against his people" (5:25), mainly in "the violence of war" (42:25). The wicked actually set themselves on fire, devising schemes that bring about their own destruction (1:31; 50:11). Their own breath is a fire that consumes them (33:11).

God Himself is a consuming fire (33:14), and His breath is a stream of burning sulfur that destroys the wicked (30:33). When God comes to judge Assyria, He is called "the Light of Israel" (10:17). The final judgment also portrays the Lord as "coming with fire" and hurling flames against His foes (66:15–16).

The fires of judgment cannot be extinguished. The smoke from Edom "will rise forever" (34:9–10), and the fire that consumes all who rebel against God cannot be quenched (66:24). The experience of the redeemed will be different; they will walk through the fire and not be burned (43:2)!

Rocks and Stones

A rock or cornerstone portrays stability and a solid foundation. God Himself is called "the Rock" a number of times. He is the fortress (17:10), the *Rock eternal* (26:4), the only God and King (44:8). In 28:16 the Lord is the "precious cornerstone" laid in Zion who deserves the trust of the people. In 19:13 the plural "cornerstones" refers to the leaders of Egypt. But Egypt's political and religious leaders were not able to save the nation in the Day of Judgment. The rock or quarry from which Israel was cut probably refers to Abraham (51:1–2).

Rocks and stones also symbolize obstacles in one's pathway. The Lord would prove to be a stumbling stone for Israel and Judah because they refused to revere Him (8:13–14). After the Exile, however, the remnant would be able to return to Jerusalem. No obstacle would stand in their way because all the stones that blocked the highway would be removed (57:14; 62:10).

The Highway

The theme of the highway has both literal and metaphorical significance. Isaiah was especially concerned about building a straight highway so that the exiles could return to Jerusalem (cf. 11:16). Physical obstacles—such as mountains, rocks, and lack of water—could indeed have blocked the way, but the real problems were of a political and spiritual nature. Thus when Isaiah emphasized the smooth road through the wilderness (40:3–4; 42:16; 49:11; 57:14; and 62:10), he had in mind the chain of events that would result in Cyrus's decree that permitted the exiles to return. God would in fact make all of Cyrus's ways straight (45:13). God would enable him to reach his goals of conquest and of freeing the exiles (cf. 45:2).

Earlier in the book, Isaiah noted that God makes the way of the righteous level and smooth (26:7). Those who walk "in the way of your laws" (26:8) can avoid the pitfalls of sin and lead productive and happy lives.

Animals and Birds

The two best-known examples of animal symbolism are also the most difficult to interpret. Leviathan is called the "gliding serpent . . . the monster of the sea" (27:1). In Job 41:1 Leviathan seems to be equated with the crocodile. Clearly, Leviathan represents an evil power, perhaps Egypt. Another powerful monster named Rahab is mentioned in 30:7 and in 51:9. This time the identification with Egypt is more explicit, but the nature of the animal is more obscure. Perhaps the crocodile or a sea creature is referred to.

The armies of foreign powers are called "beasts of the

field" in 56:9. The "wild oxen" who are judged in 34:7 may be the leaders of Edom. Cyrus is the "bird of prey" summoned by God to punish Babylon (46:11). The symbolism of a powerful bird also is found in 8:8, where the "outspread wings" of the armies of Assyria cover the land of Judah.

Israel's watchmen are compared with mute dogs that have voracious appetites (56:10–11). Sinners are like sheep that have gone astray (53:6), and their plans are as deadly as the eggs of vipers (59:5). According to 53:7, the Servant of the Lord "was led like a lamb to the slaughter" and was silent before his shearers. The young men of Jerusalem fainted in battle and lay in the streets "like antelope caught in a net" (51:20).

Parts of the Body

Starting with the first chapter (where Israel is portrayed as a person full of wounds and welts from head to toe—1:6), Isaiah used the body to illustrate man's moral and spiritual condition. The eyes, the ears, and the heart are especially emphasized. Those who are blind are walking in the darkness of sin (6:10; 29:18; 59:10). The deaf have refused to respond to the Word of God (29:18; 48:8), and those with calloused hearts do not understand His ways (6:10). "Heart" (*lēb*) is sometimes translated "mind," for a hardened heart is probably best rendered in English as a "closed mind" (cf. 44:18). In the messianic age, however, spiritual responsiveness is reflected in restored sight and hearing (cf. 32:3–4; 35:5).

The mouth of the Messiah is compared to a sword (49:2) or a rod (11:4) because of the authority of His word. His determination is reflected in the statement that He set His face like flint (50:7). A bronze forehead and iron neck, however, symbolized Israel's stubbornness (48:4).

It was Israel's shoulder that bore the yoke of Assyrian oppression, but that burdensome yoke would be broken off (9:4; 10:27). The shoulder signified the bearing of governmental responsibility for the Wonderful Counselor and for Eliakim (9:6; 22:22).

Another important symbol is the hand, or arm, of the Lord. God was angry with Israel, so His hand was raised to strike them down (5:25). From 9:12 to 10:4 there are four references to God's upraised hand (cf. 9:17, 21). It was the Lord's powerful arm that destroyed Egypt when He ransomed His people (50:2; 51:9; cf. Deut. 4:34), and Isaiah promised that this same arm would rescue the remnant from Babylon (52:10; 59:1). In His mercy the Lord protects the Servant "in the shadow of his hand" (49:2), and Israel as a whole is strengthened and upheld by God's "righteous right hand" (41:10).

Marriage and Childbirth

The covenant relationship between God and Israel was like a marriage, so Israel's unfaithfulness is described as adultery. She loved other "husbands," the idols of surrounding nations, and she burned with lust and worshiped them (57:3, 5–6). Jerusalem, the once-faithful city, had "become a harlot" (1:21). The deteriorating relationship between God and Israel was compared to divorce (50:1). The Babylonian captivity was like a separation or divorce; God sent His people away from Judah, just as He had sent the northern kingdom into captivity in Assyria (cf. Jer. 3:8). During those years in captivity, Judah was like a widow, alone and humiliated (54:4; cf. 47:8–9), but the restoration of the land would renew the marriage. The Lord would be Judah's husband (54:5), and the nation would be called "Beulah" land, a land that is married (62:4). Strangely, Isaiah 62:5 states that Judah's sons would marry her. This probably means that the people would return from exile and take possession of the once-deserted land.

Just as the birth of children brings joy into a marriage, so Zion, the city of Jerusalem, would rejoice over the many children she would suddenly possess. The Exile had made Jerusalem a barren woman, but the return from Babylon would increase her family at such an astonishing rate that Jerusalem would not remember being in labor. She would have so many children that her borders would need to be extended (49:20–21; 54:1–2). In 66:7–8 Jerusalem's population explosion is compared to a mother who gives birth before her labor pains begin! Those who rejoice over Jerusalem are able to draw resources from her as a baby who nurses at her breasts (66:10–11). This symbolism is reversed in 60:16. There Jerusalem drinks the milk of the nations; the riches of the nations will be brought to her (60:5).

Often in Isaiah the pain associated with childbirth is a symbol of great distress. When the judgment of the Lord strikes the nations, men are filled with pain and anguish and "writhe like a woman in labor" (13:8). Isaiah himself was racked with pain when he heard about Babylon's collapse (21:3). The dilemma faced by King Hezekiah during Sennacherib's advance against Jerusalem in 701 B.C. is likened to the crisis of a woman in labor who has no strength to deliver (37:3).

Garments and Adornment

Clothes usually reflect one's status and state of mind. In Isaiah sackcloth signifies mourning and distress, and beautiful clothes signify joy and prosperity. At times finery could indicate pride, as in the case of the haughty women of Zion whose lovely garments and expensive jewelry would be replaced by sackcloth and baldness (cf. 3:16–24). The beautiful city of Samaria was like a wreath of flowers that would fade and be trampled underfoot (28:1–4). Clothes also wore out or were eaten by moths, and even "the earth will wear out like a garment" (51:6). So-called "righteous acts," which were really hypocritical, are compared with filthy rags—probably menstrual rags—because they were unclean (64:6).

The most important symbolic value of clothes is strength. The Lord clothed Himself in "garments of vengeance" as He marched forth to defeat the enemy (59:17). In the day of victory the Lord "will be a glorious crown . . . for the remnant of his people" and "a source of strength" for the warriors in Israel (28:5–6). Isaiah 52:1 states the issue most clearly. Captive Jerusalem is told: "Clothe yourself with strength. Put on your garments of splendor." Like a priest with his headdress or like a bride adorned with her jewels, Israel was to rejoice in her rescue from Babylon (61:10). The same verse mentions the "garments of salvation" and the "robe of righteousness" (cf. 61:3). The returning Jews would be like ornaments (49:18), and even the restored city of Jerusalem will have "gates of sparkling jewels" and "walls of precious stones" (54:12). Similarly Jerusalem will be "a crown of splendor in the Lord's hand" (62:3). Such beauty will symbolize the salvation and righteousness that will characterize the land in that day.

Vineyards and Wine

Israel was a land full of vineyards, and Isaiah made many references to the vines and their products. In 3:14 and in 5:1–7, the nation of Israel is portrayed as the vineyard of the Lord— well cared for but ruined by sin and corruption. The picture changes in 27:2–6 where Israel becomes a fruitful vineyard that will "fill all the world with fruit" (v. 6).

Treading the winepress was normally a joyous time at the grape harvest (cf. 16:10), but in 63:2–6 the Lord tramples the nations in judgment. The grapes represent the blood that is spattered on His garments. God's judgment is also linked with wine that the Lord gives to Israel and the nations to make them drunk. Those who drink from this "cup of wrath" stagger and fall (51:17, 22). In 19:14 "a spirit of dizziness" makes the leaders of Egypt stagger about like drunkards, and in 29:9 the prophets of Judah are overcome by a spiritual stupor. The earth itself "reels like a drunkard" as the judgment of God is unleashed (24:20; cf. 63:6).

Wine also appears as a symbol of deep spiritual blessing. The great messianic banquet will feature "the best of meats and the finest of wines" (25:6), and those who are spiritually thirsty can enjoy wine and milk and "delight in the richest of fare" (55:1–2). When God creates the new heavens and new earth, joy and prosperity will be reflected in the planting of vineyards and the eating of their fruit (65:21).

Occupations and Instruments

Like the Book of Psalms, the Book of Isaiah often refers to the shepherd and his work. God is the shepherd who tends the flock of Israel and leads them back home (40:11). During the first Exodus, Moses brought Israel through the sea as "the shepherd of his flock" (63:11). The Gentile ruler who would be

God's instrument of deliverance in the New Exodus was Cyrus, King of Persia (44:28). But the shepherd symbol could be used negatively to refer to the false prophets of Israel, blind watchmen who were called "shepherds who lack understanding" (56:11).

Since rulers were commonly called shepherds (cf. Jer. 23:2–4), the shepherd's rod could be referred to as the ruler's staff, a symbol of power. Six times the words "rod" and "scepter" (also translated as "club" or "bar"), *šēḇeṭ* and *maṭṭêh*, occur in parallelism. God used Assyria as a rod or club to punish the nations (10:5, 24), but the Lord's scepter would eventually shatter that nation (9:4; 10:15; 30:31–32). Babylon would follow Assyria and strike down many nations, but the Lord would break her rod as well (14:5). The authority of Israel's ruler is also represented by the "key to the house of David," mentioned only in 22:22.

A number of passages refer to the shepherd's tent. As Creator, God stretched out the heavens like a tent (40:22; cf. 42:5; 44:24; 45:12; 48:13; 51:13), and His coming is compared to tearing the curtains of the sky (64:1). The human body is called "a shepherd's tent" (38:12), and twice Jerusalem is described in terms of a tent (33:20; 54:2). David's "tent" in 16:5 refers to his family, which would produce a descendant to continue his dynasty (cf. 7:2, 13; 22:22).

God's work as creator is also related to the work of a potter. He is the potter and man is the clay, a mere potsherd that cannot complain about the way he was made or demean the reputation of the potter (29:16; 45:9; 64:8).

The life of the farmer is reflected in the imagery of threshing at harvest time. Israel's punishment is compared to being "crushed on the threshing floor" (21:10), and her regathering involves some judgment against the nations (27:12). Whatever the level of punishment should be, God will thresh in the proper way at the proper time (28:27–28). In the future, Israel will become a mighty threshing sledge that will crush the nations and reduce them to chaff (41:15).

The same verse that describes death as taking down a shepherd's tent (38:12) also speaks of it as being cut off from the loom. Life is like a cloth that a weaver rolls up and then severs from the loom. Hezekiah feared that the last thread had been woven into the fabric of his life.

Cities and Countries

Several names in Isaiah seem to represent more than their usual geographical entities. The easiest to identify are Sodom and Gomorrah, used to signify Jerusalem in 1:10. Unfortunately Jerusalem's sin was as defiant as Sodom's (3:9), and her punishment was to be almost as severe. Two of Israel's closest neighbors also play a symbolic role in Isaiah. Moab and Edom were bitter enemies of Israel and Judah, a fact that helped to bring God's judgment on them (cf. 15:1–16:14). In the more apocalyptic sections, Moab and Edom represent a world system opposed to God. The city that is ruined and battered (cf. 24:10, 12; 25:2) is not a literal city in Moab (cf. 25:10), and the judgment that devastates Edom and Bozrah (cf. 34:5–10; 63:1–6) is a judgment against all the nations.

A clearer symbolic meaning is attached to the country of Babylon. The Chaldean kingdom of Nebuchadnezzar ruled the world from 605–539 B.C., but its collapse did not mean the end of Babylon as an enemy of God. Revelation 17 and 18 describe the destruction of the New Babylon, a nation, or empire, that will rise up to oppose God when Christ returns.

Warfare

When war broke out, troops were sometimes summoned by raising banners on a hill (cf. 5:26; 13:2; 18:3). The use of the banner as a rallying point is applied by Isaiah to the gathering of the exiles. In 11:10 the Messiah, "the Root of Jesse," serves as a banner for the peoples, and Isaiah refers to this banner for the nations three more times (11:12; 49:22; 62:10). The Gentiles would help the Jews return to Jerusalem. Another signal, used on occasion in conjunction with the banner, was the trumpet (cf. 18:3). According to 27:13, "a great trumpet will sound" and will summon the Jews back home.

Horses and chariots gave armies mobility and striking power, so the swiftness and effectiveness of the Lord's judgment is compared to chariots that come like a whirlwind (66:15; cf. 19:1). The whip that urged on the horses probably stands behind the symbolism of the "overwhelming scourge" ("whip," *šôṭ*) that struck Jerusalem (28:15, 18; cf. Nah. 3:2). The armies of Assyria and Babylon inflicted punishment on her. Before long, however, God would lash Assyria with a whip, and her power would be broken (10:26).

Victorious armies divided the plunder of the enemy and rejoiced in their triumph. The great victory of the Servant of the Lord over sin and Satan is compared with dividing spoils among the strong (53:12).

Part II

AN ANALYSIS
OF ISAIAH

5

OPENING MESSAGES AND THE CALL OF ISAIAH
1:1–6:13

THE INTRODUCTION (1:1–31)

One could reasonably argue that the first six chapters of the Book of Isaiah are introductory in nature. Chapter 1 forms a fitting introduction to the entire book. It contains a summary of the major themes developed by Isaiah—the sinfulness of the nation (vv. 1–15), God's invitation to repentance (vv. 18–20), and the prediction of both judgment and salvation (vv. 24–31). The fact that chapter 2 begins with a new heading is another indication that chapter 1 stands alone as an introduction.

We have already discussed the title in 1:1. Three of the four kings mentioned were classified as basically good. The fourth, Ahaz, was the opposite. Even during Isaiah's ministry under godly kings, the majority of the people lived pagan lives.

The Pitiful Condition of Israel (1:1–9)

Chapter 1 follows the pattern of a lawsuit. God calls heaven and earth as witnesses of His indictment against Israel (cf. Deut. 30:19). The nation owed God the respect and honor of a father, but instead they rebelled against Him. Three different words are used in the chapter to portray rebellion. The idea of "political revolt" is basic to the term found in verses 2 and 28 (pāšaʻ). "Turning aside," or "deviation," best translates the word used in verses 5 and 23 (*sûr*), and "bitterness" is the root behind "rebel" in verse 20 (*mārâ*).

Rebellion is one of the most frequently mentioned sins in Isaiah. According to the law, a father had the power to bring a rebellious son before the elders and to recommend that he be stoned to death (Deut. 21:18–21). Israel's position was precarious indeed. Compared with ignorant animals, the nation showed a total lack of understanding. She refused to acknowledge her Lord and Master.

The picture painted in verses 4–6 is not a pretty one. "Loaded" with guilt literally means "heavy," just as Abram was "heavy" or "rich" in livestock, silver, and gold (Gen. 13:2). But the resources of his descendants consisted of a superabundance of sin and corruption. Enmeshed in evil, they abandoned the God of their fathers. In the last half of verse 4, the figure changes to the marriage relationship. Like an unfaithful wife, Israel had become estranged from "the Holy One of Israel." This is the first of twenty-six occurrences of this distinctive name for God in the Book of Isaiah.

Israel's sin had resulted in severe punishment and had left the nation in a pitiable condition. Only a "heart transplant" could restore her to health. As I noted earlier, several of the terms employed in verses 5 and 6 occur again in chapter 53. The Suffering Servant was afflicted and beaten that He might redeem mankind from their moral and spiritual plight.

The sinfulness of the nation left its mark on the surface of the land. Punishment involved invasion and devastation at the hands of cruel foreigners like the Assyrians. It may well be that the isolation implied in verse 8 reflects Sennacherib's capture of most of Judah in 701 B.C. The "shelter" and "hut" were frail structures that were unable to withstand a storm (24:20).

The Sins of the Nation (1:10–17)

By referring to Sodom and Gomorrah in verses 9 and 10, Isaiah hoped to impress on the people the seriousness of their situation. Their superficial attempt at being religious could not save them. They continued to bring large numbers of sacrifices, but their lack of true devotion vitiated the intended effect of the offerings. God requires His worshipers to have clean hands and a pure heart, and they had neither (Ps. 24:4). The quality of one's worship—not the quantity of outward deeds—is most important. As God said in verse 11, "I have had more than enough of burnt offerings." The same word is translated "satisfied" (*śāba'*) in 53:11. God was *satiated* with Israel's sacrifices, but the one sacrifice of Christ fully satisfied His demands.

There was nothing intrinsically wrong with the sacrificial system or with the special holy days mentioned in verses 13 and 14. God had ordained these days in the law, but the activities of the people on those days had become as detestable as the sacrifice of a dog or a pig (cf. 66:3). Even the prayers of God's people were futile and would go unanswered (1:15).

Verses 15b–17 partially explain why God refused to accept Israel's worship. In particular the leaders of the nation were guilty of oppressing the poor and of refusing to aid the helpless. The excesses of these leaders had even led to bloodshed. Throughout the book, Isaiah condemned those who perverted justice (10:1–2; 58:6–7). Nine short, successive imperatival statements exhorted the people to change their ways.

The Choice Between Repentance and Judgment (1:18–31)

The situation was not hopeless, however, and verses 18 through 20 reveal the possibility of forgiveness. Israel's blood-stained hands could be made clean if she repented. The people had to choose between obedience and rebellion, between eating the produce of the land and being "eaten" by the sword. In chapter 53 we learn that the obedience of the Servant provides the basis for all cleansing from sin.

Verses 21–23 contain a short lament over the condition of Jerusalem. She was a prostitute because she had abandoned the Lord and turned to the worship of idols (cf. vv. 4, 29–30). To make matters worse, dishonesty, bribery, and murder had seriously diluted the quality of life for the Jews.

In view of Jerusalem's sinful state, the Lord had no recourse but to pronounce judgment against her. He would take drastic steps to purify the land. Verse 24 provides one of the greatest concentrations of divine names in Isaiah (cf. 54:5), thus underscoring the authority of the Judge. "Lord" ('ādôn) stresses God's sovereignty. "Lord Almighty" (YHWH ṣᵉbā'ôt) combines the covenant name for God ("He who is with us") with a word meaning "hosts" or "armies," referring either to the armies of Israel or to the angels. "Mighty One" ('ᵃbîr) is an epithet also used of a powerful animal. As a divine name, it appears in Genesis 49:24 where God intervened for the patriarchs, and it also appears in Isaiah 49:26 and in 60:16. In these other verses the phrase is always "the Mighty One of Jacob."

The enemies of this mighty God were the Israelites themselves. God was going to punish them to restore the nation. In the future, Jerusalem would no longer be called a harlot because she would be faithful to the Lord. Verses 27 and 28 draw a contrast between the redemption of Zion (Jerusalem) as a whole and the perishing of individuals in Zion who refuse to repent. This is elaborated on more in 65:8–15.

The final verses of chapter 1 condemn the idolatry in which many Jews had become involved. According to 65:3 and 66:17, pagan sacrifices were offered in the gardens that were mentioned in 1:29, and 57:5 implies that sexual immorality accompanied rites under the oak trees. Such worship would be judged with unending fire. The use of fire as a means of punishment or cleansing is also seen in 4:4; 10:17; 26:11; 34:9–10; and in 66:24.

THE PEACE OF THE MESSIANIC AGE (2:1–4)

Isaiah's prophetic message proper begins with chapter 2, the first of four chapters that date from the earliest period of his ministry. These chapters contain messages given after Isaiah's call (ch. 6), but they set the stage to make the description of that call most effective.

The opening section has an introduction (2:1–4) and a conclusion (4:2–6). Both paragraphs deal with the future, stressing restoration and peace. The intervening material primarily refers to the contemporary situation, directing attention to the Day of the Lord (2:12). The phrase "in that day" occurs seven times in these chapters (2:11, 17, 20; 3:7, 18; 4:1, 2). The introduction (2:1–4) also appears in Micah 4:1–3, and it is difficult to know who first wrote these famous words. The paragraph is a more integral part of the text of Micah, and it may well be that Isaiah adapted this passage from his contemporary's prophecy. Similarly, Amos began his prophecy (Amos 1:2) with a quotation from Joel 3:16.

The theme of the "mountain of the Lord" is an important one in Isaiah. Often the prophet refers to the "holy mountain" in passages that depict the coming of Jews and Gentiles to Jerusalem in the last days (11:9; 27:13; 56:7; 57:13; 65:11, 25; 66:20). Most of these verses occur in contexts that describe the peace and prosperity of the future age. One writer calls this movement of Gentiles to Jerusalem the "pilgrimage of the nations."[1]

Sometimes *last days* refers in a general way to "future days" (Gen. 49:1), but the New Testament makes it clear that in a technical, eschatological sense, the *last days* began with the first coming of Christ (Acts 2:17; Heb 1:2). Most of the events portrayed in 2:1–4, however, await His second coming for their fulfillment. At that time, nations will be judged, worldwide peace will be a reality, and Jerusalem will be the governing center of the world.

In its attempt to foster peace among nations, the United Nations uses verse 4 as a motto. From a different perspective, Israel sometimes displays part of verse 3 in front of the sacred Western Wall in Jerusalem: "The law will go out from Zion, the word of the Lord from Jerusalem." Both dreams will be fully realized only during the millennial rule of Christ.

THE DAY OF THE LORD (2:5–22)

In verse 5 Isaiah returns his readers to the present. Since very little in the content of verses 2–4 was true of eighth-century Judah, Isaiah exhorted the people to return to the Lord and to obey His word.

The rest of the chapter describes the actual situation of Judah and her impending judgment. Verses 6–9 are a prayer to

[1] Otto Kaiser, *Isaiah 1–12*, trans. R. A. Wilson (London: SCM, 1972), p. 27.

the Lord. By means of their many sins (cf. 1:4), Israel had forsaken Him. Therefore He abandoned them. The nation was "full" of four different things that indicated her reliance on foreign gods, foreign alliances, military might, and money. Each of these items was specifically forbidden in Deuteronomy 17:16–17 and 18:10–11. Isaiah 30 is a sad commentary on the futility of such resources, most of which entered Israel as the result of trade with foreigners.

A number of refrains occur in this chapter as the horrible consequences of the nation's sin build to a climax in verse 21. Verses 8, 18, and 20 refer to idols that eventually would prove completely useless to their owners (cf. 30:22; 31:7). Verses 9, 11, and 17 refer to the divine humbling of men, and this humbling is spoken of as a corollary of God's exaltation.

The most developed refrain occurs in verses 10, 19, and 21 where flight from judgment is described. Lines 3 and 4 of each verse remain constant: "From dread of the Lord and the splendor of his majesty"; but the opening two lines are expanded until the "rocks" and "ground" of verse 10 become "caverns in the rocks" and "overhanging crags" in verse 21. Verses 19 and 21 also add an extra line: "When he rises to shake the earth." The picture is one of increasing desperation as men try to avoid God's judgment.

This description of the Day of the Lord is derived from times of severe oppression when the Israelites literally took refuge in caves and holes in the ground. Centuries earlier both the Midianites and the Philistines had terrorized Israel in this fashion (Judg. 6:1–6; 1 Sam. 13:6). From Isaiah's standpoint the coming judgment was related to God's use of Assyria and Babylon against Israel, but the culmination of God's judgment will occur during the Tribulation (Rev. 6:15).

Isaiah probably included the judgment of world powers as part of the "near fulfillment." The reference to the proud cedars of Lebanon is close to the description of Assyria and its king in 10:12–14. At the end of chapter ten, the collapse of the Assyrian empire is compared with the felling of a cedar tree (10:33–34).

The severity of God's judgment against man's pride emphasizes the seriousness of that sin. God regards pride as an attempt on man's part to assume the prerogatives of deity (cf.

14:13–14). In fact the word translated "majesty" (*gā'ôn*) in verses 10, 19, and 21 is the normal word that is translated "pride" when applied to men. In his fallen nature man longs to be independent of God's control (Ps. 2:2–3).

Verse 22 shows the folly of relying on leaders of one's own country or of foreign lands. Human rulers cannot take the place of God because they are all mortal and will come under His judgment. Far too often Israel looked for help to Egypt or Assyria, only to be disappointed.

JUDGMENT AGAINST A DEFIANT NATION
(3:1–4:1)

The Condemnation of the Leaders (3:1–15)

The previous verse (2:22) serves as a transition to chapter 3 and its condemnation of the leaders of Judah. In the coming judgment, the rulers of the land will be removed through death or deportation. Every kind of "supply and support" will be taken away. Isaiah arranged these items in five pairs, plus a sixth group with three terms. The first pair mentions the shortage of the basic necessities of life and may reflect conditions during a siege. Each of the other groups includes military, political, or religious leaders. When Nebuchadnezzar won the submission of Jerusalem in 597 B.C., captains, warriors, and craftsmen were among his ten thousand captives (2 Kings 24:14).

The reference to the "soothsayer" and "enchanter" (vv. 2–3) does not mean that they were considered legitimate leaders. The point is that all kinds of assistance—legitimate and illegitimate—would be unavailable (Hos. 3:4). Unhappily, however, the people resorted to the latter much too frequently (cf. 8:19).

Without leadership, the country would suffer under inept rule or anarchy. Society would be in upheaval, and no one even partially qualified would want to rule. Otto Kaiser remarks that such a chaotic condition resembled the state of affairs in Germany after World War II.[2] The "heap of ruins" in verse 6 is

---

[2]Ibid., p. 42.

cognate to the word "overthrown" in 1:7. Both times it is used, the following context refers to Sodom (1:9–10; 3:9), the classic example of an overthrown city.

Verses 8–26 list additional reasons for the coming calamity. Like the Sodomites, the people of Judah were defiant and made no attempt to hide their sin. Oppression was common. Men in authority took advantage of the poor and deceived the people. God said that these were the leaders who "ruined my vineyard" (v. 14)—the first time the significant symbol of the vineyard was used to refer to the nation of Israel (cf. 5:1–7).

The Condemnation of the Women (3:16–4:1)

Isaiah placed part of the blame for Israel's plight on the behavior of her women (vv. 16–26) because the behavior of a country's women powerfully influences that country's morals and spiritual condition. The "daughters of Zion"—like the leaders of chapter 2—were guilty of pride, of "walking," we would say, "with their noses in the air." In an Eastern culture the way a woman walked portrayed her attitude.

The women of Israel were proud of their clothes and jewelry, which they sought to display ostentatiously. They were obsessed with looking beautiful, and they used their charms to flirt with men. Perhaps the "crescent" ornaments mentioned in verse 18 were a sign of idolatry because they were popular with the Midianites and other worshipers of the moon god "Nanna," or "Sin" (Judg. 8:21, 26). In Canaan crescent-shaped ornaments were the symbol of the goddess Astarte.

Special judgment would fall on the heads of the women. They would be disgraced by baldness (vv. 17, 24), and verses 18–23 list twenty-one articles of clothing, jewelry, and other accessories that would be taken from them. In verse 24 Isaiah made five contrasts between the attractiveness of the women and their future destitution. The effective stylistic use of "instead" is repeated in 61:3 where despair is turned into joy and beauty.

According to verse 25, the great change in the status of women will be due to Israel's military defeat (cf. vv. 1–3). The women who were not dragged off into exile would find a shortage of men. Their desire to "take hold" of one man (4:1) is similar to the seizing of a potential leader in 3:6. Both are contrary to normal patterns and are signs of a society in turmoil. The "disgrace" of 4:1 is that of childlessness and widowhood. To improve their situation even slightly, the desperate women would be willing to support themselves if they could be married. What a change from the luxury and smug complacency described in 3:16–23!

A DAY OF CLEANSING AND PEACE (4:2–6)

Isaiah's opening message ends with five verses of hope (4:2–6). For the first time *in that day* introduces a scene of joy and peace. After judgment comes salvation because God will purge away sin and filth on behalf of the holy remnant. The pride and vanity of men and women will be replaced with a legitimate pride in the purified land and its ruler. There will be a proper sense of beauty and adornment.

The word "Branch" (v. 2; *ṣemaḥ*) is a messianic title related to other terms for "branch" and "shoot" in 11:1 (*ḥōṭer, nēṣer*) and in 53:2 (*yônēg*). Further references to the fruitfulness of the "family tree" of David are found in Jeremiah 23:5 and in Zechariah 3:8 and 6:12. Under the rule of Christ, justice will again prevail in Jerusalem.

The terminology in verses 5 and 6 is based on Israel's wilderness experience when the pillar of cloud and fire protected them from the enemy day and night. The provision of refuge and shelter contrasts sharply with the flight to the caves and rocks described in chapter 2. Although *shelter* (*sukkâ*) signified loneliness and flimsy protection in 1:8, the meaning is quite different in 4:6. The Israelites lived in shelters or booths during their wanderings in the wilderness. The phrase *Feast of Tabernacles* contains the same word (Lev. 23:40–43).

This short but important paragraph (4:2–6) has significant parallels in 28:5–8, 15–17, and in 65:18.

THE SONG OF THE VINEYARD AND THE INDICTMENT OF ISRAEL (5:1–30)

The Song (5:1–7)

The prophets used a variety of means to communicate their messages. In chapter 5 Isaiah used a song to compare Israel and a vineyard, as is done in the Psalms (80:8–12; cf. Isa. 3:14). The first verse of the song contains several examples of inner rhyme, or assonance.* It was a love song, and the imagery of vineyards was natural to a romantic setting (cf. Song of Sol. 4:10; 8:11–12; Ezek. 33:32). The vineyard Isaiah described was given extraordinary care. It received plenty of sunlight and was planted with the best vines available (the valley of Sorek is named after this kind of vine). The most distinctive feature about the vineyard was the watchtower, though a more modest "shelter" was usually employed for keeping watch (cf. 1:8). With a tower, the watchmen were well-protected and fully able to care for the vineyard. The mention of a tower in Matthew 21:33 proves that Christ's parable of the vineyard was based on Isaiah's song—a fact that the chief priests and Pharisees immediately understood (Matt. 21:33–41; Luke 20:9–16).

The song comes to an abrupt and unromantic end in verse 2 with the revelation of the disappointing harvest. The owner of the vineyard speaks in verses 3–6, revealing how he will destroy his vineyard. The vineyard will be abandoned, its walls and hedges gone. It will be fit for nothing more than briers and thorns (the alliterated pair "briers and thorns" [*šāmîr* and *šayit*] occurs five more times—7:23–25; 9:18; 27:4).

The vineyard represents Israel, and the vineyard's owner is God. Verse 7 makes that clear and contains what may be the best examples of wordplay, or paronomasia, found in the Old Testament. The word for "justice" (*mišpāt*) sounds almost the same as "bloodshed" (*mišpāh*), and "righteousness" (*sᵉdāqâ*) is very close to "cries of distress" (*sᵉʿāqâ*). The nation may have appeared to be a land of justice, but the truth was precisely the opposite.

---

*Note *'āšîrâ* and *šîrat*, *lîdîdî* and *dôdî*.

The Six Woes Against the Nation (5:8–30)

The extent of Judah's corruption is explained in the remaining verses of the chapter. Six woes are pronounced (vv. 8, 11, 18, 20, 21, 22), two of which (vv. 11, 22) condemn drunkenness and the perversions it brings. The reference to the misuse of wine in verses 10–12 and in verse 22 may be related to the vineyard theme of the song. The judgment sections in verses 9 and 10, 13–15, and in 24 and 25 correspond to the "woes," the last four of which are given in rapid succession and fall between the second and third judgment passages.

Verse 8 presents the *first woe*, one that is directed against the wealthy landowners. According to the law, land could only be leased—never sold on a permanent basis (Num. 27:7–11). Covetous individuals evidently tried to work around this law and to buy the property of the poor. First Kings 21:1–6 records the diligent efforts of Naboth to retain his family inheritance, though King Ahab pressured him to sell it.

The judgment on the greedy was twofold: they would not get to occupy their estates for very long, and their lands would produce meager harvests. The first judgment was probably related to the coming exile (v. 13), and the second judgment was a common occurrence in times of national sin (cf. Hag. 2:16–17). The poor crops may also have been due to the curse of verse 6. Both examples in verse 10 use a ten to one ratio: ten acres produce one bath (about six gallons) of wine, and one homer (about six bushels) of seed will yield an ephah (one-tenth of a homer) of grain. This "reverse tithe" is a hint that the covetous men involved were not the least bit interested in bringing contributions to the sanctuary. In both cases the harvests were only a tiny fraction of what could normally be expected.

The *second woe* (v. 11) decries the drunken condition of the nation. A similar charge is leveled against the leaders in Ecclesiastes 10:16–17. Completely oblivious to the purposes of God, such people continue to drink and to listen to raucous music (cf. Amos 6:5–6).

As in the case of Belshazzar's feast (Dan. 5), the partying will end in death or in exile. Sheol, with its insatiable appetite (cf. Hab. 2:5), will swallow up the revelers from all classes of people. By bringing about such a judgment, the Lord will reveal that His holy standards cannot be ignored without dire consequences. Verses 15 and 16a borrow a refrain from Isaiah 2:9, 11, and 17. The punishment of the proud shows that God is indeed the sovereign one.

The imagery behind the *third woe* (v. 18) is obscure. Men seemed to be enslaved by their own sin, bogged down by wicked methods and goals (cf. Hos. 11:4). As such they were unable to assume the pose that they accused God of assuming (v. 19), that of dragging His heels. As I noted earlier, this verse is important because it combines elements of the name "Maher-Shalal-Hash-Baz" (cf. 8:1) with the title "Holy One." The mocking attitude of the men stirred Isaiah to tell about the awesomeness of the Holy God (ch. 6).

Woe four (v. 20) is aimed at those who perverted reality by twisting the truth to their own liking. They were those who would acquit the wicked and condemn the righteous (Prov. 17:15). Among their number were those who called Baal "God" and who called the arrogant "blessed" (Mal. 3:15).

Woes five and *six* (vv. 21–23) are closely related to the *fourth woe*, which may be the reason why no words of judgment intervene. Those who invent new definitions for *good* and *evil* think that they are wiser than God. They do not hesitate to take bribes and are not concerned if drunkenness impairs their judgment. Such men excel only in mixing drinks, a reference to the various spices used to make wine and beer more stimulating (v. 22).

Verses 24 and 25 move back to the theme of judgment, portraying the burning anger of God that consumes His people. The language of verse 24 is close to 1:4, but this time it is the *word* of the Holy One that is spurned. Rejecting the Lord involves ignoring His word.

The power of this judgment is emphasized by God's upraised hand. In fact *hand* can often be translated as power. God struck His people repeatedly (cf. 1:5), but additional punishment lay ahead. The last two lines of verse 25 are a refrain that is used 4 times in chapters 9 and 10.

In verses 26–30 the armies of Assyria are described as

God's agent for inflicting punishment. They were summoned by the raised banner, an expression used throughout Isaiah (11:10, 12; 13:2; 18:3; 49:22). A pole with a banner or flag was placed on a hill as a signal for the troops to gather. Sometimes the banner summoned the nations for more positive purposes, such as bringing the Jews back to Jerusalem (49:22). Here, however, the purpose was war, and a powerful army swung into motion. The speed with which they advanced corresponds to the mockers' taunt that challenged God to take swift action (v. 19).

The army would be in peak condition when it reached its target area. The long journey would not tire out the troops or blunt their motivation. Their strength would be a sure sign that God was on their side (cf. 40:29–31). Like a lion, the Assyrian army would fearlessly attack the foe and fight until they were victorious.

The outlook for Israel was gloomy. The turning of light into darkness would be the punishment for those who had glibly interchanged the two (cf. v. 20). The picture of deep distress is repeated in 8:22.

ISAIAH'S CALL (6:1–13)

Isaiah is a book of contrasts. It moves from a chapter about darkness and sin to one about glory and holiness. Some scholars believe that chapter 6 is a recommissioning experience, but there are good reasons for regarding it as the account of Isaiah's original prophetic call. First, since Isaiah ministered until 700 B.C. and probably longer, it is unlikely that his prophetic work began much before the year Uzziah died (739 B.C.). Second, the response of Isaiah in verse 5 and the commission given in verses 9 and 10 are best understood as a description of his initial call. Third, several features in this chapter resemble the descriptions of the calls of Jeremiah and Ezekiel. All three accounts refer to being sent, to the word of God, and to the stubbornness of the recipients of the prophetic message (cf. Jer. 1 and Ezek. 2). The touching of Isaiah's mouth (v. 7) is identical with the experience of Jeremiah (Jer. 1:9). Fourth, as I have indicated, Isaiah had a definite reason for not presenting his call earlier.

Chapter 6 is the only true vision found in the book. The prophet was transported into the presence of God in the heavenly temple, a scene similar to that viewed by the apostle John in Revelation 4. The exaltation of the Holy God underscores Isaiah's pronouncement in 5:16 (cf. 2:11 and 17). "High" and "exalted" are also used of the Servant in 52:13.

The long, flowing robe is reminiscent of the garb of the high priest (Exod. 39:24) and of the description of the "son of man" in Revelation 1:13. Kings and other important officials customarily wore long robes as a sign of their authority.[3] In John 12:41, a passage closely related to Isaiah 6, John said that Isaiah saw the glory of Christ. All three persons of the Trinity are, in fact, associated with this chapter.

The seraphs around the throne are not mentioned elsewhere. "Seraph" means "burn," and it is used of a "darting, venomous serpent" in 14:29 and in 30:6. The seraphs correspond to the four "living creatures" of Revelation 4:8, who also have six wings and who repeat "Holy, holy, holy." Because these angelic creatures—like mankind—cannot gaze directly at the blinding glory of God, they use two of their wings to cover their faces.

The threefold repetition of "holy" expresses the infinite holiness of God. Although the number three may be an adumbration of the Trinity (cf. v. 8), it is also used to signify completeness. Compare this with the triple use of "The temple of the Lord" in Jeremiah 7:4 to indicate the people's full confidence in that sanctuary. This Holy God has chosen to reveal His glory through His handiwork in creation and in miracles. Twice (Num. 14:21–22; Ps. 72:19) the world-wide glory of God is linked with the performance of signs and wonders. In view of His vast power, the whole earth should be filled with awe.

Often the appearance of God is accompanied by an earthquake. The heavenly temple is shaken at His presence and at the power of the voices that proclaim His glory. At Mount Sinai the children of Israel were so terrified by the voice of God

[3] Albert Barnes, *Notes on the Old Testament, Isaiah,* 2 vols. (1845; reprint, Grand Rapids: Baker, 1950), 1:138.

that they begged Him to speak only with Moses (Exod. 20:18–19).

Smoke is usually present during a theophany (Exod. 19:18), and the most holy place of the earthly temple was filled with the cloud of glory (1 Kings 8:10–11). When the high priest entered the Holy of Holies on the Day of Atonement, a cloud of incense was to shroud the mercy seat.

Isaiah's reaction to the awesome sight was one of dismay because anyone who saw God expected to die on the spot (cf. Judg. 13:22). Isaiah's cry of woe resembles the six "woes" of chapter 5. So impressive was the vision that he was overwhelmed with his own sinfulness and with that of the people. The ruin he anticipated is used to refer to a devastated city in 15:1.

The emphasis on the Lord as the true King of Israel may be related to the death of Uzziah. That once great king had intruded into the priests' office and as punishment had to endure the stigma of being a leper for the rest of his life. No wonder Isaiah felt that he lived among an unclean people! At the time of Uzziah's death, Jotham had already been coregent with his father for over ten years.

Isaiah's sense of unworthiness was countered by the symbolic application of a live coal to his lips. Coals of fire from the altar were taken inside the most holy place on the Day of Atonement (Lev. 16:12), and so Isaiah was reminded that sacrifice had been made for his sins. His lips, the instrument of his prophetic ministry, were now pure. In Jeremiah's case it was the Lord's hand that touched his mouth (Jer. 1:9).

The realization that his sins were forgiven made Isaiah willing to respond to the Lord's call (v. 8), even before he knew what the task was. The invitation to serve his majestic God was a privilege he did not want to miss. Isaiah's determination did not waver when he learned how unresponsive his audience would be. Like most of the prophets, his mission was to condemn and to pronounce judgment—not a very popular assignment. Through an effective chiastic arrangement, the Lord revealed how He would make the hearts of the people "fat," their ears "heavy," and their eyes "smeared over." Just as the Lord hardened Pharaoh's heart when he refused to listen to

God's message spoken through Moses (Exod. 4:21; 7:14), so the Israelites would eventually find themselves unable to repent.

Israel's blind and deaf condition is mentioned several more times in the book (29:9; 42:19; 43:8). In the course of his ministry Isaiah learned that the Lord's assessment of Israel's spiritual state was indeed accurate. Some passages, however, anticipate a reversal of this sad situation (29:18; 35:5). One should not conclude that God had given up on all the individuals in the nation because time after time, God called on them to repent (31:6).

Verses 9 and 10 are cited in each of the synoptic Gospels in connection with the parable of the sower (Matt. 13:14–15; Mark 4:12; Luke 8:10). Christ used parables so that only His disciples would be able to understand the message. In John 12:40 the apostle used this passage to bemoan the unbelieving condition of Israel, but verse 42 notes that many individuals did believe. The blindness and deafness of the nation was not total. At the end of Acts, Paul quoted Isaiah 6:9–10 as he observed the unbelief of the Jews in Rome (28:26–27).

The last three verses of chapter 6 reveal the fate of the nation. Israel's sin would bring devastation and deportation. Although this sad truth must have deeply discouraged Isaiah, the chapter ends on a note of hope: a remnant would survive the destruction. The number preserved would be less than a tenth, and this group is compared to a stump. In 11:1 and in 53:2 the same imagery is used in a messianic sense.

The remnant may be called "holy" because the tithe was considered "holy" to the Lord. At Mount Sinai the entire nation was set apart as a "kingdom of priests" and a "holy nation" (Exod. 19:6), but only a fraction of their number lived in accord with that position. In a chapter that stresses the holiness of God, the term "holy seed" is a lofty title.

6

THE RULE OF ASSYRIA AND THE MESSIAH
7:1–12:6

The prediction that the people would ignore the preaching and advice of Isaiah was fulfilled in the prophet's encounter with Ahaz. This important event occurred in 734 B.C. when Syria and Israel tried to draw Judah into an alliance against Assyria. Since Ahaz was unwilling to cooperate, his northern neighbors attempted to overthrow him in what is usually called the Syro-Ephraimite war (see ch. 1 of this volume).

Syria and Israel were justifiably disturbed over the expansionist tendencies of Assyria, a country that was intent on creating an empire. Isaiah predicted that after initial success, the armies of Assyria would suffer total destruction (chs. 9–10). Another, more powerful kingdom would arise, and a child who would reign forever on David's throne would be born. The Spirit of the Lord would dwell on Him, and He would rule the world with justice, uphold the poor and needy, and crush the wicked. In chapters 10 and 11 Isaiah showed how Assyria would fall and how the kingdom of the Messiah would flourish.

THE SIGN OF IMMANUEL (7:1–17)

Ahaz was deeply distressed by his predicament, and his heart and the hearts of his people were badly shaken (v. 2). The same word for shake (*nûa'*) was used in 6:4, where the heavenly voices shook the doorposts and thresholds of the temple. Ahaz feared man more than God, and the word of God did not move him. His solution to his nation's problems was to appeal to the King of Assyria for help.

One day the king was at the aqueduct of the Upper Pool, probably to inspect the water supplies of the city in the light of an impending siege (v. 3). The aqueduct may have been near En-Rogel, an important spring at the southern end of Jerusalem. Isaiah and his son Shear-Jashub were sent to meet Ahaz and to calm his fears. "Shear-Jashub" means "a remnant will return," a name which incorporated both the warning and the promise of 6:11–13. Someday Judah would go into captivity, but not at the hands of her current enemies, Ephraim (Israel) and Syria, whose kings were "smoldering stubs" on the verge of losing their power.

Through Isaiah God revealed that the invasion of Judah would be unsuccessful. Neither Rezin nor Pekah possessed the might to accomplish their goals. Within sixty-five years the deportation policies of Assyria would mean the virtual elimination of Ephraim as a people, and so Isaiah urged Ahaz to "stand firm" in his faith or he would "not stand at all" (v. 9). By means of this clever wordplay, the prophet challenged the king to trust God rather than to panic.

To bolster Ahaz's faith, the Lord promised to show him a sign (vv. 10–16). But Ahaz refused to ask for a sign because he did not want to believe God's Word. His mind was already made up; he wanted to appeal to Assyria. Ahaz hid his hypocrisy behind a pious façade by pretending to be concerned to obey the command not to put God to the test (Deut. 6:16). Since God had volunteered to give him a sign, however, it would not have been sinful for Ahaz to request it.

Isaiah condemned Ahaz's attitude in no uncertain terms. The use of "my God" for "your God" in verse 13 indicates Ahaz's separation from the Lord. Ahaz exhausted God's patience, just as the festivals and feasts of the nation had wearied Him (1:14). Therefore God would give Ahaz a sign, and the king would have to listen to it. A virgin would become pregnant and give birth to a son named Immanuel—"God is with us" (7:14). Before the boy would know the difference between right and wrong, Ahaz's two enemies would be destroyed by Assyria (v. 16). But because Ahaz refused to trust

God, Assyria would invade Judah and cause great damage (v. 17).

That is the context of the famous prophecy in 7:14, a verse that has suffered greatly at the hands of interpreters. Conservatives have rightly emphasized the prophecy's messianic relationship to Christ and the Virgin Mary, but they have failed to fit the verse into its historical context. Liberals have correctly looked for a historical fulfillment in Ahaz's day, but they have misused the translation "young woman" by ignoring the messianic implications of the prophecy.

The solution to the problem may lie in the use of *virgin* (*'almâ*) in Ugaritic literature. Ugarit was a city-state located on the Mediterranean coast opposite Cyprus. Like Hebrew, Ugaritic was a Canaanite language that has been helpful in understanding Hebrew words and culture. In Ugaritic literature there is a passage that says "a virgin will give birth" (*tld btlt* is parallel to *hl ǵlmt tld bn*).[1] In its context the phrase means that a particular virgin would soon be engaged and that after her marriage she would become the mother of a son. At the time the prediction was made, she was a virgin. This kind of announcement was a blessing on the upcoming marriage.

A close study of Isaiah 7 and 8 reveals the same picture. Isaiah was about to be engaged to a prophetess. The first three verses of chapter 8 describe the engagement and marriage. After the wedding Isaiah's wife became pregnant and subsequently had a son named Maher-Shalal-Hash-Baz. The boy may have been referred to as "Immanuel" in 8:8 (cf. v. 10)—though this cannot be conclusively demonstrated—and he was to be a sign for Ahaz and his generation. In the New Testament, Isaiah 7:14 was used in a fuller sense and applied to Mary and Jesus. Mary, unlike the virgin in Isaiah's day, was still a virgin even after becoming pregnant.

This interpretation relieves the problem of making the sign of Jesus' birth somehow relate to King Ahaz. A sign must be fulfilled within a few years or it ceases to be a sign (cf. 37:30;

---

[1] Text 77:5, 7 in Cyrus H. Gordon, *Ugaritic Textbook,* 2 vols. (Rome: Pontifical Biblical Institute, 1965), 1:183. This is translated by Gordon in *Ugaritic Literature* (Rome: Pontifical Biblical Institute, 1949), pp. 63–64.

Exod. 3:12). Ahaz would have realized that soon after the birth of Isaiah's son the prophecy would be fulfilled.

The name "Immanuel" was a rebuke to Ahaz. If "God is with us," why should he have feared the enemy? In Numbers 14:9 the expression "the Lord is with us" was meant to counteract Israel's fear of the Canaanites. At that crucial juncture in their history, the nation, like Ahaz in the eighth century, chose the path of unbelief.

THE DESTRUCTIVE INVASION OF ASSYRIA
(7:18–8:10)

King Ahaz failed to recognize that the real enemy was Assyria (cf. vv. 17, 20). The Assyrians might provide temporary relief as an ally, but one day they would threaten Judah with unparalleled destruction. The terminology of verses 18–25 leans heavily on that of chapter 5. Whistling for Assyria was mentioned in 5:26. The quantity of flies and bees summoned to Judah would make escape even in crevices of the rocks impossible. Mention of the rocks and ravines, along with the phrase "in that day" (vv. 18, 20, 23), suggests that this judgment was to be be a foretaste of the "day of the Lord" (cf. 2:10–12, 19–21).

"That day" would bring disgrace and poverty. The shaving off of the beard was considered a great insult (2 Sam. 10:4–5), and the Assyrian razor would be even more cruel (v. 21). Verses 20 and 21 depict a return to the simple and "miserable food" of nomadic life.[2] Curds are much like yogurt, and both curds and honey also were mentioned in verse 15. The invasion would bring to a temporary halt all agricultural pursuits.

Verses 23–25 sound like the fulfillment of the Song of the Vineyard (5:1–7). Vineyards would be turned into "briers and thorns," which are mentioned in three successive verses (cf. 5:6). Cultivation would be impossible, and the animals would roam freely as the protective wall of 5:5 is broken down.

---

[2] Franz Delitzsch, *Biblical Commentary on the Prophecies of Isaiah,* trans. James Martin, 3d ed., 2 vols. (1877; reprint, Grand Rapids: Eerdmans, 1967), 1:221.

The opening verses of chapter 8 are related to 7:14–16, as has been shown above. Verses 1–3 are terse, and their inner connection is difficult. The function of the "reliable witnesses" holds the key to the interpretation. Witnesses were usually present when a covenant (Ps. 50:5; Josh. 24:2) or legal transaction was made, and the closest parallel to the wording in verse 2 is found in Jeremiah 32:10, 25, and 44 where Jeremiah was involved in the purchase of a field. Otto Kaiser believes that Isaiah drew up a deed registered in the name of "Quick to the plunder, swift to the spoil" (Maher-Shalal-Hash-Baz) as a symbolic act that God had given Syria and Palestine to Assyria.[3]

I agree that a legal transaction had been made, but I favor the view that a marriage contract was being attested. Marriage contracts contained references to children (Maher-Shalal-Hash-Baz, v. 1), and the marriage was considered to be fully legal only after intercourse (v. 3). This interpretation ties together an otherwise disjointed three verses. The name of the boy symbolized the looting that would ruin Judah's enemies, but the name also contained the threat of Judah's eventual plundering (vv. 5–8). Isaiah named his son in verse 3, and the child's mother apparently named him "Immanuel," according to 7:14. Other children in the Old Testament who had two names were "Benjamin," named "Ben-oni" by his mother (Gen. 35:18), and "Solomon," called "Jedidiah" by Nathan (2 Sam. 12:25). If this interpretation is correct, the time element in 8:4 would be identical with that of 7:16 (see the section on Christology for a more complete discussion of the relationship between 7:14 and 8:1ff.).[4]

Verses 5–8 present a more poetic version of the Assyrian invasion than do the corresponding verses in 7:17–20. Verses 5–8 contrast the gentle waters of Shiloah and the flooding Euphrates River. The former body of water probably is the Gihon Spring, the major source of Jerusalem's water supply.

---

[3] Otto Kaiser, *Isaiah 1–12*, trans. R. A. Wilson (London: SCM, 1972), p. 111.

[4] A somewhat technical discussion of the issues involved in an analysis of 7:14–8:22 is found in my article, "A Solution to the Immanuel Prophecy in Isaiah 7:14–8:22," *Journal of Biblical Literature* 91 (1972): 449–56.

The "gentle waters of Shiloah" may also refer symbolically to the Lord. The Euphrates River represents Assyria; a flooding river often depicted a powerful invading force (cf. Dan. 11:40). Although Judah rejoiced over Assyria's defeat of Damascus and Ephraim, Assyria would later overwhelm Judah. The reference is probably to Sennacherib's future conquest of all of Judah, with the exception of Jerusalem.

Verse 8 abruptly changes the figure to that of a large bird of prey. Then, surprisingly, Isaiah referred to Immanuel as the owner of the land. In contrast to 7:14, Immanuel now appears to be present, and this supports the identification of Maher-Shalal-Hash-Baz with Immanuel. The child was symbolic of God's presence with the nation, just as Shear-Jashub symbolized the return of the remnant to the land of Israel.

"Immanuel" occurs one more time in the phrase "for God is with us" (8:10). With words taken from 7:7–8, Isaiah emphasized God's control over the nations of the world. Just as Ephraim would be shattered, so any nation that opposed the Lord would eventually fall. This would include Assyria and Babylon, the tools of God's punishment against His own people. Only God's word and purposes would ultimately stand (40:8). E. J. Young regards chapters 13–27 as an exposition and enlargement of 8:9–10.[5]

A WARNING TO FEAR GOD (8:11–22)

For the fourth time in the chapter the Lord spoke to Isaiah (v. 11). He warned the prophet to disassociate himself from the prevailing views of the people. Jeremiah was accused of being a traitor for advocating surrender to Babylon, and Isaiah may have been castigated for his political stance regarding Assyria. But God, not Ahaz or the people, was the one Isaiah was to fear. By being faithful to the Lord, the prophet would find safety, but the Lord Himself would be a stone that both Judah and Israel would stumble over. In 1 Peter 2:6 and 8 this stone is linked with the "precious cornerstone" of Isaiah 28:16.

[5] E. J. Young, *The Book of Isaiah*, 3 vols. (Grand Rapids: Eerdmans, 1965–72), 1:413.

Verses 16–22 sum up Isaiah's important teaching in chapters 7 and 8. The sixteenth verse refers back to the legal transaction at the beginning of chapter 8. "Testimony," or "attestation," occurs only in verses 16 and 20 and in Ruth 4:7 where the removal of one's sandal before witnesses confirmed a legal transaction. The binding up of this testimony probably refers to the tying and sealing of the deed witnessed in verses 1 and 2. In the parallel passage in Jeremiah 32:14, Baruch, Jeremiah's associate, was asked to preserve in a clay jar the deeds recording his purchase of property.[6] Similarly Isaiah's disciples were requested to preserve his teaching about the coming invasion. It would be a time when God would withdraw His favor from Israel (v. 17), but Isaiah would continue to trust in Him.

Isaiah and his children were important signs for the nation (8:18), just as the virgin's son was to be a "sign" (7:14)—a further indication that Immanuel was Isaiah's second son, Maher-Shalal-Hash-Baz. His first son, Shear-Jashub, bore a name with obvious implications for the whole nation.

Sadly, though, Israel would not accept Isaiah's message. The people sought information about the future from mediums and from spiritists. Even King Saul had consulted a medium in a desperate attempt to learn the outcome of a battle, and Isaiah's contemporaries were no different (cf. 3:2). Mediums usually worked at night (1 Sam. 28:8), which may account for the emphasis on darkness in verses 20–22. Isaiah's testimony, or word, was Maher-Shalal-Hash-Baz, "Quick to the Plunder, Swift to the Spoil." As 5:19 shows, the people did not believe God would judge them, but chapter 5—like chapter 8—ends with a frightful description of the darkness and distress that would be associated with the Assyrian invasion (cf. 5:30 with 8:22). Israel's refusal to trust God brought her deep agony and despair.

Ahaz had been instructed to look upward and to ask for a sign (7:10), but in these verses Isaiah showed that the nation was

---

[6] The community at Qumran (famous for the Dead Sea Scrolls) also used jars to preserve their precious manuscripts. Cf. Frank Cross, *The Ancient Library of Qumran* (Garden City, N.Y.: Doubleday, 1961), p. 7.

looking upward and cursing God. Anyone who cursed either the king or God would be punished severely (Exod. 22:28; Lev. 24:15). It is little wonder, then, that God called the nation "these people" (v. 12) and not "my people."

THE BIRTH AND RULE OF THE MESSIAH (9:1–7)

Isaiah is a book of contrasts, moving from the discouragement and darkness of chapter 8 to the brilliant hope of chapter 9. Once more, in chapter 9 a child is the focus of attention. In 7:14 the prophet had introduced Immanuel, a veiled prophecy of the Messiah. God was with His people in the eighth century B.C. but not in the same way as when Christ, God incarnate, walked the streets of Galilee. Isaiah understood this fuller sense of "Immanuel" and depicted the glory and joy of His coming and rule.

The tribes of Zebulun and Naphtali were the first to suffer when Tiglath-Pileser III attacked Israel in 735 and 732 B.C. (2 Kings 15:29). Located in the northern part of Israel, these tribal areas were always susceptible to foreign influence. In fact Solomon had given King Hiram of Tyre twenty cities of Galilee in exchange for timber and gold (1 Kings 9:11). Even in New Testament times, cities like Nazareth did not have a good reputation, but it was to that very city that the light of Jesus came. Capernaum was another important city in Galilee where Jesus ministered (Matt. 4:13–16).

Isaiah compared God to the sun in 60:1–3, 19–20, and the concept of the Servant being a "light for the Gentiles" is prominent in 42:6 and in 49:6. Each of these passages goes back to 9:2, which predicts the coming of Christ and the light of salvation He would bring.

Like many of Isaiah's prophecies, verses 1–7 are written in the past tense. Not until the last verb in verse 7 did Isaiah use the future tense. Using the past tense as a so-called "prophetic perfect" was a technique that stressed the certainty of the fulfillment. The prophet was so sure that his predictions would come true that he spoke of them as if they had already happened.

The light of Christ would bring a reversal of the situation

in chapter 8. In place of anger, defeat, and famine there would be joy, victory, and abundance. The yoke that oppressed Israel would be removed completely, just as Gideon broke Midian's stranglehold (Judg. 7). The terminology of verse 4 is used in 10:26, a passage that predicted the fall of Assyria. Ultimately, however, the peace and joy spoken of in 9:2–7 would be fulfilled during the millennial rule of Christ. Military weapons and equipment will no longer be needed at that time (v. 5), because nations will "beat their swords into plowshares and their spears into pruning hooks" (2:4).

In verse 6 the light is finally identified: the glorious future Isaiah predicted would come through a child, a son. Isaiah's language is precise. The Son is given, for He is the eternal Son of God. He will also be a son of David (cf. v. 7), and for this reason He will have the right to shoulder the responsibilities of government. In 3:1–7 Isaiah had predicted that Judah would have a leadership crisis. Due to coming invasions, all the rulers would be exiled, including the king. Would this mean the end of the Davidic dynasty? The answer was an emphatic "No" for one was coming who would reign on David's throne.

In verse 6 four names are given to this son. Unlike "Immanuel," these names ordinarily would not have been given to Hebrew boys. Each of the names consists of two elements, one of which tends to stress the son's divine nature. "Wonderful Counselor" is literally "a Wonder of a Counselor." Miracles are often called "wonders," and in Judges 13:18 the Angel of the Lord—perhaps the preincarnate Christ—gives "Wonderful" as His name. A counselor was often necessary to help a king determine policies and to give specific advice in critical situations. David's key advisor, Ahithophel, was regarded as highly as a messenger of God would have been (2 Sam. 16:23). The Messiah, however, would not have to depend on anyone else to give Him advice.

"Mighty God" emphasizes the deity of this Ruler and His military ability. Psalm 24:8 depicts this relationship in the words "The LORD strong and mighty, the LORD mighty in battle." In Isaiah 10:21 the "Mighty God" is identified with the Holy One of Israel.

"Everlasting Father" emphasizes the eternality of the Son.

This idea is repeated two more times in verse 7, so that this incredible truth will sink in. "Father" suggests the tenderness and compassion that characterize human fathers and the protection afforded by government officials (cf. 22:21), but it also raises a trinitarian question about the distinction between the Father and the Son. Since the phrase could be translated "father of eternity," some scholars think it means "possessor" or "originator" of eternity (cf. Gen. 4:20–21). Yet Jesus Himself said, "Anyone who has seen me has seen the Father" (John 14:9). The relationship between the persons of the Trinity is intimate and mysterious.

"Prince of Peace" means that Christ will be a "peaceful prince," not a tyrant. His rule will bring a cessation of war and a wholeness, or health, to society. This aspect of His government is also mentioned in verse 7 because peace involves a reign of justice and righteousness, two elements that were sadly lacking in the lives and reigns of the contemporary kings of Israel and Judah (5:7).

All of this will be accomplished because God is jealous and zealous for His people. God will vindicate His purposes because of His deep love for Israel, a holy love that must first, however, punish sin. The last sentence of verse 7 is repeated in 37:32.

GOD'S ANGER AGAINST ISRAEL (9:8–10:4)

The sharp break in thought between verses 7 and 8 resembles the connection between 2:2–4 and 2:5–7. In 9:8 the transition is even more abrupt. Perhaps the prophet was brought back to the present by the mention of "justice and righteousness" in verse 7 because government was anything but just in his own day. Or the word "zeal" (v. 7) may have recalled the anger of the Lord against Israel's sin. The entire section is organized around a refrain that emphasizes God's wrath (9:12, 17, 21; 10:4), a refrain that first appeared in 5:25.

In these four paragraphs Isaiah condemned various sins of Israel. Verses 8–12 inveigh against the pride and arrogance of the nation. The second paragraph (vv. 13–17) decries the corrupt leadership that allowed wickedness to permeate the whole society. Civil war and cruelty against one's brother are the focal point of verses 18–21, and oppression and injustice are the cause for judgment in 10:1–4. From verses 8 and 9 one might conclude that the northern kingdom bore the brunt of these condemning words, but the mention of the Philistines in verse 12 and of Judah in verse 21 indicates that the whole nation may be in view.

The sin of pride was dealt with in detail in chapter 2. In their arrogance, citizens of Ephraim asserted that if the clay bricks crumbled, they would build with dressed stone; if the common sycamore trees were gone, they would acquire the cedars of Lebanon. Earlier in the same century, Amos had predicted that the people of Samaria would not get to live in their beautiful houses of dressed stone.

To punish the people for their pride, the Lord was helping "Rezin's foes" (v. 11), a reference to the feared Assyrians. Bands of Syrians and Philistines would also make damaging incursions against Israel, but this would only be the beginning. God's hand was poised to strike again.

Unfortunately punishment did not produce repentance, especially among the leaders. Therefore they in particular would suffer for their sins. The mention of "head and tail" and "palm branch and reed" (v. 14) expresses totality by the use of opposites. Chapter 3 used a similar style (vv. 1–3) in another passage directed against leaders. Isaiah referred to prophets as "the tail" because many of them simply parroted what the rulers wanted to hear. Isaiah 19:15 uses the same two pairs of terms to refer to Egyptian officials.

Misrule was a serious offense because of its impact on the total populace. In this instance even the fatherless and the widows were caught up in evil. Because of their own sinfulness, they received no pity from the Lord. Their words and deeds paraded their godlessness.

Such a society was spiritually as dry as tinder and ready for the fires of judgment. Verses 18–21 present a gruesome picture of hatred and strife. In verse 5 the uniforms of soldiers were "fuel for the fire," and verse 19 says that "the people will be fuel for the fire." What a change from peace to war! The scene is one of family strife (vv. 19–20) and civil war. The mention of Manasseh's battle with Ephraim may allude to the war between

Jephthah and the Ephraimites during the period of the judges. Forty-two thousand Ephraimites died in the struggle between the descendants of the two sons of Joseph! By Isaiah's time those northern tribes had joined forces to invade Judah (cf. 7:1); the battle between north and south had continued intermittently since the division of the kingdom (cf. 1 Kings 14:30).

The fourth paragraph (10:1–4) pronounces woe on those who opposed the helpless, a frequent theme in the Book of Isaiah (cf. 1:17; 5:23). Their illegally obtained wealth would be useless when disaster struck, and they would have to choose between captivity and death. Verse 4 is the clearest reference in this section to the Assyrian invasion.

THE JUDGMENT OF ASSYRIA (10:5–34)

The Folly of Assyria's Arrogance (10:5–19)

A second woe in this chapter is directed against Assyria, the nation that served as God's rod of anger (v. 5). When Assyria's judgmental work was finished, the Lord's anger would shift from Israel to Assyria.* The days of taking plunder and loot would be over (v. 6), and a remnant would return to Israel (v. 21). In other words the symbolism of "Maher-Shalal-Hash-Baz" would fade into the background, and that of "Shear-Jashub" would come to the foreground.

Assyria functioned as an instrument of judgment on behalf of God. Under the leadership of their king, this powerful nation was like a club that beat Israel's back. God's people had become godless (cf. 9:17), and they deserved to be trampled down. Therefore God sent Assyria, just as He had sent a message against Israel in 9:8. Although the Assyrian general in 36:10 was boasting when he claimed that Sennacherib had been commissioned by the Lord to destroy Judah, it was true that up to that point Assyria had been God's tool.

When the kings of Assyria conquered other nations, they

---

*A similar shift in the object of divine punishment occurred in the case of the Babylonians. God raised up the Babylonian armies between 605 and 586 B.C. to punish Judah (Hab. 1:6–11), and then He announced judgment on Babylon (Hab. 2:6–17; Isa. 14:5).

were totally unaware that they were carrying out God's wishes. They thought that their own plans and power had brought them victory. The cities mentioned in verses 9 and 10 came under Assyrian control between 740 and 721 B.C., and none of the gods of these areas had provided the slightest help. It was assumed that the "idols" (v. 10) of Jerusalem were equally impotent.

Verses 12–19 reveal that the God of Jerusalem was far more powerful than the king of Assyria. Throughout the empire period, Assyrian monarchs were known for their excessive pride, an arrogance similar to the descriptions in 2:11 and 17. The Assyrian annals were filled with inflated statistics and boasts about the Assyrians' accomplishments. In verses 13 and 14 the Assyrian king bragged about his might and wisdom, referring to himself no less than nine times. Conquering the nations was as easy as picking up eggs from an unprotected nest.

By means of an effective rhetorical question in verse 15, Isaiah showed the folly of Assyria's boasts. By naming four different tools, Isaiah emphasized Assyria's role as God's instrument. Unable to talk back to the one who made use of her, Assyria would soon discover her finitude. God's judgment is described in terms of a wasting disease and a fire. The diseased condition of the soldiers—mentioned in verses 16 and 18—contrasts with the picture of vigor and strength attributed to Assyria in 5:27f. A fast-spreading plague may have been God's method of killing 185,000 Assyrian warriors in one night (cf. 37:36).

The comparison between lofty trees and proud nations had been used in 2:13, and it appears again in 10:33–34. The fires of judgment, fed by thorns and briers, would consume the splendid forests of Assyria. Only a small remnant would be left.

The Day of Victory Over Assyria (10:20–34)

The mention of an Assyrian remnant introduces the subject of the remnant of Israel (vv. 20–23). The day was coming when Israel would not rely on Assyria—a nation that would attack them—but on the true God. This was partially fulfilled when

Hezekiah trusted the Lord during the crisis of 701 B.C., and the remnant in Jerusalem (37:4) truly did return to Him.

Yet "the remnant" normally refers to those who had been scattered in other countries (11:11, 16) as a result of the "destruction decreed" (v. 22) on Israel. Exile was to follow the Assyrian and Babylonian invasions, and only a small number of Israelites would survive to return to Palestine. It may be significant that verse 21 has the name of one of Isaiah's sons, Shear-Jashub ("a remnant will return"), and one of the messianic names, "Mighty God" (cf. 9:6).

The expression "destruction decreed" (v. 22) occurs elsewhere only in 28:22 and in Daniel 9:27, a passage that deals with judgment during the Tribulation. Paul quoted 10:22–23 in Romans 9:27–28 to indicate that comparatively few Jews would be saved.

Although verses 20–23 offer hope to the remnant from a perspective that is more future, verses 24–34 deal with deliverance from the immediate enemy, Assyria. Victory is compared with two great events of the past: the triumph over Egypt at the Red Sea and Gideon's stunning defeat of the Midianites. In 9:4 Isaiah had referred to Midian's fall, and this verse also mentions the removal of the yoke and the burden. Assyria was sent by God to beat Israel with a rod and a club (v. 5), but it was now Assyria's turn to feel the whip on her back (vv. 25–26). A comparison of verses 25 and 27 shows that "that day" would come "very soon."

At first glance the promise of victory does not seem compatible with the approach of the Assyrian army (vv. 28–32). According to Isaiah's description, panic set in as the unstoppable Assyrians closed in on Jerusalem. With a deft poetic touch, Isaiah told how the enemy moved through twelve different locations, coming ever closer to the capital. Not all of the places can be identified, but the direction is from the north, starting at least 10 miles from Jerusalem. Micmash is about seven and a half miles away, Gibeah four miles, and Anathoth only three. The Assyrians last stop was at Nob, on the slopes of Mount Scopus, within sight of the temple on Mount Zion.

All seemed lost as the Assyrians shook their fists at Jerusalem. But the ax had defied the one who swings it for the last time, and the Lord felled the cedars of Lebanon with a mighty blow. The forest imagery renews the figure used in verse 18 and in 2:3.

The sudden collapse of Assyria took place when the bulk of Sennacherib's army was wiped out by the Angel of the Lord in 701 B.C. (cf. 37:36). It marked the last time that an army from Mesopotamia directly threatened Jerusalem for almost 100 years.* The actual approach route used by the Assyrians was from the west, though they entered Palestine from the north. Thus the picture drawn by Isaiah made use of poetic license, somewhat like the command in 48:20 to "flee from the Babylonians." Because of the kindness of Cyrus, the return from Babylonian exile was sanctioned by the government, and flight was unnecessary (cf. 52:12).

THE RULE OF THE MESSIAH (11:1–16)

By the end of chapter 10 both Israel and Assyria had been severely punished. They lay on the ground like two felled trees. But the tree of Israel would sprout again, and David the son of Jesse would one day have a powerful descendant. This Messiah would have a small beginning. He is called a "shoot" (*ḥōter*), "Branch" (*nēṣer*), and "Root" (*šōreš*; vv. 1, 10). Similar terminology is used of Him in 4:2 and in 53:2. After this modest start, the messianic "Branch" would grow into the most powerful ruler the world has ever known.

The second verse presents the spiritual empowerment the Messiah possesses. He is endowed with the sevenfold ministry of the Spirit of God. Like the prophets and the first two kings of Israel, Saul and David, the coming of the Spirit would designate Him as the one who had been chosen by God (cf. John 1:33). It is not certain if "Spirit" should be capitalized throughout the verse. The three pairs of attributes characterize the Holy Spirit and are also gifts given to the Messiah by the Spirit. The words

*We cannot be sure what happened during Manasseh's reign when large Assyrian armies under Esarhaddon and Ashurbanipal successfully invaded and conquered Egypt. But at least we know that the Bible mentions no siege of Jerusalem until the invasion of Pharaoh Neco in 609 B.C. (2 Chron. 36:3–4).

"counselor" and "mighty" appeared in the titles of 9:6. The "fear of the Lord" is mentioned in verses 2 and 3, perhaps because this quality was the very foundation of sound government. According to Proverbs 1:7, "the fear of the Lord is the beginning of knowledge." The rule of the Son was to be carried out in the closest possible relationship with the Father (cf. John 14:10).

Verses 3–5 describe the character of the Messiah's rule. In contrast to the situation in Isaiah's day, justice and righteousness will prevail when the Messiah rules. At that time decisions will not be based on hearsay but on truth. Just as a wide belt was used to tie together one's flowing garments when a man prepared for action, so righteousness and faithfulness will be the key elements of the Messiah's rule (v. 5). Christ's authority is emphasized in verse 4, once again using "rod" (šēḇeṭ), which was so prominent in chapter 10 (vv. 5, 24, 26). Assyria was to mete out cruel punishment, like a man wielding a rod or club, and the Messiah would use His powerful word to strike down the wicked. Revelation 19:15 expands on the iron rule of the Messiah.

A picture of conditions during the millennial reign is given in verses 6–9. By using illustrations from the animal world, Isaiah portrayed a scene of unparalleled peace and safety. The lack of hostility between the animals reflects a return to a Paradise where sin and its effects are absent. The animals are grouped largely in pairs that join a normally wild animal with a tame one. Isaiah emphasized the complete safety of infants and children, those who often suffer most in this sin-cursed earth.

One must exercise caution in pressing the details of so ideal an environment because the poet may have used figurative language to make his point. A similar description appears in 65:20–25, a passage that blends the kingdom period with the new heaven and new earth. Verse 25 has close verbal parallels with 11:6–9.

In verse 9 the main lesson is presented as the transition is made from animals back to men. Evil and corruption, which always produce harm and destruction, will not be tolerated in the future age. The whole world will know the Lord and what He requires.

Verses 10–16 explain how people will be gathered to this "holy mountain" (v. 9) where the Messiah will rule. In verse 10 attention is drawn to the Gentiles and in verses 11–16 to the Jews. Both verse 10 and verse 11 begin with the phrase "in that day."

The designation "root" (v. 10) is closely connected with "shoot" and "branch" (v. 1). Although it occurs again only in Isaiah 53:2, in the New Testament this title for Christ appears three times (Rom. 15:12; Rev. 5:5; 22:16). In the last citation, John identified Jesus as "the Root and the Offspring of David."

The root is now lifted high as a banner for the nations. Previously a banner had been raised to summon armies against Israel (5:26), but now the Gentiles are invited to participate in Christ's glorious kingdom (cf. 2:2–4). The banner for the nations is mentioned again in verse 12. According to 49:22, the Gentiles would assist the Jews when they returned from exile, a theme that is also discussed in 66:20.

The return of the remnant to Israel would originate from a broad geographical spectrum. Verse 11 mentions all four directions, including the major regions where Israel either fled or was taken captive. The wide scattering seems to reflect a more extensive dispersion than the one that resulted from the Babylonian captivity. Therefore some interpreters believe that "a second time" (v. 11) refers to a regathering subsequent to the destruction of Jerusalem in A.D. 70. The first time would then be the return from Babylon in 538 B.C. But verse 16 compares the return from Assyria (= Babylon) to the exodus from Egypt, the first deliverance. The best solution may be to see a partial fulfillment of the "second time" in the regathering from Babylon and a future fulfillment prior to the second coming of Christ. This future fulfillment is to some extent now underway in the return of thousands to the nation of Israel.

When the remnant comes back to Israel, there will be a reversal of the conditions that existed in the eighth century B.C. In place of perpetual war between northern and southern kingdoms (9:21), there will be genuine unity. Instead of defeat and harassment at the hands of surrounding nations (cf. 9:12), victory will be the rule. The enemies named in verse 14 warred against Israel through many centuries. The political domination of restored Israel is also referred to in 60:12.

Verses 15 and 16 describe the return of the remnant in terms of the Exodus. Just as God dried up the gulf (literally, "tongue") of the Red Sea, so the Euphrates River will be crossed easily. The drying up of the Euphrates is mentioned in Revelation 16:12 and apparently symbolizes the removal of any barriers preventing movement toward Israel. The removal of obstacles and the construction of a highway leading to Jerusalem are further described in 57:14 and in 62:10.

HYMNS OF PRAISE (12:1–6)

As the conclusion to these chapters on Assyria and the Messiah and to chapters 1–12, Isaiah presented two short songs of praise. These hymns offer thanks to the Lord for His deliverance in the past and for His great promises of blessing for the future.

The expression "In that day you will say" occurs in verses 1 and 4 and probably divides the chapter into separate hymns. On the basis of pronouns, however, the switch from singular to plural comes in verse 3 and continues through verse 6.

The speaker in verses 1–2 is the nation, conceived of as a unit and offering praise from the standpoint of the future. Because deliverance is certain to come, "in that day" these songs will be readily available. The turning away of anger recalls the refrain of 9:12–10:4. In the years ahead, God's anger would be directed against Assyria and Babylon, not Zion.

The last half of verse 2 quotes Exodus 15:2, a song that celebrates God's victory over Pharaoh at the Red Sea. Often in Isaiah, God's future triumphs are compared to the Exodus. The beautiful line "the Lord is my strength and my song" (*zimrat* — v. 2) is translated by some scholars "my strength and my might." A good case can be made for either interpretation.[7]

---

[7] For *zimrat* as "might" see Koehler and Baumgartner, *Lexicon in Veteris Libros*, p. 260. Also see F. M. Cross and D. N. Freedman, "The Song of Miriam," *Journal of Near Eastern Studies* 14 (1955): 243, and Gordon, *Ugaritic Textbook*, 2:388 (no. 727).

Equally beautiful is the figure of "the wells of salvation" (v. 3). This phrase may allude to God's gracious provision of water during the wilderness wanderings when He satisfied Israel's physical and spiritual needs. Paul linked the waters of Sinai with the abundance of salvation through Christ (1 Cor. 10:4).

Verses 4–6 develop the theme of joy that was introduced in verse 3 and encourage the proclamation of God's greatness to the entire world. The exaltation of the Lord—referred to in verses 4 and 5 ("glorious," or "majestic" things)—is the fulfillment of 2:11 and 17, verses that also look ahead to "that day." God's mighty works on behalf of Israel are proof of His greatness.

The two imperatives in the concluding call to praise (v. 6) occur together again in 54:1.

7

ORACLES AGAINST THE NATIONS
13:1–23:18

Most of the prophetic books contain sections that pronounce judgment against Gentile nations. Although Isaiah was primarily a prophet to Judah and Jerusalem (cf. 1:1), his words about other countries were timely and powerful. The title in 13:1 serves as an introduction to this entire section (see *Authorship* and *Structure*).

Oracle (*maśśā'*) comes from the verb "to lift up" (*naśā'*), and so it can mean "to carry" or "to lift up the voice." From the first meaning comes the translation "burden," or "load"; and from the second meaning we get the translation "oracle," or "utterance." Usually an oracle contains a message of doom, but it can more generally refer to any word from the Lord (cf. Lam 2:14).

BABYLON (13:1–14:23)

The name *Babylon* plays an important role in Isaiah, and its frequent occurrence has aroused skepticism about the authorship of the book. Babylon was not the major power of the day, but the Chaldeans displayed considerable vigor during Isaiah's lifetime. Throughout Scripture *Babylon* symbolizes an empire, or a world city, that is opposed to God. From the Tower of Babylon (Babel) to the judgment of Babylon (Rev. 17–18), the name stands for a political and religious system in conflict with God. Moreover, Babylon was to replace Assyria as the major world power and to bring about the downfall of Jerusalem and the captivity of her residents. For these important reasons, Babylon comes first in the roll call of the nations.

The Destruction of Babylon (13:1–14:2)

The oracle begins with a description of the mustering of an army against Babylon (vv. 1–5). The banner on the hilltop is similar to the one raised in 5:26, that summoned the Assyrians against Israel. Here the Medes and Persians are the "holy ones" who are being assembled. They are holy in the sense of being set apart to carry out God's will. In ancient days war was a religious activity, and a specifically sanctioned war received the title of a "holy war" (cf. Num. 31:1–6).

Verse 4 literally says, "The LORD of armies is mustering an army." Yahweh was at the head of the armies of Israel and the angelic hosts of heaven, and here He stands in full control of the armies of Cyrus. Assyria served as the rod of God's anger (10:5); the Medes and Persians are called the "weapons of his wrath" (13:5).

The destruction in store for Babylon is described in terms of the "day of the LORD" in verses 6–16. Twice the full expression is used (vv. 6, 9), and the "day of his burning anger" occurs in verse 13. "Burning anger" and "wrath" are also mentioned in verse 9. Isaiah 2:10–21 portrays the judgmental nature of this "day of the LORD." In its ultimate fulfillment this day looks ahead to the judgment on the world during the Great Tribulation and the second coming of Christ. The near fulfillment has in view the campaign against Babylon in 539 B.C.

Apocalyptic elements are found in this description, especially in verses 10 and 13. The darkening of the sun and moon and the shaking of heaven and earth are mentioned in Joel 2:10 and in Revelation 6:12–14. Isaiah 34:4 is a close parallel. Darkness and earthquakes often accompany a theophany, such as God's descent on Mount Sinai in Exodus 19:16–18.

The intense fear associated with judgment and war is frequently compared to the pain and anguish of childbirth (v. 8; cf. 26:17). Likewise the aftermath of defeat involves the cruelty depicted in verse 16. Many of the people who had migrated to the fertile regions of Babylonia would flee the land in terror (v. 14). In Babylon itself death would take its toll on the male population (cf. 4:1).

The primary object of divine judgment is to punish sin. Verses 9 and 11 show how God's wrath is directed particularly against man's pride and arrogance. Such pride characterized Babylon and the nations of the world in general (cf. 2:11, 17).

In verses 17–22 Isaiah focused specifically on the destruction of Babylon. The Medes are named for they, along with the Persians, captured Babylon in 539 B.C. Attempts to bribe them would be fruitless because their objective was to control the entire Babylonian Empire. The Medes may have been singled out here because of their reputation for cruelty (v. 18), but the Persians under King Cyrus were known for their humane treatment of their enemies.

Babylon became one of the most beautiful and famous cities in the world, claiming among its temples and palaces the hanging gardens of Nebuchadnezzar, one of the seven wonders of the ancient world. Isaiah described the glory and pride of Babylon (v. 19) with the same words that he had used to describe "the Branch of the LORD" in 4:2. The Chaldean kingdom or the Messiah of Israel—which was more powerful?

Verses 19b–22 render a clear verdict. Babylon would become another Sodom and Gomorrah (cf. 1:9). Her wide streets and luxurious palaces would be turned over to wild animals and unclean birds. Not even nomads would camp within her walls overnight. In buildings once filled with music and merriment, hyenas would utter eerie howls. The "wild goats" (v. 21) are sometimes associated with demons in goat form that are called "satyrs" (Lev. 17:7; 2 Chron. 11:15). Revelation 11:2 describes the fallen Babylon the Great—the end-times world power—as a home for demons and evil spirits. This implies that Satanic beings frequented the ruins of ancient Babylon also.

When Cyrus conquered Babylon, he did not devastate the city. The walls were left standing until 518 B.C., and general desolation did not set in until the third century B.C. Babylon gradually fell into decay, and the prophecy of Isaiah was fulfilled. Babylon became completely depopulated by the time of the Muslim conquest in the seventh century A.D., and to this day it lies deserted.

The fall of Babylon would mean the rise of Israel because Babylon was to become the captor and oppressor of Judah. Therefore, in 14:1–2 Isaiah inserted the joyous themes of God's compassion on His people and their return home. These great changes in the life of Israel comprise the heart of the prophet's message in chapters 40–66. Nations that once dominated God's people would serve them and join in the worship of their God (cf. 11:10–12).

A Taunt Song Against the King of Babylon (14:3–23)

The anticipation of Babylon's demise led Isaiah to compose a taunt song to be used in commemorating that occasion. In chapter 12 Israel had been given songs of praise with which to celebrate future deliverance. Verses 4–8 express the joy that accompanied the destruction of Babylon, a joy as great as that experienced during the Exodus. In fact the account of Israel's cruel bondage in verse 3 sounds like a replay of their experience in Egypt.

"The king of Babylon" (v. 4) probably does not refer to a specific ruler. Rather the "king" is viewed as an ideal person, a representative of the entire line of rulers. The whole Near East rejoiced over Babylon's fall because her rule was harsh and oppressive. She beat the nations with a rod the way Assyria did (10:24), but that rod finally would be broken by the Lord (cf. 9:4). The joy expressed by the nations is paralleled by the rejoicing of the cedars of Lebanon (v. 8). Isaiah repeatedly personified nature and was especially fond of trees. Since the twelfth century B.C. the kings of Mesopotamia had imported lumber from Lebanon. Nebuchadnezzar used large supplies of such choice timbers in his extensive building efforts in Babylon after 605 B.C.

Verses 9–15 describe Babylon's fall from the standpoint of Sheol. Three times (vv. 9, 11, 15) "sheol," or "the grave," is used as Isaiah depicts the final destiny of the king of Babylon (cf. 30:33). Although all would be peace and quiet on earth, the arrival of the noted monarch would cause a commotion in

Sheol. Conditions among the dead are pictured in terms of their roles on earth, and deceased leaders seem stunned at the fate of so great a king. The heavy responsibility of kings is reflected in the word for "leaders" (v. 9), which literally means "he-goats" (ʿattûḏîm). A male goat normally led a flock of sheep, just as a king was to be a shepherd to the people of his nation (cf. Jer. 50:8; Zech. 10:3).

The former status and ambitions of the king of Babylon are sharply contrasted with his position in Sheol. Pride and pomp have given way to abject humiliation, and purple robes have been replaced by a covering of maggots. His desire to gain the heights of heaven has failed to keep him from plunging into the depths of Sheol.

Verses 12–14 seem to exaggerate the ambitions of the king of Babylon since neither the rulers of Assyria nor Babylon claimed to be divine. One could appeal to the use of hyperbole and to the fact that the stars grow dark (13:10) and fall from heaven (Rev. 6:13) in apocalyptic descriptions of war. Yet the assertions in verses 13 and 14 are too explicit to make hyperbole the only solution. The "mount of assembly," or "Mount Zaphon," is the same as Mount Cassius, located about twenty-five miles northeast of Ugarit and equivalent to Mount Olympus among the Greeks. To the Canaanites, Mount Zaphon was the home and meeting place of the gods, who were led by Baal or El. The king of Babylon hoped to challenge the position of the chief deity.

Such an arrogant claim, coupled with the title "morning star" (v. 12—"Lucifer" in the Vulgate), has led some interpreters to see in this passage a reference to Satan. He is the ultimate power behind the world city symbolized by Babylon throughout the Bible, and the statements in verses 13 and 14 would fit him perfectly.

Another possibility is to understand the king of Babylon as a type of the Man of Sin, or Beast, who will lead the Babylon of the last days (Rev. 17:3). In 2 Thessalonians 2:4 this blasphemous leader sets himself up as God, and Revelation 13:4 says that the world will worship him. The identification of the king of Tyre in Ezekiel 28 presents problems similar to the ones in Isaiah 14.

In verses 16–26 the ideal king of the Chaldean Empire is once more in view. This time the scene shifts back to the earth's surface where men gaze in astonishment at his dead body. His reputation as a world power was an awesome one, and all nations feared the policy of deportation effectively used by Babylon. But now a terrible thing had happened; he was not given the honorable burial deemed so important for monarchs. Even the common man regarded proper burial as essential. A blasphemous king of Judah named Jehoiakim learned through the prophet Jeremiah that his body would be discarded outside the walls of Jerusalem (Jer. 22:19); it was one of the worst curses imaginable.

According to verse 19, the corpse of the king of Babylon would be thrown out like a rejected branch (*nēṣer*). What a contrast to the Branch from the stump of Jesse that would bear abundant fruit (11:1)! Because of Babylon's great wickedness, her descendants would never prosper or regain control over the earth. Even the people of Babylon would agree with this verdict because they had suffered greatly under the policies of their king. Thus the king of Babylon possessed neither of the two memorials available to him. If a man had no children, his name was preserved on his grave (2 Sam. 18:18), but this wretched king had neither tombstone nor children.

The resolution of the Lord to crush Babylon is set forth emphatically in verses 22 and 23. Three times the expression "declares the LORD" is used to show that God is unalterably opposed to Babylon. Her sons would not "rise" to inherit the land (v. 21) because God would "rise up" (v. 22) to wipe them out. Two alliterated pairs of terms emphasize the completeness of the judgment. There would be no remnant for Babylon. Her cities would belong to owls or hedgehogs and her farmland would become swamps. The southern regions of Babylonia, where the Chaldean tribes originally settled, were filled with marshlands. Soon the entire land would be treacherous and unfruitful.

ASSYRIA (14:24–27)

The major military power of Isaiah's day was the nation of Assyria, and though there are many references to God's judgment on Assyria outside of chapters 13–23 (cf. 10:5–34), it is fitting that at least a few verses are included here. These verses also function as a summary of the prophecy against Babylon. A similar paragraph concludes the lengthy oracle against Moab in 16:13–14. Assyria preceded Babylon as a world ruler from Mesopotamia, and so Isaiah repeated the announcement of Assyria's downfall to reinforce his predictions regarding Babylon. As surely as Sennacherib's army would be destroyed in 701 B.C., so Babylon would collapse more than a century later.

The terminology in these verses reflects several earlier passages, especially 8:10. In that verse God promised to frustrate the strategy of the nations that opposed Judah. In this verse the nations discover that God's plans and purposes cannot be thwarted. The hand once raised against Israel (9:12, 17, etc.) is extended to strike the Gentiles. Twice previously Isaiah referred to removing the burdensome yoke from Israel's shoulders (9:4; 10:27). Before Assyria's demise, however, God would use her as a tool to punish other nations. Several of these countries are listed in the following oracles.

THE PHILISTINES (14:28–32)

Having pronounced judgment against the world powers, Isaiah dealt with the fate of Israel's neighbors. The Philistines are considered first, perhaps because they lived within Palestine itself* and were a perennial enemy of Judah. Since the days of Samson, these residents of what is now called the Gaza Strip had oppressed and harassed the Israelites. David effectively subdued the Philistines by 1000 B.C., but after Solomon's reign only Jehoshaphat and Uzziah enjoyed success against them. Ahaz was one of several kings who were unable to control them.

The oracle against the Philistines is the only one to which Isaiah gave a precise date, though opinions differ as to when Ahaz died. The earliest possibility is 727 B.C., also the year of

*The name "Palestine" is derived from the word "Philistine," pᵉlištîm in Hebrew.

the death of Tiglath-Pileser III, and the latest is 715 B.C. The "rod" stands for some Assyrian king, but Philistia was warned that a descendant of that king would inflict even greater damage. The strange imagery of a "root" coming from a snake has a parallel in the Root of Jesse, though that Root comes more naturally from the stump of Jesse (11:1, 10). Both Sargon (719 B.C. and 711 B.C.) and Sennacherib (701 B.C.) invaded Philistia to put down revolts in decisive ways.

The description of the Assyrian army in verse 31 is a more compact version of the one given in 5:26–29. In the face of such might, the Philistines would wail in terror. This reaction is characteristic of the fear associated with the Lord's judgment throughout the oracles (13:6; 15:2; 16:7; 23:1).

Verse 32 implies that the Assyrian invasion that would destroy the Philistines would not be successful against Judah. The reference to the establishment of Zion also seems to look ahead to the golden age that was first introduced in 2:2–4. A number of passages within the oracle chapters briefly mention Zion's future exaltation (cf. 14:1–2; 16:5; 18:7; 19:17).

MOAB (15:1–16:14)

For some reason the length of the oracles differs widely among the treatments of the various nations. Philistia and Edom are discussed very briefly, but Moab is allotted two chapters. Like the Philistines, the Moabites had been enemies of Israel for centuries. It was King Balak of Moab who hired Balaam to lead the Israelites into idolatry and immorality when Israel was about to enter the Promised Land (Num. 25). King Eglon oppressed Israel for eighteen years during the period of the judges. Under the leadership of Saul and David, Israel established firm control over Moab, but this was sharply contested during the period of the divided kingdom. On the famous Moabite Stone, King Mesha described how Moab had gained its independence when Ahab ruled Israel (ca. 860 B.C.). The Moabites retained their freedom, except during the reign of Jeroboam II, who reconquered Moab early in the eighth century B.C. As a general rule, when the Moabites were not in subjection to Israel, they enjoyed making raids across the Jordan River (2 Kings 13:20).

Chapter 15 describes the mourning that will overtake Moab after the coming invasion. Eleven times words for wailing, weeping, and crying out are used, and Isaiah mentions about fifteen different cities that would participate in the general lament. Most of these sites were originally part of Israel's territory when Moses and Joshua defeated Sihon, King of the Amorites. All the cities north of the Arnon River—such as Dibon, Heshbon (Sihon's capital), Nebo, and Medeba—once belonged to the tribe of Reuben. Throughout the years, however, the Moabites had persistently pushed the Israelites out of these regions. "Kir" is probably a reference to Kir Hareseth, which is located south of the Arnon and which was probably the capital city of Moab.

Several cities are personified as Isaiah described the plight of the country and the terrible disarray that prevailed. The word "ruined," used twice in verse 1 along with "destroyed in a night," is the same word Isaiah had applied to himself in 6:5: "Woe to me! . . . I am ruined." For the nation, however, there was no remedy to ease the situation. Along with weeping and wailing, the Moabites donned the usual mourner's sackcloth and plucked out their beards (vv. 2–3).

The invasion completely demoralized their army (v. 4) and sent the people fleeing for safety. Apparently the enemy stopped up the major springs in the land, destroying the vegetation. Verse 9 indicates that many lives were lost. "Dimon" may have meant "bloody" and is probably a reference to the similar-sounding Dibon (v. 2) not far from the Arnon River. In the midst of all this tragedy, it is little wonder that the sound of wailing covers the entire land (vv. 4, 8). Even Isaiah added his voice to this mournful cry.

The "lion" in verse 9 could signify an enemy army (cf. 5:29) or, if taken literally, it would indicate that wild animals had taken over the land (cf. 13:21).

In 16:1–5 the fugitives of Moab learn of possible refuge in Judah. On previous occasions men from Judah had sought refuge in Moab (Ruth 1:1), but now the tables are turned. Moab must renew its allegiance to Israel by sending a tribute payment to Zion. In the past such tribute had been sent to the capital of the northern kingdom at Samaria. Prior to his rebellion, Mesha had to pay 100,000 lambs a year to Ahab (2 Kings 3:4). Because Isaiah described Jerusalem and Mount Zion as the rallying point for the nations, a new payment center is specified.

The line of flight for Moab was around the southern end of the Dead Sea and through the Judean wilderness. In verses 3 and 4a the fugitives ask for the protection of Judah and for the right to settle on her soil. Would it be possible for a nation to show mercy to a neighboring land that had mistreated her for centuries? Isaiah indicated how the answer could be "Yes" (vv. 4b–5). There would be an end to oppression and destruction, and Israel would once again have a just ruler, one from the "tent of David." Verse 5 has a distinct messianic flavor when compared to 9:6 and Amos 9:11. The latter passage mentions raising up David's fallen "tabernacle," a term similar to the word "tent" in 16:5. Perhaps righteous King Hezekiah fulfilled this prediction in a limited sense, but the final reference is to the reign of Christ (cf. Acts 15:16).

The solution to Moab's plight lay in submission to Israel and to Israel's God, but verse 6 reveals why Moab could not accept that solution. Like Assyria and Babylon, Moab was extremely proud. Isaiah piled term upon term to show that the nation's relative insignificance did not make it immune to pride. According to Jeremiah 48:42, Moab's arrogance was in defiance of the Lord.

This revelation of Moab's basic sin leads to another round of mourning (vv. 7–12). The nation and the poet bemoaned the destruction of the vineyards and grape harvests that once had been so plentiful. Trampled vineyards meant an end to the joyful shouts of those who trod the grapes. There would be no more wine and tasty raisin cakes. An extended chiastic, or introverted, arrangement involves Kir Hareseth, Heshbon, the vines of Sibmah, and Jazer. Each of these sites is mentioned once in verses 7 and 8 and a second time in verses 9–11 (in reverse order). The devastation of Moab's vineyards corresponds to the Song of the Vineyard in 5:1–7, a parable that portrays the collapse of Israel. Verse 12 underscores Moab's need to submit to the God of Israel. When the Moabites earnestly prayed at the sanctuary of Chemosh, it would be a useless exercise because their god was only an idol who could not answer prayer.

The epilogue (vv. 13–14) presents an additional word from the Lord concerning Moab. Several years had probably elapsed since the main oracle was given, but now a precise date is attached to the fulfillment of the judgment. This three-year interval compares with the three-year signs mentioned in 20:3 and in 37:30. Moab's days were numbered. Soon the land would be humbled, and only a small remnant would survive.

Interpreters are undecided about the precise length of time involved in this prophecy. Apparently King Sargon of Assyria conducted a major operation against the Arabians in 715 B.C., and he may have devastated Moab en route to encountering those tribes.[1] Another theory connects Moab with the revolt of the Philistine city of Ashdod in 713 B.C. Sargon severely punished all the participants in that uprising. Judah was not involved in either of those campaigns.

DAMASCUS AND ISRAEL (17:1–14)

The fourth oracle mentions only "Damascus" in the title, but by verse 3 the northern kingdom of "Ephraim" is linked with the Syrians. Historically this reflects the period of the Syro-Ephraimite war (*ca.* 734 B.C.) when these two nations joined forces against Ahaz. Since this northern coalition suffered greatly at the hands of Tiglath-Pileser III in 732 B.C., this oracle may represent the earliest one in chapters 13–23.

Damascus was the capital of Syria and a stronghold of the Aramean tribes. Except for the Davidic period, Damascus was independent of Israel and frequently warred against the northern kingdom. Ahab engaged in a number of battles against Ben Hadad in the ninth century B.C. and was slain while fighting the Syrians at Ramoth-Gilead. Israel and Damascus constantly quarreled over control of cities east of the Jordan. Jeroboam II enjoyed success against Damascus in the eighth century B.C.

[1] Cf. Otto Kaiser, *Isaiah 13–39,* trans. R. A. Wilson (London: SCM, 1974), p. 63.

(2 Kings 14:28), and the two nations banded together to oppose the massive Assyrian threat that arose after 740 B.C.

Damascus was one of the most beautiful cities of the Near East, but Tiglath-Pileser would reduce it to a heap of ruins. The Assyrians captured Damascus in 732 B.C. and made it a province of their empire. South of Damascus the cities of Aroer would be stripped of their population, and throughout Syria and Ephraim fortified cities would be wrested from their control. Just as the "splendor," or "glory," of Moab was removed (16:14), so Syria and Israel would lose their manpower and prestige.

Using three different figures, Isaiah described the predicament of Israel (vv. 4–6). The nation would waste away like a sick man and be stripped of its grain by the reapers and gleaners. The Valley of Rephaim lay to the west of Jerusalem and was known for its fertility. It was subject to frequent raids by the Philistines (1 Chron. 14:19). The remnant of Israel is also compared to gathering olives from an olive tree. After the beating and the shaking are over, only a few olives remain on the tree. Similarly Israel would be a mere shadow of her former self.

Verse 7—as well as verses 4 and 9—begins with the phrase "in that day," a term familiar from chapters 2–4. An eschatological application may have been intended, as a comparison of verses 7 and 8 with 2:20f. may indicate. In Isaiah's day the reference may have been to the siege of Samaria when some of the Israelites realized the folly of their pagan worship and turned to the Lord. In Judah this happened during the reign of Hezekiah (cf. comments on 10:20). The "Asherah poles," or lopped-off tree trunks, were an integral part of the Canaanite high places. They represented the goddess Asherah, consort of the leading deity, Baal.

Verse 9 is difficult to interpret because we are not told who left these cities because of the Israelites. The main point, however, is clear. Fortified cities were normally the last line of defense, but they would prove useless in this conflict. Israel should have relied on the Lord, the Rock in whom true security had been found throughout her history (Deut. 32:4, 30–31). Instead she looked elsewhere and made alliances with other nations and gods. According to verse 11, it would all be singularly unfruitful.

God's agent of punishment is on the move in verse 12. By a threefold repetition of some form of "rage" and "roar" in each of the two couplets, Isaiah achieved an onomatopoeic effect. One can almost hear the enemy advancing like a mighty sea as Isaiah used a large number of "m" and "n" sounds.

Suddenly in verses 13 and 14, the great army is unexpectedly turned back; the irresistible force becomes chaff and tumbleweed. This same sequence of events occurs in 10:28–34, where the army of Sennacherib is also in view. When Assyria had completed its work as God's rod of judgment, it too would be judged. The ultimate safety of Judah is also stressed in 14:31–32, which has its own description of the powerful Assyrians.

CUSH (18:1–7)

Isaiah had already considered countries to the north and countries adjacent to Israel. In chapters 18 and 19 he turned southward and dealt with Ethiopia (Cush) and Egypt. Ancient Ethiopia was located just to the south of Egypt, and in 715 B.C. an Ethiopian named Shabako gained control of Egypt as founder of the twenty-fifth dynasty. Ethiopian domination continued until 633 B.C. when a native Egyptian regained the throne.

This oracle differs from the others in that it begins with the word "Woe," or "Ah" (*hôy*). No specific judgment is pronounced against Cush, though disaster is predicted in 20:4. Verses 2 and 7 contain almost identical descriptions of the Ethiopians. Although the prophecy is a short one, it probably ranks as the most obscure chapter in this entire section.

By characterizing Ethiopia as a land of whirring wings, Isaiah may have referred to the numerous troops who were ready to swarm against the enemy like locusts or crickets (cf. 7:18). In verse 2 the envoys of Ethiopia ride the Nile to announce the coming war. Shortly after coming to power, the Ethiopian dynasty encouraged the countries of Palestine to revolt against Assyria. According to one interpretation of verse 2, the envoys arrive in Palestine only to be told by the prophet to return home. Other commentators believe that the messengers are being sent over the waterways of Ethiopia to spread the news to their own tribes.

The central paragraph of the chapter (vv. 3–6) indicates that all this activity is unnecessary. If God had wanted to muster an army, He would have raised a banner or sounded a trumpet. Instead the Lord is biding His time until the right moment arrives. Then He will proceed to cut away the branches of the vine of Assyria, even as He was to "lop off the boughs" of that empire (10:33).

Changing figures quickly, in verse 6 Isaiah portrayed the birds and beasts of prey as feasting on the dead bodies of Assyrian soldiers. It is a picture of utter defeat, the kind experienced by Sennacherib in 701 B.C.

The Lord's rescue of Hezekiah from Sennacherib led many nations to bring gifts to the King of Judah (2 Chron. 32:23). Ethiopia may have been one of those nations, but the broader meaning of verse 7 involves the future submission of Ethiopia to the God of Mount Zion (cf. Zeph. 3:10). Moab had been instructed to send tribute to Zion (16:1–5). In 45:14 the subjection of Egypt and Ethiopia to Israel is discussed again.

EGYPT (19:1–25)

From the days of the patriarchs when the sons of Jacob found refuge from famine within her borders, Egypt had a profound effect on the nation of Israel. But Joseph's farsighted wisdom was soon forgotten by the Egyptians themselves, and the Israelites were severely oppressed during the time of their four-hundred-year tenure in Egypt. Under Solomon, relations between the two countries were very friendly; but his son Rehoboam suffered heavy losses at the hands of the Pharaoh Shishak, who belonged to a new dynasty that had overthrown Solomon's father-in-law. In the eighth century B.C. the expansion of Assyria led some of the Israelites to favor an alliance with Egypt. This was especially true in the reign of Hezekiah as the pressure from the north increased. But here in chapter 19, and later in chapters 30 and 31, Isaiah warned against making any alliance with Egypt.

The Judgment of Egypt and Its Leaders (19:1–15)

Egypt's doom is sealed by the announcement that the Lord is riding on a storm cloud and heading for Egypt. The last time God's presence had been felt in Egypt—at the Exodus—it had been a disaster for the gods and people of the land. The judgment in store for Egypt is described in verses 2 through 10. Like Israel, Egypt would be plagued with disunity and civil war (cf. 9:21). In their desperation they too would turn to mediums and spiritists to find guidance for the future (cf. 8:19–20) but to no avail. The Assyrians would conquer Egypt. The "fierce king" (v. 4) may denote "Assyria" in an ideal sense, or it could refer to the great victories of Esarhaddon in 670 B.C. when he completely conquered Egypt. After 740 B.C. one Assyrian king after another defeated Egypt on the battlefield.

Verses 5–10 predict economic catastrophe in terms of the drying up of the Nile River. This great waterway was the lifeline of Egypt, and any change in its flood patterns had immediate and drastic effects. According to one theory, the ten plagues recorded in the Book of Exodus were caused in part by an excessive overflow of the Nile, but here the situation is far worse. As the Nile recedes, the fish die quickly. Water is unavailable for irrigation, and so before long the crops are ruined. Because large amounts of water were needed for growing and processing flax, all the garment workers were thrown out of work. Consequently they made a great lamentation. Verses 11–15 placed part of the blame for this disaster at the feet of the nation's leaders. Egypt was renowned for her class of wise men (1 Kings 4:30), but they would not be able to cope with this judgment from the Lord. Twice (vv. 11, 13) her leaders are called "officials of Zoan," a northern capital in the region where the Israelites lived during their Egyptian enslavement. The rulers of Egypt were confused. As a result they misled the people, just as the leaders of Israel had done (3:12). They behaved like drunkards and were unfit to fulfill their roles (v. 14; cf. 28:7).

The "cornerstones" (v. 13) probably include the prophets and priests of Egypt. Religious personnel are condemned along with political leaders—as in 9:14–15, a close parallel to this passage. The two pairs of opposites used in 19:15 also occur in 9:14.

The Restoration of Egypt and Her Submission to Judah (19:16–25)

Verses 16–25 move from the judgment of Egypt to the topic of her restoration and submission to Judah. It is the longest and most remarkable passage of this kind in this section on the nations and also one of the most difficult to interpret. At the beginning of five verses (vv. 16, 18, 19, 23, 24), the common phrase "in that day" is used to turn the reader's attention to the future. All of these verses are in prose, in contrast to the first part of the chapter.

The transition from judgment to restoration is made in verses 16 and 17. Great fear would fill the Egyptians as the hand of the Lord moved over their land once again (cf. 11:15). Because of the power of her God, the Egyptians would know that they should respect the kingdom of Judah.

In verse 18 the conversion of Egypt is linked with five cities where Hebrew is spoken. It is not certain whether this refers symbolically to Egypt's allegiance to the Lord or whether it signifies the presence of Jews in Egypt. After the Babylonian invasion, a number of Jews fled to Egypt and were allowed to reside there (Jer. 44:1). In the time of the Maccabees, the high priest Onias IV was forced to flee to Egypt, and there he built a temple that was similar to the one in Jerusalem. Some commentators relate the "altar" of verse 19 to this structure.

The meaning of the "City of Destruction" (heres) in verse 18 adds to the problem of interpretation. A number of versions and ancient texts, including the Dead Sea Scrolls, have the reading "City of the Sun" (heres), i.e., Heliopolis. A very slight change in one letter distinguishes the two words. Isaiah may be playing on the name "Sun," just as he used "Dimon" to represent "Dibon" in 15:9. Heliopolis was an important center for the worship of the sun god, but that worship would be destroyed when Israel's God took action (cf. v. 1). Joseph was associated with Heliopolis (Gen. 41:45), and the temple of Onias IV in Leontopolis was in the province of Heliopolis.[2]

The reference to an "altar" and "monument" in verse 19 reflects the patriarchal period of Israel's history, and the sending of a "savior" to "rescue them" (v. 20) sounds like the days of the judges. Verse 22 is a sharp reversal of the period of the Exodus. In the future when God strikes Egypt with a plague, the Egyptians will turn to Him.

The description of Egypt's participation in the worship of the Lord (v. 21) resembles the descriptions in 18:7 and in 60:7 (cf. Zeph. 3:10). Zechariah 14:16–19 presents a similar picture, though there the Egyptians seem less eager to serve God.

The allegiance of foreign powers to the God of Israel reaches a climax in verses 23–25 where Assyria joins Egypt and Israel in worshiping the Lord. These ancient enemies are pictured as standing at opposite ends of a highway through Israel, a road often used for transporting hostile armies. In 11:16 Isaiah had spoken about a highway from Egypt and Assyria that would make possible the return of Israel from captivity. But the highway in 19:23–25 is for the Assyrians and the Egyptians who, incredibly, are called "my people," "my handiwork," and "my inheritance." They will achieve equal status with Israel, though Israel will still be "a blessing on the earth" (v. 24).

When will this blissful peace be fulfilled? Politically the three nations are still at odds with one another. There has been only a slight improvement in the relationship between Israel and Egypt. One could argue that Isaiah was describing the church in which the wall between Jew and Gentile has been broken down and Christ can be worshiped by all (cf. Eph. 2:14–18). Other commentators point to Egypt's conversion to the Christian faith some centuries before the Muslim conquest. A more complete and adequate fulfillment, however, awaits the millennial age when the rule of Christ will be political as well as spiritual (cf. 2:2–4). The peace between Israel, Assyria, and Egypt will correspond to the peace between the natural enemies in the animal world (11:6–9).

[2]Ibid., pp. 107–8.

A SIGN AGAINST EGYPT AND CUSH (20:1–6)

The prediction given in 19:23–25 was a long way from being fulfilled in Isaiah's day, and 20:1–6 portrays the hatred between the Assyrians and the Egyptians. It stands almost as an epilogue to chapters 18 and 19, serving the same function as 14:24–27 and 16:13–14. The length of the sign in 20:3 even matches the time span given in 16:14.

In 711 B.C. Sargon of Assyria sent troops against the Philistine city of Ashdod, which had begun an uprising in 713 B.C. under King Azuri. Judah may have sympathized with the revolt, but Isaiah left no doubt that the rebels could expect no lasting help from Egypt and Ethiopia, in spite of the promises that emanated from the south.

To communicate the message, Isaiah was to strip off his clothes and walk around looking like a captive of Assyria. He may have been completely naked because that was the disgrace normally suffered by captives. Without clothes and without sandals, they had no protection from the blazing sun or the stones that dug into their feet over the endless miles. Other prophets were asked to go through equally difficult experiences as signs to Israel. Hosea endured a trying marriage, and Ezekiel's wife died as an illustration for the nation (Ezek. 24:16–24).

Even if Isaiah was allowed to wear some clothing, his attire would still have been considered indecent. But the people needed a shock to halt their reliance on Egypt and Ethiopia. The Lord, not some undependable foreign power, should have been the object of their trust.

One need not imagine that Isaiah walked around stripped for the entire three years or that Ezekiel lay on his side for 390 days without getting up (Ezek. 4:9). Perhaps part of each day was used for those designated purposes. Isaiah's ministry as a "sign and portent" (v. 3) compares with that of his sons in 8:18.

BABYLON—THE DESERT BY THE SEA (21:1–10)

This is the first of two oracles (the other is 22:1) that do not use a direct name for the nation involved, though from verse 9 it is clear that Babylon is intended. The cryptic "Desert by the Sea" may be a derogatory title. With its great rivers and many canals, Babylonia was a fertile farmland, but the coming judgment would turn this country on the northern edge of the Persian Gulf into a desert. The later salinization of the soil through irrigation eventually ruined its agricultural usefulness. Babylon's significance in the history of Israel may account for this additional oracle. Isaiah's treatment of Babylon occupies the most space in this section of the prophecy (cf. chs. 13–14).

Babylon's invaders would come against her like a storm from the desert. In verse 2 we are told that Elam and Media would cross the wilderness east of Babylon and make their attack. Only the Medes were mentioned in 13:17, but now Babylon's immediate neighbors across the Tigris join in. In 546 B.C. the Elamites did make a surprise raid into southern Babylonia, a move that apparently brought King Nabonidus back to Babylon after a long absence. Seven years later the Elamites were part of the larger Persian army that conquered the land.

The kings of Babylon had caused great suffering (v. 2), yet in verses 3 and 4 Isaiah staggered as he contemplated Babylon's fall. At the judgment of Moab, the prophet wept sympathetically (15:5; 16:9), but here the reaction is more traumatic. Verse 5 reveals that the Babylonians were banqueting when they should have been fighting. According to Daniel 5, the very night Babylon was captured Belshazzar held a feast—a birthday celebration for the king, according to Herodotus.

In verses 6–9 the scene shifts to a point east of the city. Isaiah was told to post a watchman to report any military movement. Because he is an ideal (not a real) watchman, he stays on the job day and night, looking for signs of the Persian army. Apparently the donkeys and camels were used in battle, not just to carry the supplies. The Midianites had once terrorized the Israelites with their fast-moving camels (Judg. 6:5).

Finally a man who had witnessed the battle is pictured as coming to tell the lookout the long-awaited news: "Babylon has fallen, has fallen!" (v. 9). This collapse would discredit Babylon's gods. This famous line was adapted by John in Revelation

14:8 and 18:2 where Babylon's demise means the end of the Satanic forces that oppose the Lord.

Babylon's fall meant Israel's release from captivity and ignominious suffering. Babylon would thresh the people of God, but her days were numbered. This is the good news that is fully developed in chapters 40–66.

EDOM (21:11–12)

This short oracle is titled "concerning Dumah," or "silence," another example of Isaiah's penchant for wordplays. "Dumah" sounds very much like "Edom," and since "Seir" (v. 11) is a synonym for "Edom," Judah's neighbor to the south must have been intended (cf. the use of "Dimon" for "Dibon" in 15:9).★

Edom descended from Jacob's brother Esau, and like Moab they remained a bitter enemy of Israel from the time of the Exodus. The Edomites were constantly warring with Judah. Whenever the southern kingdom showed signs of weakness, Edom was sure to take advantage of it. Edom plays an important role in the key prophetic passages of chapters 34 and 63, but it is difficult to explain why only two verses are allotted to the nation in chapters 13–23.

As in the previous oracle, a watchman is the important figure in this one. His response, however, is enigmatic. What he may be saying is that the long night of Assyrian oppression is almost over, and the night of Babylonian rule would follow a brief "morning" of respite.[3]

ARABIA (21:13–17)

In a chapter that emphasizes oracles about the desert (cf. 21:1), some mention of Arab tribes is expected. Edom often worked in close conjunction with the descendants of Ishmael,

★"Seir" was actually the name of the central mountain range that dominated the region of Edom.

[3]Franz Delitzsch, Biblical Commentary on the Prophecies of Isaiah, trans. James Martin, 3d ed., 2 vols. (1877; reprint, Grand Rapids: Eerdmans, 1967), 1:385.

particularly with the Dedanites (cf. Ezek. 25:13). The tribes of Arabia did not escape Assyrian domination, which began in the year 732 B.C. Sargon conducted several campaigns against them (726 and 715 B.C.). The simple bows of the Arabs were no match for the swords and composite bows of the Assyrians. Consequently the important caravan trade was badly disrupted.

Tema (v. 14) was an oasis in northern Arabia where the Babylonian king Nabonidus later spent ten years (549–539 B.C.). Because of Tema's abundant resources, the Temanites were asked to give aid to the many fugitives who fled from the armies of Assyria.

The prose warning given to Kedar (vv. 16–17) follows the same form as the warning in 16:13–14. Both passages specify a precise time, as measured by a hired man, before the splendor of the nation would come to an end. In the case of Kedar, only one year remained until judgment. The two passages also mention that Moab and Kedar would have few survivors.

JERUSALEM (22:1–25)

It is strange to find a prophecy against Judah and Jerusalem in a section that deals with the nations. But since Judah had chosen to behave like her neighbors and to desert the Lord, she deserved to be judged. This is an oracle about "the Valley of Vision," a title used again in verse 5. Jerusalem was the place where God had revealed Himself to the prophets and to Isaiah through visions. It was surrounded on three sides by valleys, but those valleys would soon be filled with chariots and troops (v. 7). Joel spoke of "the Valley of Jehosphaphat" as a place where God would judge the nations (Joel 3:2). Jerusalem went through the deep valley of judgment when Nebuchadnezzar's armies surrounded her in 588 B.C., and that final siege is the likely fulfillment of this chapter.

The Siege of Jerusalem (22:1–14)

In some ways Jerusalem was like Babylon. Both capitals were filled with revelry and feasting (vv. 2, 13; cf. 21:5). In the light of Judah's moral and spiritual corruption, the people should have been weeping and mourning, but the opposite was true. Perhaps the partying in Jerusalem continued almost to the very end, as it did in Babylon. If not, then verse 2 describes Jerusalem as it once had been.

Generally speaking, verses 1–4 fit the actual conditions that prevailed when the end came for Jerusalem in 587 B.C. Many people in the city died from famine and disease, not from combat wounds. Zedekiah and other leaders fled eastward until they were captured on the plains of Jericho. Some of the people went to their housetops, either to wail (cf. 15:3) or to worship the astral deities. Isaiah himself was overcome with grief at the prospect of the collapse of his beloved people. He had wept earlier over the fall of Moab (16:9–11), but he was inconsolable at the thought of Jerusalem's demise.

Verse 5 describes the attack against Jerusalem as the Day of the Lord, and the characteristic "in that day" occurs in verses 8, 12, 20, and 25. A powerful, threefold alliteration begins this colorful passage (v. 5). Unprecedented tumult and confusion fills the air as troops from Elam and Kir close in. Elam had been mentioned in 21:2 as one of the enemies of Babylon. Because Elam, Babylon's neighbor to the east, had strongly supported the Babylonians and the Chaldeans in the struggle against Assyria, the Elamites were probably allies of the Babylonians.[4]

Prior to the invasion, the people of Jerusalem had made some military preparations. They had taken the available weapons that were stored in the palace that Solomon had built from Lebanese cedars (1 Kings 7:2–6). They also attempted to increase the water supply in case of a long siege, as Hezekiah had done before Sennacherib's arrival (2 Chron. 32:30). At the same time they used the rubble from some expendable houses to make Jerusalem's walls more solid.

These were all excellent defensive measures, yet in themselves they were not sufficient. Above all, Judah needed to rely on the Lord. He alone, regardless of the might of the enemy, had the power to protect the Judeans (cf. 31:5). It was the sinful attitudes and actions of the people that kept them from turning

[4]Kaiser, *Isaiah 13–39*, p. 140.

to the Lord. In their shortsighted, materialistic frame of mind they would "eat and drink" today and die tomorrow (v. 13). For such stubbornness there was no forgiveness (v. 14).

The Fall of Shebna and the Rise of Eliakim (22:15–25)

The second half of the chapter (vv. 15–25) is a pronouncement of judgment on a specific individual named Shebna. Perhaps this government official exemplified the attitudes so detrimental to the life of the nation as a whole. In some respects this section corresponds to the prophecy against the king of Babylon in chapter 14. The king of Judah at this time was Hezekiah—a good king—so the condemnatory judgment fell on the next person in line. Shebna and the populace in general did not share the godly principles of King Hezekiah.

Shebna was apparently second in rank to the king. His job as palace administrator was held a few decades earlier by Jotham, a coregent with Uzziah. According to 2 Kings 15:5, the job involved major judicial responsibilities, and from Isaiah 36:3 we learn that important diplomatic assignments were also included. Whenever Shebna is mentioned, his father's name is omitted, and that suggests that he was a foreigner or a member of a low social class. Many believe that he was of Egyptian extraction and that he encouraged Hezekiah to make a firm alliance with Egypt.

Shebna was guilty of pride and the love of luxury. In good Egyptian style, he wanted to build a prominent grave that would bring him special honor. A tomb from the time of Hezekiah, found in the village of Siloam, provides an interesting example of the kind of tombs that were built in that day (cf. the discussion of graves and memorials in 14:19).[5] The Pharaohs of Egypt spent most of their time and money building their tombs, the pyramids. Shebna was also condemned for his "splendid chariots" (v. 18), another indication of the royal standing he thought he deserved. Apparently he abused his authority in the interests of personal gain.

[5] See N. Avigad, "The Epitaph of a Royal Steward from Siloam Village," *Israel Exploration Journal* 3 (1953): 137–52.

Like the king of Babylon (14:19–20), Shebna was demoted and deprived of an honorable burial. He would be thrown like a ball into a spacious country where he could keep rolling for miles. All his lofty ambitions would be shattered.

Shebna was to be replaced by Eliakim, son of Hilkiah, who was given the significant title "My servant" (v. 20). Isaiah himself was so designated in 20:3, and in chapters 42–53 the Servant Songs make full use of this title. It strongly implies that Eliakim was a godly and effective ruler.

Eliakim was to receive the distinctive dress and authority of his position. Unlike Shebna, he would not abuse his office. As a "father" (v. 21) he would genuinely care for and protect the people he ruled. Eliakim's close relationship with the king is indicated by his holding the key to the house of David (v. 22). In many matters of government, Eliakim would have the final word because the king would delegate authority to him. The imagery of the key of David is applied to Christ in Revelation 3:7. On His shoulders will rest all the powers of government (cf. 9:6).

A second figure is used in verses 23–25. There Eliakim is compared to a peg that eventually gives way. Just as one peg cannot bear the weight of an unlimited number of bowls and jars, so Eliakim would someday collapse under the load placed on him. This may be a picture of the problems caused by nepotism, though Drechsler believes that his descendants—not Eliakim himself—are the ones who were to fall.[6] In either case Eliakim's effectiveness was only temporary at best. By the year 701 B.C., Isaiah's prophecy at least had been partially fulfilled. Eliakim had risen to the position of palace administrator, and Shebna occupied the slightly lower office of "secretary" (36:3).

TYRE (23:1–18)

The final oracle against the nations is fittingly reserved for Tyre, the queen of the seas. Because of their excellent harbors and seamanship, the Phoenician cities of Tyre and Sidon had

[6] Cited by E. J. Young, The Book of Isaiah, 3 vols. (Grand Rapids: Eerdmans, 1965–72), 2:117.

carved out a commercial empire far beyond that which their size deserved. Tyre was the "Babylon" of the sea, and Revelation 18 seems to combine some of the qualities of ancient Babylon and Tyre to portray the commercial "Babylon" of the end times.

Tyre was a city in two parts, one on the coast and one on two rocky islands about half a mile from the shore. It was the island fortress that defied capture until Alexander the Great captured it (332 B.C.), and perhaps this lengthy delay in judgment explains why the oracle comes last.

During the reign of David and Solomon, King Hiram of Tyre provided cedars and craftsmen for construction and sailors for Solomon's commercial ventures. This valuable contact was offset by the marriage of Jezebel, the daughter of Ethbaal, King of Tyre, to Ahab in 870 B.C. Jezebel brought with her a militant Baalism that made heavy inroads into Israel's religious life.

Several Assyrian kings exacted heavy tribute from the Phoenicians, but Nebuchadnezzar was the first to capture the mainland city of Tyre (572 B.C.) after a thirteen-year siege. He was unable, however, to capture the offshore fortress itself. Alexander succeeded in destroying the island city of Tyre by building a two-hundred-foot-wide causeway half a mile out into the water. Alexander leveled the city completely, slaughtered most of its leaders, and sold about 30,000 of the residents into slavery. Mainland Tyre regained its independence in 126 B.C., but it never attained the prominence it once had enjoyed. Over the years the island city was nearly covered with water as its coastline sank below the level of the Mediterranean Sea.

Chapter 23 features a number of imperatives at the start of each of the paragraphs (vv. 1, 2, 4, 6, 10, 12b, 14). The command "Wail, O ships of Tarshish!" occurs at the beginning and the end of this series, and "Tarshish" is mentioned again in verses 6 and 10. Ships from Tarshish were far-ranging, ocean-going vessels used by Solomon and other kings in their commercial ventures (cf. 2:16; 1 Kings 10:22; 22:48). Thus far attempts to locate the city of Tarshish have centered on Tartessus in Spain, the island of Sardinia, or else somewhere along the coast of North Africa.

The fall of Tyre would affect the economy of the entire Mediterranean world, a fact that explains the multiple references to Cyprus, Egypt, and other areas. Without Phoenician sailors the harvest of the Nile could not reach the world markets as easily (vv. 3, 5). Sidon, Tyre's sister city, also would suffer at the collapse of her neighbor (vv. 2, 4, 12). She is called the "Virgin Daughter of Sidon" in verse 12 because until the time of the prophecy, she had escaped the domination of foreigners (cf. 37:22). Tyre and Sidon represent the whole region of Phoenicia.

Verses 6–12 explain why Tyre would fall. Like Jerusalem (22:2) Tyre was a city of revelry and was renowned for her pride. Therefore the Lord would stretch out His hand and strike her down. This was His plan and purpose (vv. 9, 11) and no one could resist His order (cf. 14:24–27). The great pride of Tyre and her ruler is also the subject of Ezekiel 28.

The meaning and function of verse 13 is the most difficult part of this chapter. One school of thought believes that the Chaldeans are another illustration of a people who suffer destruction. The Assyrian monarch Sennacherib did destroy the city of Babylon in 689 B.C. and prevented the Chaldeans from emerging as a major power for another sixty-five years. Other commentators believe that the Chaldeans are introduced in verse 13 because they were the ones who eventually conquered Tyre. The Chaldeans would raise their siege towers and strip the palaces of Tyre. In the context this interpretation makes better sense, but it is more difficult to derive from the syntax of the verse.

The last section (vv. 15–18) describes the restoration of Tyre after a seventy-year period. This length of time corresponds to the years of Judah's captivity. (Sennacherib initiated a seventy-year desolation of Babylon.) After this period Tyre will resume her role as a commercial "prostitute" (v. 15), but her earnings will be given to the Lord. This strange figure of speech stems from the pagan custom of having temple prostitutes devote their services to a particular deity, a custom that supposedly transformed sexual immorality into a religious offering. In international affairs a prostitute was a nation that sacrificed honest practices for commercial advantage (Rev. 18:3).

Once again Tyre will use questionable methods to make a

profit, but this time God will not allow her to amass a fortune. Part of her profits will be turned over to the people of God (cf. 60:5–7, 11–12). The language of verse 18 may imply that someday Tyre will give up her harlotry and will truly serve the Lord (cf. 18:7). In later centuries Tyre became the seat of a Christian bishopric.

8

THE APOCALYPSE
24:1–27:13

As we noted earlier, chapters 24–27 are often considered to be the grand finale to the Oracles Against the Nations. These four chapters look ahead to the final judgment that will come on the world before the Lord begins His reign on Mount Zion. Although it is true that many of the themes of chapters 24–27 expand on sections of chapters 13–23 (cf. 13:2–16; 19:23–25), the overall theme of the Day of the Lord was first discussed in chapters 2–4. There, as in chapters 24–27, the expression "in that day" occurs repeatedly (24:21; 25:9; 26:1; 27:1, 2, 12, 13) and reaches a climax in the fourfold use of that phrase in chapter 27. As the judgment of God falls on sinful nations, the righteous break forth with singing and rejoicing (24:16; 25:9; 26:1, 19; 27:2). The song of the ungodly reveler (24:9) and of the ruthless oppressor (25:5) will be stilled.

Some of the elements of these chapters are apocalyptic. This genre of literature, best illustrated in the Bible by the Book of Revelation, emphasizes the last days and a dualistic struggle between the forces of God and the forces of Satan. The outlook of chapters 24–27 is eschatological; they contain no clear reference to the prophet's own day. Isaiah 25:6–8 anticipates the bliss of the eternal state (cf. Rev. 7:17; 21:4). The battle between God and the forces of evil is mentioned in 24:21 and in 27:1, and in the latter verse the serpent Leviathan is a symbol of Satan. In apocalyptic literature animals are often used symbolically (cf. Dan. 7).

Although this section of Isaiah contains the largest concentration of apocalyptic elements, earlier passages also employed this literary genre (cf. 13:10; 14:12). Chapter 34, with its description of a cataclysmic, world-wide judgment, is a close parallel to chapter 24.

THE DESTRUCTION OF THE EARTH (24:1–23)

The opening chapter of the apocalypse depicts the total devastation of the earth. "Earth" itself occurs fifteen times, and a ruined city is mentioned in verses 10 and 12. Even the forces of heaven are punished as the great judgment strikes (vv. 21–22). The first three verses describe the extent of the judgment and its great leveling effect on society. In verse 2 Isaiah listed six pairs of persons who had opposite positions in life—a technique similar to the one reflected in the pairs of terms that are used in 3:1–3. When the Lord lays the earth waste, society will be turned upside down. All classes of people will be affected.

Verses 4–13 portray some of the particular effects of the judgment and the reasons for it. The situation is summed up graphically by verse 4, with its repetition of "withers" and "languish" (cf. 34:4). Sin brought this curse on the earth because man disobeyed God's laws and broke His everlasting covenant. This is most likely a reference to the Noahic Covenant where God promised never again to destroy the world with a flood (Gen. 9:11, 16). Yet in verses 18 and 19 Isaiah described the judgment of God figuratively in terms of that very flood. Man's rebellion against God's requirements was so total that God had to consume the earth.

The scene of mourning and gloom is emphasized by the "withering" of the vine (v. 7). Without wine there is no music and no joy. A dreadful pall comes over the city; entertainment and partying have disappeared completely. The description is reminiscent of Babylon (21:5) and Jerusalem (22:2), and it may be that the city so prominent in these chapters (25:2; 27:10) reflects a composite picture. It is a worldly city, one that is opposed to the righteous principles of God. At various points in history it was represented by Babylon, Nineveh, Jerusalem, and Rome—or by several cities concurrently.[1] If Jerusalem is involved, she too must be destroyed (cf. 27:10).

Not all mankind will be destroyed, however, for verse 13 tells about the gleanings from an olive tree or a grape harvest. The same imagery is used of the remnant of Israel in 17:6. Probably it is this righteous remnant that speaks out in verses 14–16a. While the wicked wail and groan, the remnant shouts for joy and glorifies the God of Israel. The pride of man will be abased and the majesty of God acclaimed (cf. 2:10f.).

Lest this note of hope be overemphasized, Isaiah returned to the theme of judgment (v. 16b), and his words resemble those he used in 6:5 to describe his response to seeing God's glory. Isaiah viewed the "treacherous" (v. 16) either as the enemies of Jerusalem or as the wicked within Judah. Based on the occurrence of the same word in 21:2 and in 33:1, the first interpretation seems more likely. With a powerful, threefold alliteration, Isaiah showed just how inescapable the coming judgment will be. In a similar way, Amos referred to three different animals—one of which was sure to claim its victim (5:19).

The catastrophe reaches even greater proportions in the last part of verse 18 where there is a clear allusion to the Flood. Just as the Lord once opened the windows of heaven and broke up the fountains of the deep (Gen. 7:11), so He would again unleash a terrible destruction on the world. The description in verses 18–20 emphasizes the power of earthquakes. In 1:8 the fragile hut refers to an isolated Jerusalem. Here in verse 20 it is a picture of total collapse—the earth has withered away completely (cf. v. 4).

Verses 21–23 broaden the scope of the judgment to include the heavens. This is the first occurrence in this section of the phrase "in that day," a strong indication that the end times are in view. To complete the judgment of the earth, God must deal

---

[1] Note that the "great city" of Revelation 11:8 may represent Sodom, Egypt, Jerusalem, and Rome—a kind of "transhistorical city of Satan." See Alan F. Johnson, "Revelation," in *The Expositor's Bible Commentary*, ed. Frank E. Gaebelein (Grand Rapids: Zondervan, 1981), 12:506.

with the evil forces that foment rebellion against Him, namely Satan and his army of angels. The imprisonment of these powerful beings has significant parallels with the confinement of Satan that is recorded in Revelation 20:1–10. After being restrained for a thousand years, Satan will be released for a brief time and then thrown into the lake of fire. The kings of the earth appear in Sheol in Isaiah 14:9–10.

With the defeat of all His enemies in heaven and on earth, the Lord will reign supreme on Mount Zion, thus fulfilling the prophecy of 2:2–4. No longer will the light of the sun or the moon be needed. The glory of the Lord will outshine them both (cf. 60:19–20; Rev. 21:23–25; 22:5). At Mount Sinai, Moses, Aaron, and the elders of Israel caught a glimpse of that same divine glory (Exod. 24:9–10). The personification of the sun and the moon in verse 23 and of the earth in verse 20 is characteristic of Isaiah's poetic style.

REJOICING OVER THE FALL OF GOD'S ENEMIES
(25:1–12)

The theme of the exaltation of Mount Zion continues in chapter 25. Three times the phrase "on this mountain" is used (vv. 6, 7, 10). In the first 5 verses, however, Isaiah interjected a psalm in praise of the victories described in chapter 24. God's triumph over the fortified city was truly a marvelous thing (v. 21). The ruthless had oppressed the poor and the needy (vv. 4, 5), but those same ruthless nations will have to bow before the Lord (v. 3). Four times in verse 4 God offers refuge and protection for the helpless. Their enemies will be silenced, and the city they feared will never be rebuilt (v. 2). Almost the same terminology was applied to the earth in 24:20. It will fall, "never to rise again."

In verses 6–8 Isaiah resumed his description of the New Jerusalem that he had begun in 24:23. When the Lord reigns on Mount Zion, He will prepare a lavish banquet to celebrate His coronation (cf. 1 Kings 1:19, 25). All the righteous will participate in this feast, which has important parallels with the marriage supper of the Lamb in Revelation 19:9. It will be an occasion of true rejoicing over the downfall of God's enemies.

How different is the drunken revelry that only for a brief time blots out the problems of sinners (cf. 22:13)!

Since Adam's fall man's final enemy has been death. But even death will be destroyed by the Lord Almighty. Death, or Sheol, has always swallowed up everything in its path, but now death itself will be swallowed up! The apostle Paul rejoiced in this victory that ultimately will be accomplished through Christ (1 Cor. 15:54). When death is vanquished, suffering and sorrow will also be removed. Twice before, Isaiah had mentioned weeping (15:3; 23:14). In the Near East weeping was not considered to be effeminate or a sign of weakness, and it was much more common than in our culture. Some day pain and mourning will be gone, and so there will no longer be a need to cry (cf. 35:10; Rev. 21:4).

God's triumph over His foes will bring an end to Israel's disgrace. Because of the sin of that nation, God allowed foreign invaders to defeat His people and to take them into exile. All this will be changed as the righteous remnant sees God vindicated and her position of blessing restored (cf. 54:4).

Again Isaiah paused to praise the Lord. In verses 1–5 an individual was speaking, but in verse 9 the plural reflects the voice of the people, who were mentioned in verse 8. When the Lord brings into being the blessings of verses 6–8, the redeemed will have ample reason to rejoice in His salvation.

Verses 10–12 return to the subject of the fall of the fortified city. This time the mountain of Zion is contrasted with Moab, her neighbor across the Jordan. Moab, like Edom in chapter 34, symbolizes the enemies of God. Throughout its history Moab had been a thorn in Israel's flesh (see the comments on chapter 15), and so it serves as an appropriate symbol of the world city. The pride that characterized Moab (16:4) befits the lofty walls of this fortified city—walls that will utterly collapse under God's judgment (v. 12).

The picture of Moab's judgment (vv. 10–11) is not a pretty one. The nation will suffer the utter degradation of a person who drowns in a pile of manure. Such graphic and earthy imagery emphasizes the severity of the coming judgment, a severity that is portrayed with even greater vividness in the final verse of Isaiah's prophecy (66:24).

JUDAH'S SONG OF PRAISE (26:1–21)

For the second time in this apocalyptic section, praise to the Lord is associated with the phrase "in that day" (cf. 25:9). In 12:1 and 4 Isaiah used the same expression to introduce songs. The song of praise in chapter 26 probably extends through verse 6, and verses 7–19 constitute a prayer to God to take action soon. These verses contain several elements that are characteristic of a hymn of lament (cf. 63:7–64:12).

The Song of Judah (26:1–6)

The opening song is a direct response to the closing verses of chapter 25. The walls of Moab's fortified city will come crashing down to the ground, but the city of Judah is strong and safe. According to verse 2, only the righteous may enter its gates, a thought similar to Psalm 24:3–4. Perfect peace (šālôm šālôm, "genuine peace") is in store for those who are firmly committed to and who fully trust the Lord (cf. Ps. 112:7–8). The word for "mind" (v. 3) connotes a frame of mind or a plan, or purpose. Man's attitudes and goals must be thoroughly aligned with God's will. This deep sense of trust in the Lord— repeated in verse 4—was the very quality that Judah did not possess in Isaiah's time. They trusted in the occult (8:19) and ridiculed the plans of the "Holy One of Israel" (5:19). Ahaz trusted in Assyria, though he should have known that the Lord was the eternal Rock (v. 4), the only true source of confidence.

The terminology of verse 5 is heavily dependent on 25:12. So complete will the downfall of the lofty city be that those who once were oppressed will trample it down. The former plight of the helpless in the fortified city was related in 25:4.

The Prayer of Judah (26:7–21)

Verse 7 marks a shift in thought as the nation pleads with God to make the promises of chapters 25 and 26 a reality. The song now takes on the character of a lament, with the prayer that God will judge the earth and vindicate the righteous. Verses 7–11 contain several features common to Wisdom

Literature, of which Proverbs is the best known example. Isaiah contrasted the righteous and the wicked in terms of their different reactions to God's leading. The Lord always provides a smooth road for the righteous, as He would for those who were exiled in Babylon (cf. 40:3–4). Obedience to God's law and a deep longing to see God honored characterize the righteous. These assertions of loyalty to the Lord constitute a confession of trust within the lament. Verses 12, 13, and 19 provide additional examples. By expressing their trust in the Lord, the righteous hope to motivate Him to answer their prayer.[2] Psalm 44:17–22 illustrates how in a national hymn of lament a motivational passage prepares the way for the petition.

The wicked go along life's way oblivious to the rights of the just. They do not heed the warning of God's uplifted hand and must feel judgment before they learn. Thus in verses 9 through 11, the righteous plead with God to show His zeal for His people by consuming their enemies. God's zeal was first mentioned in 9:7, and it appears again in 63:15 in the midst of a powerful lament.

Laments often contain a reference to the past, and this one is no exception. Verses 12–18 review some of Israel's past defeats and triumphs, recognizing that God was fully responsible for the latter. Perhaps Isaiah includes Babylon and Assyria among the "lords" of verse 13. The punishment accorded them resembles the fate of the king of Babylon (14:9–10). The nation's enlargement (v. 15) recalls 9:3 and the victory over Midian. Whenever Israel triumphed over her enemies, her borders were restored and her joy increased. The return from exile is described in similar terms in 54:2–3.

Hidden behind the word "ruled" (v. 13) is the Hebrew noun *ba'al*, which means master or husband. The implication may be that the prevalent worship of the god "Baal" lay at the root of many of Israel's troubles.

The severe distress mentioned in verses 16–18 may correspond to the situation described in 5:30 and in 8:21–22 where the Assyrian invasion was predicted. In 37:3 Hezekiah

---

[2]Claus Westermann, *The Praise of God in the Psalms,* trans. Keith R. Crim (Richmond, Vir.: John Knox, 1965), p. 55.

used the imagery of childbearing when making his appeal to the Lord in the face of Sennacherib's threat. One could also relate verse 19 to that same crucial episode. Assyria's soldiers lay dead on the field (37:36), but *your* dead will rise again, God promised.

The time of distress, however, could apply equally well to the period of the judges when Israel was repeatedly humiliated. During that era Israel's oppression was prolonged and intense. The change from the third person (v. 16) to the first person (vv. 17–18) underscores the agony of the nation. Israel might have been a source of blessing for the world at large, but the people of Israel admitted their failure (v. 18). They were designed to be "a light for the Gentiles" (42:6) but turned out to be a stumbling block and a bone of contention.

The chapter reaches a climax in verse 19, where Isaiah gave a startling assertion about a resurrection; but is it the prophet or the nation that is speaking? In verses 20 and 21, Isaiah spoke to the nation. Perhaps verse 19 is the transition. If so, the "your" of "your dead" would refer to Israel and not to God. There is a contrast between the dead who will rise (v. 19) and the departed spirits who do not rise (v. 14). Verse 14 does not deny the resurrection of both the righteous and the wicked; the specific subject of the resurrection of the body is not introduced until verse 19. Some passages about the resurrection (e.g., Ezek. 37) refer to the revival of Israel as a nation; others (e.g., Dan. 12:2) clearly teach the resurrection of the body of every dead person (believer or not). Isaiah 26:19 belongs to the latter category and develops the earlier promise that death would be swallowed up (25:7–8). The refreshing morning dew stands in striking contrast to the dust of death. What a picture of productivity compared to the futility and fruitlessness of verse 18!

The answer to Israel's prayer is given in verses 20 and 21. Soon God would begin to pour out His wrath and to punish the world for its sin. The time of "wrath" could include additional suffering for Israel, such as the Exile, or it could refer more directly to the Great Tribulation. During that period (Rev. 7:14) the fury of the nations will be turned loose against Israel until God judges the world in His wrath (see 66:14–16 for a fuller account of this judgment).

ISRAEL'S SALVATION (27:1–13)

After Israel's enemies are punished, the nation will enjoy God's blessing and protection as never before. Israel will be forgiven, made fruitful, and restored to her own soil. The first two verses and the last two verses begin with "in that day," and in each pair the first verse emphasizes punishment (vv. 1, 12).

Verse 1 is a transition verse that is closely linked with the end of chapter 26. In symbolic language it depicts the destruction of evil, which is described as a serpent or a monster. The terminology itself is derived from mythology. Passages from Ugaritic literature talk about "Lotan the fleeing serpent . . . the tortuous serpent."[3] "Lotan," a seven-headed monster, is another form of "Leviathan," and the adjectives used to describe him are identical with "gliding" and "coiling" here in verse 1 (*brḥ* and *'qltn*). In 51:9 Egypt is compared to another monster called "Rahab," and in Ezekiel 29:3 and 32:2 Egypt is referred to as a monster by the sea. Thus the reference in verse 1 could be to foreign nations. In the light of Revelation 12:9, however, it is difficult to deny that Satan is the ultimate reference behind the figure of the serpent.[4] The Devil is referred to both as a "dragon" and as a "serpent" in the same verse, and this symbolism represents his wisdom and destructive power.

When the forces of evil are destroyed, Israel's position will be established. This is portrayed in a second Song of the Vineyard, which has an outcome far different from the song in 5:1–7. Under the Lord's watchful eye, the vineyard, which represents Israel, becomes remarkably fruitful. Whereas the vineyard in chapter 5 was overrun by thorns, not a brier or thorn can be found in this vineyard. God allows no one to

---

[3] Text 67:I, lines 1–2. See Cyrus H. Gordon, *Ugaritic Textbook,* 2 vols. (Rome: Pontifical Biblical Institute, 1965), 1:178, and J. B. Pritchard, *Ancient Near Eastern Texts* (Princeton, N. J.: Princeton University Press, 1955), pp. 137–38.

[4] See E. Wallis Budge, *The Gods of the Egyptians* (New York: Dover Publications, 1969), pp. 278–79.

"harm" it (v. 3). The same word is translated "punish" in 26:21 and in 27:1. Those who oppose the vineyard must submit to the Lord or face destruction. Once Israel had been fruitless among the nations (26:18), but someday she is going to be a blessing, filling the whole world with fruit (27:6).

Such a glorious picture was a far cry from the actual status of Israel from the eighth to the sixth centuries B.C. Before the vineyard could bud and blossom, it had to be devastated, though Israel's punishment would not be as severe as that which other nations would face. Verses 7–11 describe the judgment that was to come on Israel prior to her future exaltation. Wars and exile will come, and the fortified city will be abandoned (vv. 8, 10). Here the world city is Jerusalem. She must suffer the same fate as Nineveh and Babylon because her sins are the same as theirs (cf. comments on 24:4–12). Verse 11 recalls the charge that was leveled against Israel in the opening verses of the Book of Isaiah. The nation had turned her back on God and had chosen the altars of Baal and the Asherah poles. These pagan symbols mentioned in verse 9 were condemned earlier in 17:8, a passage that also depicts the underbrush and thickets that will take over Israel's cities (cf. 17:9; 27:10–11).

The last two verses of this apocalyptic section return to the theme of 27:1–6. "In that day" Israel will come back to Jerusalem from Assyria and Egypt. The picture is similar to that of 19:23–25 where a highway from Assyria to Egypt made it possible for these nations to worship with Israel. Here in 27:12–13, however, the focus is on the remnant of Israel.

Threshing (v. 12) is normally associated with judgment and is an indication that the nations may be reluctant to give up their Israelite captives. The Euphrates and the Wadi of Egypt— the Wadi el-Arish—represent the northern and southern borders of the Promised Land in its widest extent (Gen. 15:18). The threshing will separate the Jews from the Gentiles, and the former will resume their worship on Mount Zion (cf. 2:2–4). Ultimately these verses refer to the return to Israel in the last days, but the return from Babylon afforded a partial fulfillment (see 11:11 and comments).

9

BOOK OF WOES
AND RESTORATION
28:1–35:10

Beginning with chapter 28, Isaiah again described the judgment that would come on Israel and Judah, directing most of his remarks in chapters 28–35 to the southern kingdom. Although five of the first six chapters in this section begin with *woe,* Isaiah also emphasized the theme of hope, and his presentation alternates between the themes of judgment and salvation. This section of the Book of Isaiah is brought to a climax in chapters 34 and 35, which are a short, powerful apocalypse.

Except for chapters 34 and 35, the material in this section is closely related to the historical setting in Isaiah's own day. The fall of Samaria was imminent, and Judah was about to be punished. During Hezekiah's reign the leaders of Judah entered alliances with Egypt in an effort to throw off the Assyrian yoke, and Isaiah directly addressed this issue.

A PROPHECY AGAINST SAMARIA (28:1–29)

The chapters in this unit occur in pairs. The first two deal with the capital cities of the northern and southern kingdoms respectively.

The Pride and Unbelief of the People (28:1–10)

Chapter 28 begins with a description of the fall of Samaria, a city whose power was fading in Isaiah's day. Samaria was built on a prominent, well-rounded hill by Ahab's father, King Omri. It stood out dramatically from the surrounding terrain, and the people of the northern kingdom of Israel (Ephraim) were proud of its beauty and strong fortifications. But Israel had been devastated by the Assyrian invasion of 732 B.C.; and at the time Isaiah was writing (probably about 725 B.C.), Samaria's collapse was not far off.

During the early part of the eighth century B.C., Samaria was known for its luxury. The prophet Amos especially condemned the materialism and drunkenness of the people (Amos 6:4–7), and Isaiah implied that such practices continued even after they had lost their wealth. God would judge the people's pride and drunkenness by sending a great storm against them, the overflowing waters of Assyria, Isaiah prophesied (cf. 8:7). Samaria would be trampled down, just like the vineyard of Judah (5:5).

Words like "glorious," "beautiful," and "pride" reminded Isaiah of his description of the Messiah, the "pride and glory" of Israel (4:2). In the messianic future Israel will once again have a just ruler, one who will have the power to resist military aggression (cf. 11:2).

After this brief interlude, Isaiah returned to the problem at hand. Were all the drunkards confined to Samaria? No! Judah had the same problem, and the religious leaders were the most guilty. Those who should have been filled with the Spirit were filled with wine. Through the alternation of the words "stagger" and "reel," one can almost visualize the tipsy scene. The repulsive description in verse 8 is comparable to that described in 25:10–11.

Verses 9 and 10 portray the sarcastic reaction these Judean leaders had to Isaiah's words of rebuke. They were tired of Isaiah's strictness and of his recurring application of God's laws. The string of monosyllables in verse 10 may mean that the Judean leaders regarded Isaiah's message as meaningless or as child's play. Their mocking tone recalls the words of 5:19.

The Lord's Opposition to His Own People (28:11–29)

God promised that the Judean leaders would hear stranger sounds yet (vv. 11–13). The Assyrians were coming, and the people would not be able to understand them at all. Their rules and regulations would be harsh. God wanted His people to have peace and rest (v. 12), but they stumbled over His word and were injured and captured. The last four verbs in verse 13 are also found in the important parallel passage in 8:15.

Although the people had rejected the word of the Lord, Isaiah presented it to them anyway (vv. 14–22). The nation had taken steps—so it thought—to insure the safety of the people. They were acting as if death could not touch them. Perhaps this refers to the alliance with Egypt that was supposed to protect the nation from Assyrian aggression (cf. 20:6). Reliance on other gods was also involved.

Israel's true security lay in the Lord. He was a sure foundation, a solid rock who could be trusted (cf. 26:4) and who would never disappoint. In 8:14 the Lord is compared to a sanctuary and to a stone of stumbling, but for Israel the stone became a stumbling block (cf. 28:13), as it later did when the Jews rejected their Messiah (cf. 1 Pet. 2:6–8).

In verse 17 God uses His measuring line and plumb line to test the "refuge" in which the people trusted. Because it did not measure up to His standards, the Lord sent a storm to sweep it away. "The overwhelming scourge" (v. 18) combines two figures. "Overwhelming," or "overflowing," (vv. 15, 17, 18) refers to a flooding river that destroys everything in its path. A "scourge" is a whip and is also used to depict judgment against a nation (cf. 10:26). For the northern kingdom the "overwhelming scourge" was Assyria (cf. 28:2), but for Judah it was a combination of Assyria and Babylon. As often as the Mesopotamian powers came by, they would take captives from Judah (v. 19). God had offered the people rest, but they had refused (v. 12). According to the proverb given in verse 20, they would discover that their military and spiritual preparations were inadequate. Their bed would be too short and their blanket too narrow to afford any relief from an Assyrian invasion.

Verse 21 cites two illustrations that reinforce God's threat. The first comes from 2 Samuel 5:20. There David praised the Lord for breaking through the Philistines like a flood and for giving him victory. The second illustration refers to a hailstorm that helped Joshua defeat the five kings on the long day of Gibeon (Josh. 10:11). On both of these occasions, God was on Israel's side, storming against her foes. But according to Isaiah, this time the Lord would fight against His chosen people. In the light of these sobering words, Isaiah warned the people to stop scoffing. Their covenant with death★ would be annulled; destruction had been decreed against Judah (cf. 10:22–23). The fall of Samaria, predicted in verses 1–4, was the guarantee that God's judgment also would reach Judah.

The chapter ends with a two-stanza wisdom poem that describes farming (vv. 23–26, 27–29). The poem begins with a fourfold imperative, and each stanza ends with a verse that refers to God as the author of wisdom (vv. 26, 29). Verses 24 and 25 make effective use of questions. The poem discusses the various procedures and methods used by farmers as they plow their fields, plant various seeds, and thresh at harvest time. Because of the emphasis placed on threshing, the lesson may concern God's judgment on Israel. In 27:12 Isaiah linked threshing with the regathering of Israel, using the same word that is translated "beaten" in 28:27. God had to punish His people, but His judgment would not be overly harsh. Just as the farmer was careful to do the right thing at the right time, so God's timing would be perfect.

The phrase "wonderful in counsel" (v. 29) contains the same two roots found in "Wonderful Counselor" (9:6). The Messiah's rule would be characterized by the wise administration of justice, and God's handling of the nation of Israel also displayed that infinite wisdom. He used the proper instrument and procedure at the proper time to accomplish His purposes among His stubborn people.

A PROPHECY AGAINST JERUSALEM AND HER OPPONENTS (29:1–24)

The Siege of Jerusalem and the Reasons for It (29:1–16)

Parallel to the woe against Samaria in 28:1 is the woe against Jerusalem in 29:1. Once again a symbolic expression is

---

★Perhaps a reference to Ahaz's alliance with Assyria against the northern coalition.

used to describe the character of the city. "Ariel" appears five times in verses 1, 2, and 7. Verse 2 makes it clear that in this context "ariel" means "an altar hearth." The fighting and bloodshed around Jerusalem would make the city like a giant place of sacrifice. The people were convinced that the normal course of life would continue year after year, but God promised that He would lead the fight against Jerusalem, the very city He had chosen as His dwelling place!

In their extreme distress, the people whisper a prayer to the Lord (cf. 26:16). The language of verse 4 is closely tied to 8:19 where God condemned His people for resorting to spiritists who whisper and mutter. As punishment, Judah would be reduced to a ghostlike status, hanging precariously between life and death.

When all seems lost, the Lord suddenly bursts on the scene to rescue Jerusalem (vv. 5–8). This is a dramatic example of the speed with which Isaiah's message turns from judgment to salvation, and it illustrates how reluctant God is to punish His people. The Lord's intervention is described in terms of a theophany, complete with thunder, earthquake, and wind (Exod. 19:16–19). Against His might the enemy will vanish like dust or chaff. The word for "hordes" of nations occurs in verses 5, 7, and 8, but these assembled armies will meet crushing defeat. It will seem like a nightmare as they experience the frustration of having victory within their grasp and see it slip away.

In some respects Isaiah's description of the attack and deliverance resembles the events of the Assyrian invasion of 701 B.C., when disaster struck the invincible northern forces. Yet the opening paragraph of the chapter implies that Jerusalem would suffer severe damage and, perhaps, defeat. Some interpreters believe that Isaiah had no specific siege of Jerusalem in view but was summarizing the opposition Jerusalem would face throughout history.[1] The reference to "hordes of nations" fits the description of the final attack against Jerusalem just before the

---

[1] See Joseph A. Alexander, *Commentary on the Prophecies of Isaiah,* 2 vols. (1875; reprint, Grand Rapids: Zondervan, 1953), 1:461, and E. J. Young, *The Book of Isaiah,* 3 vols. (Grand Rapids: Eerdmans, 1965–72), 2:310.

second coming of Christ. When Jerusalem has been besieged and captured and is on the verge of extinction, Christ will return and completely shatter the nations (cf. Zech. 14:1–5). As far as the immediate future was in view, Isaiah may have been giving a combined description of the Assyrian and Babylonian invasions.

In verses 9–16, Isaiah returned to the topic of judgment and explained its necessity. The people were drunk, but it was different from the drunkenness of chapter 28 (cf. vv. 1, 7). A spiritual stupor had come over Judah and the prophets she trusted. They staggered like blind men because the Word of God had become a closed book to them. Whether educated or illiterate, it was impossible for them to read and understand God's Word. This condition existed because the people gave God lip service, but their hearts were not committed to Him (v. 13). They had mocked the teachings of God (28:10) and had exalted man-made rules, just as later the Pharisees emphasized human tradition (cf. Matt. 15:8–9). Their leaders made plans without consulting God because in their eyes human wisdom seemed sufficient. Those who were blind actually thought that *God* was the One who could not see! Since they had completely reversed the Creator-creature relationship, it is not surprising that Isaiah pronounced woe on them (v. 15). In 45:9 Isaiah showed how ridiculous it is to suppose that a pot could talk back to the potter, and in 10:15 he compared Assyria to an ax that quarrels with the woodsman.

A Glorious Transformation (29:17–24)

Again Isaiah refused to dwell too long on negative matters and looked ahead to a glorious transformation of God's people (vv. 17–24). In the glorious future societal wrongs will be made right, and Israel will genuinely worship the Lord. As usual it is difficult to understand when these events are supposed to occur. Verse 17 begins with "in a very short time," but verse 18 begins with the more common phrase "in that day," a phrase that often points to the distant future. If the cedars of Lebanon symbolize Assyria, as they do in 10:34, then Isaiah's language may refer to the humiliation of 701 B.C., when Lebanon was reduced to the status of a fertile field (cf. 32:15). The interchange between "forest" (i.e., Lebanon) and "fertile field," however, could refer in a general way to the changes in status that are reflected by the examples in verses 18–24.

The restoration of the ability to see and to hear (v. 18) is linked with the rule of the righteous king (32:3). A messianic interpretation of verse 18 is supported by the context and by 35:5. The Lord will defend the rights of the helpless and judge those who pervert justice. Isaiah condemned the "scoffers" in 28:14 and 22, and he used "ruthless" to describe the hordes of nations in 29:5. All the ungodly—whether Jews or Gentiles—will vanish under God's hand of judgment.

To emphasize the great change in store for Israel, Isaiah remarked that verses 22–24 are a solemn pronouncement of the Lord, Israel's Redeemer—a prominent title for God in chapters 40–66. Israel faced humiliation in battle (vv. 2–4), but someday she would not have to be ashamed or frightened. Her numbers would be reduced by war and captivity, but in the future her children will be numerous. Once Israel made fun of the Holy One of Israel (5:19), but in that future day she will have a profound respect for Him. Both Ephraim and Judah were wayward and drunk, but someday they will be eager to obey God's Word. Physically, morally, and spiritually the nation will be healthy and vigorous.

Many of the concepts in verses 22–24 are found in chapter 54, a song that celebrates the end of Israel's disgrace and the repopulation of the land (54:1–7). Perhaps the restoration from captivity is at least a partial fulfillment of this grand prophecy.

THE CONDEMNATION OF JUDAH'S ALLIANCE WITH EGYPT (30:1–33)

The second pair of woes is directed against those who advocated the formation of a military alliance with Egypt. Although chapters 30 and 31 are of unequal length, they follow a similar pattern. Both begin with a denunciation of the proposed alliance, which is doomed to failure. Then the Lord reassures the nation that He will protect Zion and that He deserves the full trust of the people. Someday they will throw out the idols that have fascinated them for so long (30:22; 31:7). Each chapter ends with a description of God's destruction of Assyria.

During the reign of Hezekiah, Judah's existence was threatened by Assyria. Samaria fell in 722/21 B.C., removing the last buffer state between Judah and the Assyrian provinces. After Pharaoh Shabako came to power in 715 B.C., the small kingdoms in Palestine and Syria sought his help in resisting their Assyrian overlord. In Judah there was growing pressure to join this alliance. One of Hezekiah's leading officials, Shebna, probably had close personal ties with Egypt and may have spearheaded the move (cf. 22:15–19). Isaiah opposed it vigorously.

The Failure of the Appeal to Egypt (30:1–17)

The first five verses of chapter 30 present God's evaluation of Judah's plan. It was not His idea, and it revealed Judah's rebellious nature and her need to repent (cf. 30:9; 31:6). The people of Judah were exchanging the protection and shelter of God for the refuge that Pharaoh could supply (cf. 25:4). Spiritually this worked to their detriment, and it was also unwise from a political perspective. Verse 4 mentions "Zoan," a place that symbolized the awful slavery Israel endured during her long tenure in Egypt (cf. 19:11). How could the people expect help from a nation that had brought their ancestors such suffering? The result would be "shame" and "disgrace" (v. 3), words that recall Isaiah's object lesson about Egypt (20:3–6).

A short oracle in verses 6 and 7 reinforces the opening message. Verse 6 describes the dangerous route taken by the envoys who were sent from Judah to Egypt. The "Negev" is the desert region on the southern fringes of Judah. Perhaps the Assyrians already had control of the coastal road normally used for the journey, making it necessary to take back roads instead.

In any event the arduous trip would not be worthwhile because Egypt's help would be totally useless. Egypt had the reputation of being an arrogant storm (i.e., "Rahab," v. 7), a great monster such as a crocodile or snake, but she would turn out to be remarkably docile and inactive on Judah's behalf. The term "Rahab"—a different Hebrew word from the "Rahab" (*rāḥāḇ*) of Joshua 2—is used elsewhere as a poetic equivalent for Egypt (cf. Ps. 87:4; Isa. 51:9). "Leviathan" is used in a similar way in 27:1.

Probably it was the title "Rahab the Do-Nothing" (v. 7) that Isaiah wrote on a tablet as a witness against Judah. In 8:1 he had written the name "Maher-Shalal-Hash-Baz" because of its important symbolic content. The people were unwilling to listen to his warning or to the words of other true prophets. They wanted to hear pleasant, inoffensive messages that were not negative or depressing. Above all they were tired of hearing about "the Holy One of Israel" (v. 11) and the godly life that He required.

Not intimidated in the least, Isaiah gave the people of Judah two additional messages from "the Holy One of Israel" (vv. 12, 15). In the first message the Lord condemned the oppression that characterized Judah's domestic policy and the deceit involved in her foreign policy. Such practices would bring about the government's downfall. The total collapse of Judah's national life is vividly described by using the imagery of shattered pottery (vv. 13–14).

The second message from "the Holy One" (vv. 15–17) depicts the tragedy that would overtake Judah on the battlefield. They could have avoided catastrophe by placing their trust in the Lord. Ahaz had rejected the "gently flowing waters" of the Lord only to be struck by the flood of Assyria (8:6–7), and the pro-Egyptian party in Judah was making the same mistake. Egypt could supply them with swift horses—a potent military force—but the Lord warned that the opponents would have faster horses and would chase the fleeing horsemen of Judah. Verse 17 recalls the curse of Deuteronomy 32:30 where the Lord promised that without His help tremendous numerical advantages would not guarantee victory. Judah's warriors would be scattered and forlorn, as isolated as a flagstaff on a hilltop.

The Restoration and Deliverance of Jerusalem (30:18–33)

In spite of God's anger against Judah, He yearned to bless His people, and the remainder of the chapter develops this positive theme. Verse 18 provides the transition, stressing God's mercy and compassion. The following two paragraphs (vv. 19–22 and vv. 23–26) apparently describe a distant day when the people of Jerusalem will faithfully worship the Lord. Apocalyptic elements enter in verses 25 and 26. Most translations handle these verses as prose, though several of them manifest a degree of parallelism.

God's eagerness to respond to His people (v. 19) is comparable to His zeal on behalf of the vineyard (27:2–6). The Lord longed to put an end to His people's affliction and weeping, and He promised to give them careful guidance. The time would come when the people would listen to teachers like Isaiah (cf. vv. 10–11) and gladly follow their advice. In that day the men of Jerusalem will throw away their attractive idols as if they were filthy rags. This strong rejection closely parallels the equally vivid statement in 2:20 (cf. 31:7).

Verses 23–26 show how nature and the animal world will participate in the blessings of a restored Zion. These verses reflect the promises given in Deuteronomy 28:11–12. Abundant rains will produce plentiful harvests, and even the animals will enjoy a rich diet. Israel's enemies will be crushed in that great Day of the Lord, and Israel will be healed of her wounds (cf. 1:6). The mention of "streams of water" (v. 25) anticipates 44:3, and the description of the intensification of the light of the sun and moon looks ahead to the day when the glory of the Lord will outshine the sun (60:19–20; cf. 24:23). The language is figurative, but it depicts an age of unparalleled blessing and prosperity.

In verses 27–33, Isaiah returned to the present and illustrated how God's power would solve Judah's immediate problem. The Lord would defeat Assyria to demonstrate His great love for Judah and to show why the alliance with Egypt was unnecessary. The description is powerful and dramatic and draws attention to God's voice and breath. "Lips," "tongue," and "breath" occur in succession in verses 27 and 28. "Voice" is used in 30 and 31, and "breath" in the climactic verse (v. 33). These terms are part of the storm imagery that so often accompanies a theophany (cf. 28:2; 29:6). The "voice" is related to thunder, and one is reminded of the terror of the Israelites who heard God speak at Mount Sinai (Exod. 20:18–19). In verses 27 and 33 "breath" and "tongue" are associated with fire—perhaps a reference to lightning.

In verse 28 the coming of the Lord matches the description in 8:8 of the coming of Assyria against Judah. Both verses refer to the "rushing" or "overwhelming" torrent that rises up to the neck. The torrent of the Lord, which in verse 33 is compared to a stream of burning sulfur, would be more powerful than the rushing torrent of Assyria.

In this paragraph we also hear the voice of the people of Judah singing and rejoicing over the fall of Assyria as if on a pilgrimage to Jerusalem to celebrate a festival. Isaiah probably had the celebration of the Passover in mind because it commemorated God's judgment against the Egyptians (cf. 31:5). According to verse 32, God's punishing blows will be made "to the music of tambourines and harps." This is probably an allusion to the custom of singing and dancing to celebrate a great victory. Miriam started this tradition when she took her tambourine and led the women of Israel in a triumphal march after the defeat of Pharaoh at the Red Sea (Exod. 15:20–21; cf. 1 Sam 18:6).

In verse 33 the fall of Assyria is symbolized by a huge funeral pyre that is prepared for the cremation of its king. Topheth was located just south of Jerusalem in the valley of Hinnom where the Israelites sometimes sacrificed their children to the god Molech (Jer. 7:31–33). It later became the place where the rubbish of Jerusalem was burned. In the New Testament the word "Gehenna" was taken directly from "Valley of Hinnom" (gē' hinnōm). Just as Sheol was ready for the king of Babylon (14:9), so "Gehenna" was prepared for Assyria's monarch. The language is highly symbolic, not an attempt to predict exactly how the Assyrians or their king would meet death.

THE DELIVERANCE OF JUDAH BY GOD, NOT EGYPT (31:1–9)

Chapter 31 is almost a replica of chapter 30, compressing the same message into only nine verses. In chapter 31 Isaiah presented this message in a clearer, more propositional form, and it serves as an effective summary of his teaching about Judah's alliance with Egypt.

The first three verses roundly condemn the proposed alliance with Egypt, which Isaiah saw as a direct rejection of the Lord. Israel valued Egypt's help because the Egyptians had many horses and chariots (cf. 30:16). Centuries earlier, however, Moses had warned Israel not to go to Egypt for that purpose (Deut. 17:16). Chariots were the tanks of the ancient world, and both Assyria and Egypt had an ample supply. Yet chariots were no match for the Lord (cf. Judg. 4:15), and the men of Judah had forfeited their major source of strength by ignoring Him. They preferred to trust in human strength, even though it was weak and unreliable (v. 2). If the Lord were to stretch out His arm, both Egypt and Judah would stumble and fall.

Verses 4 and 5 use two different illustrations to describe God's ability to defend Jerusalem. In the first figure God is described as a mighty lion that cannot be frightened away from claiming his prey. Jerusalem is the prey, and the "shepherds" are nations such as Assyria that wanted to wrest the prey from God's grasp. In the Bible, the word "shepherds" often represents the rulers of a country (e.g., Jer. 3:15).

In the second figure God is compared to birds that hover over their young. This symbolism emphasizes the tender love that a mother bird displays as she shields her little ones from harm. One of the greatest demonstrations of God's protection of Israel occurred at the Exodus when the angel of the Lord passed over His people and spared the firstborn son in every home that had blood on the doorposts. Verse 5 uses the technical word for "passover" (psh) that is found in Exodus 12. Isaiah referred to that great event in Israel's history to remind the people of Judah of Egypt's historical significance in the life of the nation of Israel.

How could Judah reject such a God and seek help from Egypt or from idols? Judah's folly seemed incredible, and Isaiah urged the Judeans to repent and to stop rebelling against God. Verse 7 predicts a day when the Judeans would abandon their idols, but Isaiah encouraged them to return to the Lord before God's judgment fell (v. 6; cf. 2:20; 30:22).

As in chapter 30, the final paragraph of chapter 31 depicts the fall of Assyria, though this time in less dramatic fashion. The sword that would destroy the Assyrians belongs to the angel of the Lord, whose previous activity was alluded to in verse 5. In 37:36 the angel struck down 185,000 Assyrian soldiers in one night. God, not the Egyptians with their horses, would defeat Assyria (cf. v. 3). By 612 B.C. the stronghold of Assyria had fallen. The Medes and Babylonians captured Nineveh, and her proud warriors were humiliated.

The reference to the Lord's "fire" and "furnace" in Jerusalem (v. 9) may correspond to "Topheth" in 30:33. In her attempt to conquer Judah's capital, Assyria would encounter the fires of God's judgment.

THE RULE OF THE RIGHTEOUS KING (32:1–20)

Chapters 32 and 33 break the pattern of the description of Israel's woes. Although they contain elements of Isaiah's message of judgment, these two chapters express a greater measure of hope for the people of Judah than do the previous four chapters. In these two chapters Isaiah emphasized the righteous rule of the coming King who will bring true security to Zion. The King and His rule are described in 32:1 and in 33:17, and the Lord is called "our king" in 33:22. These factors indicate that Isaiah had a messianic King in mind, an interpretation borne out by the levels of righteousness and peace that Isaiah predicted.

The twin themes of justice and righteousness occur in 32:1 and 16 and in 33:5. Each of these verses is followed by a reference to the peace and security that Zion will enjoy under the righteous King (32:2, 17–18; 33:6). His strong protection is also emphasized in 33:20–22. These verses use terms such as "refuge," "confidence," "secure homes," "sure foundation," and "peaceful abode" to describe the tranquillity that is the dream of every nation.

The Characteristics of the Age of Righteousness (32:1–8)

Chapter 32 is the only one in this six-chapter cluster (chs. 28–33) that does not begin with "woe." Instead it begins with a description of an ideal king (vv. 1–2) who will be a "shelter" and a "refuge" for His people—words that are applied to the Lord in 25:4–5. Another apocalyptic passage, Isaiah 35:6, speaks about streams in the desert, and these are also mentioned here in verse 2. This imagery contrasts sharply with the picture of the Lord as a storm or a driving wind that lashes His people in judgment (28:2).

When the righteous King rules, great changes will occur in Israel—a transformation that is discussed in verses 3–8. This paragraph makes use of a number of motifs that are common to wisdom literature, such as the contrast between the fool and the noble man. When God called him to be a prophet, Isaiah was told that the nation would not respond to his message (6:10). Here we learn that someday the eyes, ears, and mind of the people will function properly. Tongues that once stammered because of drunkenness (cf. 28:7, 8) will be able to speak clearly.

The fools may include those rulers who advocated the alliance with Egypt. Many officials were guilty of oppression and deceit (cf. 30:12), practices that demonstrated their ungodliness. Such men were fools, but the time would come when they would be thrown out of office and those who were truly noble would be given authority.

The Coming of Peace and Security After a Time of Judgment and Mourning (32:9–20)

Before continuing his description of this era of justice, Isaiah stopped to condemn the complacent women of Israel (vv. 9–14). He probably referred to the women to dramatize the idea of mourning, not to imply that they were more guilty than the men. In 3:16–26 Isaiah brought serious charges against the women of Zion, and in 32:9 he charged them with having a false sense of security. Apparently they trusted in their material possessions and not in the Lord. Twice (vv. 9, 11) Isaiah called them "complacent" (ša'ʾnannôt) and those "who feel secure" (*bōṭᶜhôṯ*; cf. Amos 6:1). These same two words are applied in a positive sense in verse 18. There God promised His people "secure homes" and "undisturbed places of rest." In the future, Jerusalem will be a "peaceful abode" (33:20). According to Isaiah, there is nothing wrong with feeling secure and undisturbed as long as one's trust is solidly based on the Lord.

It is difficult to interpret the statement "in little more than a year" (v. 10). It may mean that about a year from the time the prophecy was made Sennacherib would come to devastate the fields and vineyards of Judah and so bring to an end her prosperous economy. The land would be overgrown with thorns and briers, and therefore there would be no celebration of abundant harvests (cf. 37:30). Instead the women would mourn and lament as the Moabites did for the vines of Sibmah (16:9). The widespread destruction in Judah would be a sign that someday Jerusalem herself would be devastated and abandoned to the animals.

Such a gloomy prospect is quickly overshadowed by the promise of hope (vv. 15–20). Jerusalem would not remain a perpetual wasteland. A transformation as great as that described in verses 3 and 4 would take place. This reversal is associated with the outpouring of the Spirit, the One who rested on the Branch of Jesse in 11:1–2. In 44:3 the pouring out of the Spirit like streams on dry ground signifies blessing for the people, a blessing not unlike the blooming of the desert described in 32:15. "Fertile field" (v. 15) is a translation of the word "carmel." Mount Carmel was a region known for its fruit trees and fine grazing land. "Forest" (v. 15) is equivalent to "Lebanon," with its splendid cedar trees (cf. 29:17 and 35:2).

A second "forest" is mentioned in verse 19, perhaps a reference to the collapse of Assyria, the "forest thickets" that God would cut down with an ax (10:34). The leveled city recalls the fortified city of the apocalyptic section (24:10; 25:2), a city that represents the world powers who were opposed to the Lord. Although the Lord would be a shelter and refuge for His people (v. 2), He would destroy the forest with a hailstorm. Verse 20 also employs apocalyptic language that depicts vast farmlands and grazing areas. The close parallel in 30:23–24 likewise refers to the future messianic age.

The picture painted in verses 15–20 contrasts point for point with that drawn in verses 9–14. A false sense of security is replaced by genuine peace and confidence—the same "quietness and trust" that was spurned by some of the rulers of Judah (30:15). Devastated crops are replaced by unparalleled fertility, and shuddering and mourning give way to true happiness.

PROSPERITY FOR JERUSALEM AFTER THE DESTRUCTION OF ASSYRIA (33:1–24)

A Prayer for Assyria's Destruction (33:1–9)

In chapter 33 Isaiah returned to the pattern of beginning chapters with "woe." This time, however, he pronounced woe on the Assyrian invaders, not on any city or power bloc in Israel. Verse 1 uses assonance effectively by repeating two different roots four times each. Pairs of terms for "destroy" and "betray" alternate in successive couplets. The "traitor/betray" root occurred in 24:16, and the word for "destroyed" is best known from one of the most powerful verses in all poetry, Judges 5:27. There the Canaanite general Sisera was the one who was destroyed. Assyria had been appointed by God to punish Israel, but when this task was completed, she too would be judged.

Verses 2–9 contain a prayer that petitions the Lord to bring about the destruction of Assyria. Because God had promised to be gracious to His people (30:18), Isaiah interceded on their behalf. No nation can stand against the "thunder" of the Lord's voice (v. 3), an expression that recalls the storm of 30:27–33. All the plunder that Assyria had amassed would eagerly be snapped up by those she had oppressed.

Isaiah's confidence in the Lord characterizes the tone of verses 6 and 7. He knew that God was in control and that He would bring justice and stability to Jerusalem. Many of the terms of verse 6 are common to the repertoire of wisdom literature and are linked with the Messiah in 11:2.

In verses 7–9, the "motivation" section of this lament, Isaiah presented several reasons why God would intervene on behalf of His people. First, the enemy would not accept and abide by any terms of peace. King Hezekiah had agreed to give Sennacherib three hundred talents of silver and thirty talents of gold, but the Assyrian, showing how treacherous he could be, accepted the indemnity and moved against Jerusalem anyway (2 Kings 18:14–17). The "envoys of peace" (v. 7) may be those negotiators mentioned in 36:3 who reported to Hezekiah amidst deep mourning (36:22). Second, Isaiah pleaded on the basis of the economic condition of the land. Since travel was unsafe (v. 8), no trading was possible. This was a further blow to the economy (cf. Judg. 5:6).

A third reason, closely related to the second, is given in verse 9. The entire region was devastated, including the farmland and many cities. This is pictured by personifying several well-known areas. Lebanon and Carmel were dealt with in 32:15. Bashan was famous for its oak trees (2:13), and Sharon, along the Mediterranean Coast, was known for its beautiful foliage and excellent grazing land (1 Chron. 27:29). All this had turned into an "Arabah" (v. 9), the desert south of the Dead Sea.

The Lord's Response and the Promise of Peace and Prosperity (33:10–24)

The Lord's reply is given in verses 10–12. By means of the threefold repetition of "now" in verse 10, the Lord indicated that the time for action had finally come. Assyria and the "peoples" who were part of her army would be destroyed. The swiftness of their destruction is emphasized by the symbolism of a fire that consumes straw and thornbushes. The completeness of their collapse is stressed by the burning to lime.

Verses 13–16 describe the proper response to God's display of power. People far and near were to acknowledge what He had done and to revere this almighty God. Because the sinners in Zion were not exempt from the fires of His judgment (cf. 4:4), Isaiah challenged all the Judeans to live pure lives. Those who refused to participate in wickedness were promised security, and this is symbolized by the figures of inaccessible heights and a steady supply of food and drink.

If a man has a blind spot for evil (v. 15), he will get to "see the king in his beauty" (v. 17). This portrayal of the Messiah is based on the description of the splendor and majesty of a Davidic king—perhaps Solomon—in Psalm 45. Jerusalem will be at the center of a vast kingdom, and gone will be those proud officials and soldiers of Assyria and their hated regulations and strange ways.

Verses 20–22 continue to emphasize the *eyes,* as the righteous are allowed to view the security of Jerusalem. Three times a year the people journeyed to Mount Zion to celebrate the feasts of Passover, Pentecost, and Tabernacles. During the Feast of Tabernacles, the people lived in tents. Someday Jerusalem will be like a tent that will never have to be moved (cf. 54:2). Zion's security depends on the Lord, and He will separate Jerusalem from her enemies by vast rivers and oceans so that no enemy ship will be able to come close to her shores.

Isaiah repeated a single word three times in verses 10 and 18, and in verse 22 "the LORD" (Yahweh) is also thrice repeated for emphasis. Israel will return to a theocratic rule that will guarantee justice and deliverance from the enemy. Again the messianic age may be the primary reference.

In verse 20 Jerusalem was compared to a tent, but in verse 23 the figure of a ship is used. Since the work of Drechsler, interpreters generally have not identified this ship as the enemy vessel of verse 21 but as Zion.[2] Judah's present condition was like a poorly outfitted ship that was barely able to sail. The word "then" in verse 23 refers to the future when Zion's ropes will have the strength referred to in verse 20. The spoils of the enemy will be carried off easily. Even the lame will join in the looting (cf. 2 Sam. 5:6). Perhaps this is an allusion to the abundant spoils that Assyria was to leave when her army was destroyed in 701 B.C. The passage, however, looks ahead to the time when Zion will be healed physically and spiritually (v. 24) and when peace and security will have reached their ultimate fulfillment.

[2] Young, *Isaiah,* 2:426.

GOD'S DAY OF VENGEANCE AGAINST THE NATIONS (34:1–17)

Chapters 34 and 35 bear the same relationship to chapters 28 through 33 as chapters 24–27 do to chapters 13–23. They form a climax to the preceding section's alternating themes of judgment and salvation. The apocalyptic description of judgment in chapter 34 is even more vivid and dramatic than the corresponding material in chapters 24 and 25. The contrast between the two chapters is a striking one. Chapter 34 is concerned with death, destruction, and wrath; and chapter 35 emphasizes health, restoration, and the glory of God.

The language of these two chapters nicely prepares the way for chapters 40–66. The opening imperatives are similar to those used in 48:16 and in 49:1. The Lord's sacrifice in Bozrah (34:6) is similar to Bozrah's symbolic winepress (63:1–3). In 34:8 and in 35:4 the coming of the Lord is associated with vengeance and retribution, and the same themes are found in 40:10; 62:11; and 63:4. Israel's return from exile lies at the heart of the last part of the Book of Isaiah. This theme is also emphasized in 35:8–10. Isaiah 34:10 is repeated verbatim in 51:11.

Verses 1–4 depict the cataclysmic judgment that will fall on the earth in the end times. Here Isaiah moves beyond the destruction of Assyria in 701 and 612 B.C. to a consideration of the similar fate that is in store for future world powers that are aligned against the Lord. God's terrible anger will result in the "total destruction" of His foes. This is the first occurrence in Isaiah of the technical term (*heherîm*) for devoting persons or things to the Lord. When Israel invaded Canaan, they were told to put to death all the people and animals. The enemy was placed under a "ban" (*hērem*), a curse that would wipe them out completely (cf. Josh. 6:17). The term is used in 34:2 and again in verse 5 with reference to Edom. Only nations whose societies were thoroughly corrupt were condemned in this fashion.

The blood and gore from this slaughter heavily colors chapter 34. The mountains and the land are "soaked," or "drenched," with blood (vv. 3, 7), and even the sword of the Lord is "bathed in blood" (v. 6).

The fourth verse shows the cosmic dimensions of this judgment, using terms parallel to those in 24:4. There the earth, not the heavens, was emphasized. Isaiah 34:4 is alluded to or quoted in Matthew 24:29 and in Revelation 6:13–14. Both passages link the cosmic dimensions of Isaiah's description of God's judgment with the judgments of the Great Tribulation and the second coming of Christ. Isaiah 13:10 uses similar imagery as it describes the Day of the Lord. Thunderstorms and earthquakes accompanied God's appearances in the Old Testament, but in the end times the heavens will be shaken as well.

Verses 5–17 relate the judgment on the nations to the destruction of Edom, just as 25:10 prophesies God's judgment on Moab. Both countries symbolize a world that is opposed to God, just as Babylon did in chapters 13 and 14. Edom fought against Israel and Judah with malicious zeal, and the Edomites were overjoyed when Jerusalem was captured. In Lamentations 4:21 Edom was warned that her elation would be short-lived, and she, too, would be severely punished. The Edomites were later pushed out of their ancestral territory by the Nabatean Arabs, perhaps as early as 500 B.C., but chapter 34 has a far broader devastation in view.

The imagery behind verses 5–7 is that of a sacrifice. Normally animals were killed as an offering to the Lord, but here the Lord Himself slays the victims. Only in verse 5 does the Lord speak in the first person, thereby showing His personal involvement in the action. The scene of the battle is "Bozrah," an important city of Edom located about twenty-five miles southeast of the Dead Sea. Its major significance for this context is its name. "Bozrah" means "grape-gathering," and that suits the blood-red description of the slaughter (cf. 63:1–3).

Animals did not escape if a region was placed under the ban, but the mention of sacrificial animals is primarily intended to refer to the slaughter of people. The "wild oxen" or "great bulls" (v. 7) could symbolize the leaders of the land. "Fat" is mentioned three times in verses 6 and 7, perhaps because it was considered the best part of the meat. This sacrifice will provide plenty of fat for the birds and beasts to enjoy (cf. Ezek. 39:17–19).

In verse 8 this period of judgment is called a "day of

vengeance," a term that is also found in 61:2 and in 63:4. "Retribution" and "vengeance" are joined in 35:4 and in 59:17–18. Edom had derided and attacked Judah for centuries, but now God would avenge this hateful attitude that is so characteristic of the world's ways.

The destruction of Edom is compared to three other notable examples of desolation. Verse 9 alludes to the fire and brimstone that fell on Sodom and Gomorrah. "Burning sulfur" and "blazing pitch" would devastate Edom's soil and streams forever. In verse 10 four terms for eternity are used in successive clauses. Similarly, Revelation 19:3 mentions the perpetual smoke that will mark the destruction of Babylon. Edom and Babylon are also linked together by Isaiah. Many of the eerie birds and wild animals found in verses 11–15 were also present in Isaiah's description of Babylon in 13:20–22. Verse 14 reflects an even greater demonic influence than that found in Babylon. Both the "goats" and the "night creatures" (*lîlît*) are associated with evil powers. "Lilitu" appears as a night demon in Babylonian literature.[3]

The third example of desolation was the earth in its unformed state. The Hebrew words for "emptiness" and "desolation" (v. 11) occur in Genesis 1:2 as descriptions of the condition of the earth at the beginning of the days of creation.

After Edom has become a wasteland, men will take out the scroll and verify that Isaiah's predictions came true. All of the creatures he named will be there because God has given them clear title to the land (vv. 16–17). The same measuring line mentioned in verse 11 is used to divide up the land in verse 17.

THE JOY AND SALVATION OF THE REDEEMED
(35:1–10)

The somber picture of death and destruction in chapter 34 is transformed into one of vibrant life and rejoicing in chapter 35. This change is symbolized by the blooming of the desert as nature enters into the joy of God's redeemed people. The

---

[3]H. W. F. Saggs, *The Greatness That Was Babylon* (New York: Hawthorne Books, 1962), pp. 485–86.

beautiful trees and foliage of Lebanon, Carmel, and Sharon were mentioned in 33:9, though there they were withering away. God's glory (v. 2) is seen in nature but more specifically in His work of salvation. In 44:23 nature responds again when Israel is redeemed.

The glory of the Lord is also associated with the presence of the Lord. Verses 3 and 4 anticipate the glorious return of the Lord to deliver His weak and struggling people (cf. 40:5). The imperatives used in these two verses recall the Lord's words to Joshua as he prepared to lead Israel into the Promised Land. Since God had promised to be with them, fear and dismay were to give way to courage (Josh. 1:9). The description of the coming of the Lord (v. 4) has several parallels with Isaiah's description of the second coming of Christ (62:11).

Three parts of the body are mentioned in verses 3 and 4, and three more appear in verses 5 and 6. All three—eyes, ears, and tongue—occur in 32:3–4, a passage that also describes the blessings that will characterize the messianic age. Israel was blind and deaf to the Word of God that Isaiah proclaimed (6:9–10), but in the future her spiritual perception will be restored. This spiritual healing is symbolized by the removal of physical disabilities and the fruitfulness of nature (cf. vv. 1–2). Christ's healing of the blind and the lame proved that He also could forgive sin (Matt. 11:5). In chapter 34 the streams of Edom were filled with pitch, and jackals roamed through the citadels. Now the jackals are gone, and streams of water irrigate the desert.

Endued with new courage and spiritual power, the Israelites are pictured as ready to make a new entrance into Palestine. The highway prepared for this purpose is described in verses 8 through 10. In Isaiah's day the roads were dangerous and deserted (cf. 33:8), but this highway of the future will be completely safe. It will be a limited-access highway, one that is restricted to those who have been ransomed by the Lord. Lions and other wild animals plagued travelers in Israel (cf. 2 Kings 17:26), but this road will be free from such menaces. In antiquity certain sacred roads were used only by those who were cultically pure. The road that connected the temples of Luxor and Karnak in Thebes is one such example.[4] Similarly, God was "the Holy One of Israel," and "His Way of Holiness" could be used only by the redeemed.

During the pilgrimage feasts, the Israelites journeyed to Jerusalem amid joy and singing (cf. 30:29). In the future this same happiness once again will characterize God's people. No animals or robbers will molest them. Instead they will be overtaken by "gladness and joy" (v. 10). The beautiful themes of verse 10 are repeated in 51:11, a passage that compares the future return from Babylon to the road that God made through the Red Sea at the Exodus. Both events depict a spiritual return to the Lord as well as a literal road to Palestine.

[4]A. L. Oppenheim, *Ancient Mesopotamia* (Chicago: University of Chicago Press, 1964), p. 139.

10

HISTORICAL INTERLUDE
36:1–39:8

Chapters 36–39—the center of the Book of Isaiah—tie together chapters 1–35 and chapters 40 through 66. Chapters 36 and 37 show the fulfillment of Isaiah's various predictions about the collapse of Assyria, and this fulfillment authenticates the other prophecies he made. Chapters 38 and 39 introduce the reader to the predominately Babylonian framework assumed in chapters 40–66. In these chapters Assyria drops out of the picture, and Babylon looms as the major threat to the people of God. Chronologically, the events in chapters 38 and 39 precede the events in chapters 36 and 37, but Isaiah's purpose dictated that he invert this material.

The content of chapters 36–39 also appears in 2 Kings 18:13–20:19, with the major omission of Hezekiah's hymn of thanksgiving (38:9–20). Although there are other, less significant variations between the two accounts, generally speaking they are close parallels. Since chapters 36–39 form such an integral part of the Book of Isaiah and since these chapters clearly reflect Isaiah's style, the writer of Kings probably used Isaiah as a source rather than vice versa.

We have seen that chapters 28–35 are grouped in pairs. The same arrangement prevails in chapters 36–39, the historical interlude, and this shows the essential continuity of these chapters with the preceding material.

THE ASSYRIAN INVASION OF 701 B.C. (36:1–22)

During the year 701 B.C., the mighty Assyrian king Sennacherib reached Palestine in an attempt to suppress a widespread rebellion. The events involved in his invasion and the suggested emendation of "fourteenth" to "twenty-fourth" (v. 1) are discussed in detail in the earlier chapter on the historical background of the Book of Isaiah. As the Assyrians swept down from the north, city after city capitulated. Soon the enemy was in Judah, and the pattern of Assyrian victories continued. Lachish was about twenty-five miles southwest of Jerusalem, and it guarded the main approach road to that city. Hezekiah had sent envoys to Lachish to acknowledge that he was wrong to have revolted against Assyria (2 Kings 18:14f.). Sennacherib accepted a sizeable tribute payment, but then decided against leaving Jerusalem unscathed.

Sennacherib sent for the "Rabshakeh," or "chief cupbearer"—a title for an important military commander—and told him to call for the complete surrender of Jerusalem. Backed by a strong army, this commander came to the very spot outside the walls of Jerusalem where many years before Ahaz had held his fateful meeting with Isaiah (cf. 7:3; 36:2). Ahaz had thought that Assyria would rescue Judah, but instead Assyria was in the process of destroying her.

Hezekiah sent out a trio of important officials to negotiate with the Assyrian emissary. Eliakim and Shebna were mentioned in 22:15–25, verses that indicate that next to the king they held the highest offices in the land. Their responsibilities approximated those of a modern-day prime minister and secretary of state.

In the ensuing confrontation, the field commander made a speech before these Judean officials and the troops who manned the wall. The Rabshakeh's speech displayed considerable finesse in the art of psychological warfare (vv. 4–20). He began by exposing the military weaknesses of Judah. She did not have the personnel or equipment to resist Assyria effectively. Her main ally was Egypt, and the commander pointed out the painful fact that the Egyptians were notoriously unreliable in living up to their commitments.

Because Hezekiah claimed to be relying on the Lord, the Rabshakeh observed that Hezekiah may have incurred God's disfavor by removing many of the high places (v. 7). These centers of worship were popular throughout Israel, and the people probably feared the results of their destruction. To neutralize their faith in God even further, the commander contended that Judah's God ("Yahweh") had commissioned Assyria to attack Judah. In the light of Isaiah's earlier messages (10:5–6), we know that Assyria did serve as a tool that God used to punish other nations, and that made the Rabshakeh's bold claim sound even more plausible.

Realizing the potential effect of his speech, the Judean officials interrupted the commander by requesting that he speak in Aramaic, not Hebrew (v. 11). Aramaic was the recognized diplomatic language, and the commander should have followed protocol. But he was trying to stir up the masses, so he—or his interpreter—continued to use Hebrew and to speak more loudly. In verses 4–10 he pretended to speak to Hezekiah, but in verses 13–20 he openly addressed all the people.

In verses 12–17 the proud general spelled out the alternatives that the residents of Jerusalem faced. They could continue to eat grapes and figs and to drink clear water (v. 16), or they could "eat their own filth and drink their own urine" (v. 12) during the famine of a long siege. Every Israelite highly prized his own vine and fig tree (cf. Mic. 4:4). Although the Judeans would eventually be taken into captivity, the Assyrians had enough grain and wine to help the Judeans forget how good things were in Judah.

The last part of the speech combines arguments from theology and history (vv. 18–20). Other gods had not been able to rescue their devotees from the king of Assyria. This was true of the Syrian deities of Hamath and Arpad and also of the gods of Samaria. Mention of the capital of the northern kingdom of Israel was designed to strike terror into the hearts of the Judeans because they worshiped the same God as the Israelites. War was viewed as a battle between the gods of respective nations, and it appeared that the gods of Assyria were winning.

At several points in his speech the commander attempted to pit the power and integrity of "the great king, the king of

Assyria" (vv. 4, 13) against the weakness and deceitfulness of king Hezekiah. Graft and corruption were common in Near Eastern governments, and the Rabshakeh strongly insinuated that Hezekiah was deceiving his people (vv. 14, 15, 16, 18).

The reaction to the speech was not what the Assyrians had hoped for. The people of Jerusalem did not panic or throw open the gates of the city. They were loyal to Hezekiah, and they gave the Assyrians the silent treatment (v. 21). The three officials realized the seriousness of the situation, and having torn their clothes in distress, they reported the contents of the speech to Hezekiah.

THE DESTRUCTION OF THE ASSYRIAN ARMY
(37:1–38)

The Assurance of Isaiah and a Letter From Sennacherib
(37:1–13)

Hezekiah had been accused of relying heavily on the Lord (36:7, 15, 18), and chapter 37 proves that this claim was true. Prayer is mentioned three times (vv. 4, 15, 21) as King Hezekiah brought Judah's fate before God. Hezekiah himself went to the temple and sent several priests, along with Eliakim and Shebna, to enlist the help of Isaiah. Prophet, priest, and king were united in seeking the face of the Lord.

In his appeal to Isaiah, Hezekiah described the crisis in terms that recall the kind of distress predicted in 5:30 and in 8:22. Earlier, Israel had given birth to wind (26:18), but now both mother and child were in danger of dying at the time of birth. The key word in verse 4 is "ridicule." Assyria had insulted the living God, and such arrogance demanded His rebuke. The word translated "ridicule," or "insult," (ḥērēp) in verse 4 occurs again in verses 17, 23, and 24.

In verse 4 Jerusalem is characterized as a "remnant." Most of Judah's cities had already been captured, and many of her citizens had been taken captive. Her desperate plight recalls Isaiah's words in 1:7–9.

When the officials reached Isaiah, he had a ready answer from the Lord. The young upstarts sent by the king of Assyria were guilty of blasphemy, and the king himself would soon return to his homeland where he would die. What an encouraging reply! And yet to believe it required great faith on Hezekiah's part because the Lord did not reveal how the prophecy would be fulfilled.

Unable to force the quick surrender of Jerusalem, the Assyrian commander and his army rejoined Sennacherib at Libnah, not far from Lachish in the western foothills. While they were there, word came that Tirhakah, King of Egypt, was approaching. Actually Tirhakah was only a prince at the time, but because he assumed the throne in 690 B.C., the title "king" is used proleptically.[1] The Egyptian threat led Sennacherib to send a letter to Hezekiah to reinforce the words of his field commander. The commander had warned the people not to be deceived by Hezekiah, and the king warned Hezekiah not to be deceived by God. Verses 11 and 12 contain an expansion of the arguments used in 36:18–20. Several names of conquered nations—mainly regions in or near Mesopotamia—were added to the list. The people of Eden comprised one of the Chaldean tribes that is often called "Bit-Adini." Verse 13 contains the same trio of names that are found in 36:19. According to 2 Kings 17:24, captives from Hamath and Sepharvaim were resettled in Samaria, and so their submission to Assyria was well-known to the men of Judah.

The Prayer of Hezekiah and the Announcement of Sennacherib's Fall (37:14–38)

Hezekiah read the letter and then once more went to the temple to pray (cf. vv. 1, 14). In 1:15 the Lord had said He would not listen to the people when they spread out their hands to pray, but when Hezekiah spread out the letter before Him (v. 14), God graciously listened. Hezekiah's prayer (vv. 15–20) shows keen theological perception and anticipates some of the key teachings in chapters 40–66. Because Israel's God was the only true God and because He was sovereign over all the

[1] Kenneth Kitchen, *Ancient Orient and Old Testament* (Chicago: InterVarsity, 1966), p. 82.

nations, Sennacherib's claim that he had vanquished the deities of other nations was false. They were nothing more than man-made, powerless idols. Because the Lord God of Israel was the Creator of heaven and earth, He had the power to deliver His people. Sennacherib had insulted the *living* God (cf. vv. 4, 17).

God's answer to Hezekiah came through Isaiah in the form of an extended taunt against the king of Assyria (vv. 22–29). The content of this taunt closely resembles Isaiah's condemna-tion of the king of Babylon in chapter 14. In this poem against the king of Assyria, the Lord promises that Jerusalem will not be destroyed or "raped" by Assyria. She would remain untouched like a virgin. Because Sennacherib was guilty of blaspheming the "Holy One of Israel," his doom was certain. Assyria's great pride is described in verses 23–25, a passage that is parallel to 10:12–14 and to 14:13–14. According to 37:23–25, the Assyrians believed that no obstacle could stand in the way of their powerful monarch, whose chariots could climb the highest mountains and whose soldiers could cross any river. They thought that he was almost a god because only a deity could dry up the streams of Egypt (v. 25).

But the Assyrians were unaware that all their victories were part of God's plan. God had decreed the collapse of kingdoms and the shattering of peoples (cf. 25:1–2). Both the style and the content of verse 26 closely resemble the language of subsequent chapters (cf. 40:21; 41:26). God, not Assyria or Babylon, was the One in control of history.

According to verse 28, God is not only omnipotent but also omniscient. He thoroughly understood Assyria's attitudes and plans, and He would punish her for her arrogance. The Assyrians frequently led away captives by attaching ropes to rings placed in the victims' noses. Perhaps this is the meaning of "hook in your nose" in verse 29. The "bit" to control animals is also mentioned in 30:28.

As proof that the Assyrians would leave Judah never to threaten Jerusalem again, the Lord gave Hezekiah a sign. This "three year" sign covers the same period of time as the one in 20:3. By the end of this period the planting and harvesting of crops would return to normal. During the Assyrian invasion, the fields were ruined by neglect and destruction, but improvement could be expected. Three years seemed like a long time since the Assyrians soon would be destroyed. The "second year" probably was due to begin within a few months of the prophecy, so the total period would have been considerably less than thirty-six months. Similarly, Christ's three days in the grave covered one full day and part of two others. Whatever the exact length of time may have been, recovery from such severe devastation was not easy.

Hezekiah had requested prayer for the remnant in Jerusalem (v. 4), and verses 31 and 32 are a promise that that remnant would be fruitful. The survivors would be able to repopulate Judah and thereby assure the continuation of the nation. The imagery of "taking root" and "bearing fruit" recalls 4:2–3 and 11:10–11, passages that describe the future situation of the remnant after the Babylonian destruction of 586 B.C. The last sentence in verse 32 is identical with the final words of 9:7. Both verses contain promises about Israel's future, a future guaranteed by God's deep love for His people and for His servant David (cf. v. 35).

In verses 33–35 the Lord repeated the promise He gave in verse 29. Sennacherib would not subject Jerusalem to the horrors of a siege. Twice Isaiah stated that "he will not enter this city" (vv. 33, 34). Using the words of 31:5, God promised to "defend," or "shield," Jerusalem and to "save" it out of the hands of the enemy. For the time being, the city of David was safe.

The dramatic fulfillment of this prophecy is given in verses 36–38. The angel of death, who had slain the firstborn of Egypt, struck again, and one of the most formidable armies of the ancient world was destroyed. As we noted earlier, the Lord may have used a bubonic plague to accomplish this. The end came swiftly and decisively; a sword from God devoured the enemy (31:8). The mighty storm had struck (30:27–33), and the "Forest of Lebanon" had fallen (10:33–34).

Sennacherib and the few troops who survived had to abandon the campaign and return to Assyria. Twenty years later (681 B.C.) two of his sons assassinated him while he was worshiping in his temple. Hezekiah had gone to the temple of his God and found help, but Sennacherib went to the house of his god and found destruction (cf. v. 7). Through it all, the God of Israel was vindicated, and Isaiah's role as a true prophet was validated.

THE ILLNESS AND RECOVERY OF HEZEKIAH
(38:1–22)

Interpreters agree that the events described in chapters 38 and 39 preceded the invasion of 701 B.C. In chapters 38 and 39, the treasures of Judah have not been sent as tribute to the king of Assyria, and the land does not appear to be under imminent attack (cf. 39:2). Many date these events in 703 B.C., but the evidence more strongly suggests a date of about 712 B.C. According to this interpretation, the "king" of 38:6 would be Sargon, not Sennacherib, unless the prophecy looked ahead to the invasion of 701 B.C. toward the end of Hezekiah's life.★ Both theories have problems, but in either case "in those days" (v. 1) refers in general to the period of Hezekiah's involvement with the Assyrian armies.

The Answer to Hezekiah's Prayer (38:1–8)

The opening verses give a succinct account of Hezekiah's illness and recovery. At age thirty-nine the king was informed that he would soon die. This information was revealed to Isaiah, just as Elisha was able to predict the death of Ben-Hadad (2 Kings 8:10). Hezekiah's reaction was a natural one, and he pleaded with the Lord to change His mind. Very few kings since David could have made the claims Hezekiah did (v. 3). Hezekiah had instituted a thorough reform that included the removal of the high places and the curtailment of idolatry (cf. 2 Kings 18:3–6). Deeply committed to the Lord, he felt he deserved to live longer. Another factor may have been the need for an heir. The next king, Manasseh, was not born until three years later (2 Kings 21:1), so Hezekiah may have been concerned about the continuation of the Davidic line.

★Note the twenty-year gap between verses 37 and 38 of chapter 37.

Hezekiah's prayers were answered, and he was given an additional fifteen years to live and the promise that Jerusalem would not fall to the Assyrians. It is no wonder that when the armies of Sennacherib closed in, Hezekiah believed that prayer changes things! He had learned through his previous crisis that God could work miracles. According to verse 21, figs were applied to boils to facilitate recovery. The use of figs for medicinal purposes is also attested at Ugarit.[2]

The king requested a sign from the Lord to confirm the word of Isaiah. Unlike the signs described in 20:3 and in 37:30, this one involved a miracle. Some scholars understand the "steps" (v. 8) to be the degrees on the sundial, but the passage makes good sense if a literal stairway is intended. Isaiah did not explain how the Lord accomplished the miracle, but most scholars suggest that the sunlight was refracted because of special atmospheric conditions.

The sign is discussed in verses 7–8 and again in verse 22. Since the content of verses 21–22 precedes verse 7 in the 2 Kings account, one wonders why a less logical order is used in this chapter. In the Saint Mark's Dead Sea Scroll, verses 21 and 22 are squeezed in. Apparently they were omitted at first by the scribe. Perhaps at one time verses 21–22 came between verses 6 and 7 and later were misplaced because of a scribal error.

Hezekiah's Hymn of Thanksgiving (38:9–22)

Verses 9–20 contain a hymn of thanksgiving that was written by Hezekiah to acknowledge God's intervention. The king had shown deep interest in the psalms of David and Asaph (2 Chron. 29:30), and so it is fitting that one of his own compositions should have been preserved. The hymn begins with a description of Hezekiah's agony in the face of imminent death (vv. 10–14). His feelings differed sharply from those of Paul, who longed "to depart and be with Christ" (Phil. 1:23).

[2] Cyrus H. Gordon, *Ugaritic Textbook,* 2 vols. (Rome: Pontifical Biblical Institute, 1965), 1:183. Cyrus H. Gordon, *Ugaritic Literature* (Rome: Pontifical Biblical Institute, 1949), p. 129.

Like David, Hezekiah possessed the more limited revelation of the old dispensation, and in the teaching of the Old Testament, Sheol is an uncertain, shadowy realm at best. Therefore it is understandable that Hezekiah thought it better to praise God among the living than to go down to Sheol!

In verse 12 death is compared to the taking down of a tent, a figure used in an opposite way in 33:20. A second image refers to the slender thread of life; Hezekiah had come to the end of the line. In 34:4 the sky was "rolled up like a scroll."

The reference to broken bones in verse 13 is typical of lament terminology. Physical, emotional, or spiritual distress is often compared with aching or broken bones (cf. Pss. 6:2; 51:8). In his agony Hezekiah begged the Lord to intervene personally on his behalf (v. 14; cf. Ps. 119:122f.). "Come to my aid" (v. 14) is literally "obligate yourself for me," or "be my security," to guarantee that you will help me (cf. Gen. 43:9).

God did intervene, and so verses 15–19 reflect on God's faithfulness. Hezekiah's health was restored, his sins were forgiven (v. 17), and he promised to praise the Lord for His gracious answer. In verse 17 the king admitted how beneficial this difficult experience had been.

In the Old Testament, individual hymns of thanksgiving often conclude with a vow of praise like the one in verse 20. The person whose prayer had been heard gives his testimony in front of the assembly, and the people join him in praising the Lord (Ps. 116:18–19). The hymn began with mourning and crying, but it ended with music and singing. Hezekiah loved the temple of the Lord, and it was his desire to spend the rest of his life near its courts (cf. Ps. 23:6).

THE VISITORS FROM BABYLON (39:1–8)

Chapter 39 records an important sequel to Hezekiah's illness. The king of Babylon, Merodach-Baladan (*Marduk-apal-iddina*—"Marduk has given a son"), chose the occasion of Hezekiah's recovery to send him a letter of congratulations and a gift. This is the second reference in the historical interlude to a letter from a Mesopotamian king, but its contents were radically different from the letter Sennacherib had sent (cf.

37:14). Merodach-Baladan was a Chaldean prince who never tired of stirring up revolts against the Assyrians. He ruled Babylon from 721–710 B.C., and it was probably toward the end of this period that he sent the envoys to Hezekiah. Sargon was priming his Assyrian troops for an attack on Babylon, and Merodach-Baladan was eager to enlist the support of other nations, including the kingdom of Judah.

Hezekiah was deeply worried about Assyria. Feeling honored by the embassy, he gladly welcomed the envoys of this archenemy of Assyria. Without consulting either the Lord or Isaiah, he showed them his vast treasures, his abundant supplies of food, and his military armaments. God had given Hezekiah great wealth, so the visitors were duly impressed (2 Chron. 32:27–29).

After their departure Isaiah questioned the king about his guests. Hezekiah admitted that he had given them a complete tour of all the treasures and resources of Judah. It was a rash display of pride, and Isaiah revealed the sad consequences (vv. 6–7). The men from Babylon would not forget about all the silver and gold they had seen, and one day they would return to lay claim to it. Moreover the people of Judah—including some of Hezekiah's own descendants—would be carried off into captivity. This is the first time in the Book of Isaiah that Babylon is named as the eventual conqueror of Jerusalem. Just as Isaiah's predictions about Assyria came true in 701 B.C., so this prophecy about Babylon also would be fulfilled (over a century later). Hezekiah's reply to this message of doom is somewhat puzzling because he must have been distressed by Isaiah's words. Perhaps the meaning of verse 8 is that there is at least one item of good news in this prophecy: the judgment will not come during Hezekiah's lifetime. Until the destruction of Sennacherib's army, however, neither the king nor his people enjoyed much peace and security.

11

DELIVERANCE FROM BABYLON
40:1–48:22

The announcement that the Babylonians would someday capture Jerusalem and take the people into exile was a bitter blow. How could Judah celebrate the downfall of Assyria when everyone knew that a more powerful invader was on the way? To encourage the people, Isaiah wrote a number of chapters that described in detail the return from exile and the rebuilding of Jerusalem. He also explained more fully why the Exile was necessary as a punishment for sin. He depicted sin, *not* the Exile, as Israel's major problem. In chapter 53 in particular, Isaiah presented God's solution to the problem of sin and guilt. The theological emphasis of the final twenty-seven chapters can be divided into nine-chapter segments. Chapters 40–48 emphasize "theology proper," especially the power of God as Creator and Redeemer. The middle segment (chs. 49–57) stresses the doctrine of salvation through the Servant, and the last nine chapters deal comprehensively with eschatology. Further discussion of the interrelationship of chapters 40–66 and of their connection with the first part of Isaiah is given in the earlier chapters on *Authorship* and *Structure*.

THE PROLOGUE (40:1–11)

The first eleven verses of chapter 40 introduce the major themes of chapters 40–66—the comforting news that the people of Judah would return from exile and the announcement of the coming of the Lord. The double imperative in verse 1 is a stylistic device that is also found in 51:9, 17; 52:11; 57:14; and in 62:10. It expresses the urgent need that the people felt for comfort. "Speak tenderly" (v. 2) literally means "speak to the heart," an idiom used in 2 Chronicles 32:7 when Hezekiah encouraged his people to trust God to rescue them from the Assyrians. Isaiah now encouraged the generation of 540 B.C. because the "hard service" (v. 2) of the Exile was almost over. The nation would have suffered sufficiently, having received "double" (v. 2) punishment for her sins. This twofold payment may be related to the "double calamities" described in 51:19.

In verses 3, 6, and 9 three different voices speak, and each one explains how the comforting promise of verses 1 and 2 will be fulfilled. The first voice reveals that a smooth road will be built to enable the exiles to return in safety to Jerusalem (vv. 3–5). Valleys will be filled in, hills will be leveled, and all the stones will be taken out of the way. This highway imagery appeared in 35:8, and it occurs again in 57:14 and in 62:10–11. In the New Testament the highway is prepared for the coming of Christ, and the voice that calls out belongs to John the Baptist (Luke 3:4–6). According to John, this preparation involved a thoroughgoing repentance on the part of the people. A comparison of all these "prepare the way" passages shows that the fulfillment involves three different events: (1) the return from Babylon, (2) the first coming of Christ, and (3) His climactic second coming. The revelation of the "glory of the LORD" (v. 5) is most easily understood in terms of Christ's second coming, but again all three events are included. God's glory would be displayed in Israel's redemption from Babylon (44:23), and He is described as accompanying the people when they return (52:12). At that time all the nations will see God's intervention on behalf of His people (52:10).

The second voice speaks in verses 6–8, a section that contrasts the frailty and transitoriness of man with the enduring qualities of God's Word. The Israelites knew something about the power of Assyria and Babylon. If Babylon would soon possess the might to conquer Judah, how could the people of Israel hope to be released from captivity? God's answer is that man is like grass, here today and gone tomorrow. When the

Lord "blows on them" (vv. 7, 24), man withers away (51:12). The plans and purposes of Babylon or of any nation will not stand (cf. 8:10); only God's Word lasts forever.

The third voice announces that God, accompanied by His people, is coming back to Judah (vv. 9–11). Usually a messenger of good news from the scene of a battle would go to the city to give the results of a crucial conflict (2 Sam. 18:26). In this instance, however, the herald climbs a mountain to tell Judah and Jerusalem that the exiles are on the way back. God has shown His superior power by defeating Babylon (cf. 52:7–11)! The same language is used to describe the return from Exile and the second coming of Christ (62:11). The "reward," or "recompense," (v. 10) probably refers to the people God is bringing with Him. They are called a "flock" in verse 11, and the Lord is depicted as a kind shepherd who is careful not to drive the sheep faster than they can go. His tenderness and compassion reflect the theme of "comfort" that was introduced in verses 1 and 2.

THE WISDOM AND POWER OF GOD (40:12–31)

When Jerusalem was captured, many Israelites must have had doubts about God's power. Why had He let His people suffer defeat if He was able to rescue them? Because they doubted God's ability to bring them back to Israel, Isaiah gave a majestic description of the limitless power of the Holy One of Israel (vv. 12–31). The effectiveness of Isaiah's description is enhanced by the use of a series of rhetorical questions at the start of the various paragraphs. The questions in verses 18 and 21 are almost identical with those in verses 25 and 28 respectively. The form of verses 12–31 is similar to the structure of many psalms of praise, which extol both the majesty of God (vv. 11–26) and His goodness to mankind (vv. 27–31).[1] Although chapter 40 emphasizes the first element, the second element occupies an important place as well.

With bold strokes Isaiah described the infinite power and

---

[1] Claus Westermann, *The Praise of God in the Psalms,* trans. Keith R. Crim (Richmond, Vir.: John Knox, 1965), p. 123.

wisdom of God (vv. 12–14). God is supreme over nature and controls the whole universe with effortless ease. No other being assisted Him in the creation or management of heaven and earth. God's superiority also extends over the nations of the world. Compared with Him, their significance is infinitesimal. In verse 15 they are regarded as "a drop in the bucket," but by verse 17 their status is reduced to less than nothing. Even if it were possible to use all the cedars of Lebanon as firewood for the sacrifice of all the animals of the forest, this vast offering would not do justice to the greatness of God.

God is not only greater than the nations, He is also superior to the idols the nations worship. Verses 18–20 begin the comparison between God and idols that continues into chapter 48. Idols can be made beautiful if several craftsmen labor over them, but even then one must be careful not to let the idols fall over. This note of sarcasm (v. 20) is developed more fully in chapter 44. Lifeless idols must be set on a pedestal, but God "sits enthroned above the circle of the earth" (v. 22). In the language of Psalm 104:2, God has stretched out the heavens like the curtains of a tent, and as Creator He rules over the entire world. Verses 15–17 emphasized God's sovereignty over the nations, and verses 22–24 stress His full control over the rulers of those nations. Whether a Sennacherib or a Nebuchadnezzar, all rulers come under His sway and will reign only as long as the Lord decrees (cf. vv. 6–7). In 37:16 Hezekiah acknowledged the sovereign rule of the God who was "enthroned between the cherubim" in the Holy of Holies.

Human beings are also prone to worship the stars in the sky; verses 25 and 26 deal with this. The Lord created all the stars and fully controls their orderly march across the heavens (Job 38:32). Not one star is missing or out of place (cf. Isa. 34:16)! Such fantastic power almost defies description, and verse 26 uses four different words to help convey God's greatness.

In the light of this description of the person of God in verses 12–26, the people of Israel should have harbored no doubts about His ability to fulfill His promises. Yet verse 27 expresses the feeling that God had overlooked Israel's plight and was unconcerned about her fate. How easy it is to believe in the infinite power of God and at the same time to feel that He is unable to meet our personal needs! Israel had to be reminded that God is indeed the eternal Creator and that His power was available for her needs (vv. 28–29). Three of the four words used for "power" or "strength" in verse 26 are repeated in verse 29.

Many of the terms in verses 25–31 have a military background. The Assyrian army was not tired or in danger of stumbling as it swept into Israel (5:27). Just as the long march did not exhaust the army, so the long journey back to Judah would not exhaust the exiles. They would be able to walk many hundreds of miles without growing weary, and they would even feel like running along the way. The mention of eagles draws attention to the speed (Jer. 4:13) and the vigor (Ps. 103:5) that would characterize the rejuvenated army of the Lord.

The key is to "hope in the LORD" (v. 31), to place one's trust in the God who never disappoints. This involves prayer (Ps. 40:1) and the careful study of God's Word (Ps. 130:5), which nourishes faith in the mighty Lord. "Renew" (v. 31) literally means "exchange strength" (heḥᵉlîp). If we look to the Lord we will exchange our weakness for God's great strength. The imagery of a new garment lies behind this idea of exchanging. In 52:1 Jerusalem is told to change her outfit, to put on "garments of splendor" and thus to "clothe" herself "with strength." Paul commands Christians, "Clothe yourselves with the Lord Jesus Christ [and with the] new self, which is being renewed . . . in the image of its Creator" (Rom. 13:14; Col. 3:10). This same divine strength is still available for those who are weak and discouraged.

DELIVERANCE ON THE WAY (41:1–29)

The Introduction of Cyrus (41:1–7)

Chapter 40 contains the great promise of the return of the exiles to Judah, and in chapter 41 we are introduced to the agent whom God would raise up to accomplish this deliverance. Isaiah had asserted God's superiority over the nations and the idols they worshiped (40:15–20), and now he challenged these rivals to God's majesty to contend this claim (41:1, 21). In a courtroomlike setting, God proved His superiority over the idolaters and their idols by describing His ability to predict the rise to power of Cyrus, the king of Persia, far in advance of this fact. Cyrus is alluded to or mentioned by name a number of times between 41:2 and 48:14, and in all of these references the emphasis is not on the magnificent success of the Persian king but on the power of God who raised him up.

The coming of Cyrus is first described in verses 2 and 3. Born east of Babylon in what is now Iran, Cyrus would move through country after country, conquering every king in his path. Shortly after 550 B.C., Cyrus was able to unify the Medes and Persians and to defeat the powerful kingdom of Lydia in Asia Minor. Then he turned south to conquer Babylon (539 B.C.). The second line in verse 2 is difficult to interpret. "Righteousness" may refer to the fulfillment of God's righteous purposes through Cyrus, or it could be understood in the less common sense of "victory." Cyrus's triumphs brought greater justice to the peoples of the Near East.

Verse 4, like 44:6 and 48:12, pictures the Lord as the Alpha and Omega, the God of history who plans all events and makes sure that they are carried out. He is the Creator and Sustainer of the universe, the eternal King of Kings.

When Cyrus began his trail of conquest, the nations would be filled with fear. "Islands" (v. 5) includes the coastlands of the Mediterranean; the whole Near East would be affected. In desperation the nations would make new idols in the belief that they would help them defeat Cyrus, and so once again Isaiah sarcastically mentioned how carefully idols must be set in place (v. 7; cf. 40:21).

God's Provision for His Servant Israel (41:8–21)

For Israel, however, the coming of Cyrus would be good news, and verses 8–20 show why God's people should not be afraid. Unlike weak idols, God is able to help His people (vv. 10, 13, 14). Isaiah contrasted the strength and encouragement that God can give (v. 10) with the feeble support the craftsmen give to one another (vv. 6, 7) as they build their lifeless idols.

Israel was like a worm (v. 14), but the Lord would transform her into a mighty threshing sledge (vv. 15–16). Like Cyrus, God's people would be able to reduce the nations to chaff (v. 15; cf. v. 2). Assyria and Babylon had shown no mercy to the Israelites, but their mighty armies would be crushed (vv. 11–12; cf. 40:17).

Verse 10 must have been a source of deep comfort to the exiles in Babylon and to all of God's people who have been oppressed or held captive by an enemy. No one can separate us from the One who takes hold of our right hand (v. 13; cf. John 10:29; Rom. 8:38–39), and because of that we need not fear and can "rejoice in the LORD" (v. 16).

In verse 8 for the first time in the Book of Isaiah, Israel is called "my servant." This is a significant term in chapters 41 through 53, and its meaning has been hotly debated. Some interpreters insist that the servant is always the nation of Israel, but even in this first occurrence there is an ambivalence between the idea of the nation and that of the individual. "Jacob" was both a person and a people. "Servant" (*'ebed*) does not always refer to a lowly slave. Kings had "servants" whom we would more naturally call "officials" because of the high government positions they held (Exod. 10:1). When used as a verb, the word "serve" (*'ābad*) can also be translated "worship." The servant of the Lord should be a true worshiper of Him (cf. 22:20).

In verses 17–20 the change in Israel's status is compared to the blooming of the desert. The abundant waters and thriving trees symbolize the blessings to come on Israel and also the provision for her journey to her homeland. All nature would rejoice when Israel was released from captivity (cf. 44:23; 55:12–13). The pine, fir, and cypress are also mentioned in connection with the beauty of Jerusalem during the messianic age (60:13; cf. 35:1–7). God's creative work on behalf of Israel would teach the nations about His power. The four verbs at the beginning of verse 20 imply that people are slow to see God's hand in history.

In verse 1 Isaiah had challenged the nations to meet Him in court, and in verses 21–24 he called on the idols themselves to produce evidence of their power. If they were genuine deities, they should have been able to point to specific predictions that they had revealed to their devotees. But the idols had not been able to predict the future, and there was very little evidence that they had been able to accomplish anything. Like the nations that made them, the idols were "less than nothing" (v. 24; cf. 40:17). Israel's God, however, had made a precise prophecy that is summed up in verses 25–29. Verse 25 repeats verse 2, though it pictures Cyrus as coming from two directions, not one. The "north" is included because the Persians conquered the lands north of Babylon before invading her borders. This time their complete domination is compared to treading clay and trampling mud (v. 25), imagery that is used of Assyria in 10:6.

The Lord looked in vain among the idols and soothsayers to see if any had foretold the coming of Cyrus. God was the first to announce the good news (through Isaiah) and only Jerusalem learned about the conqueror far in advance of his arrival. Thus the idols were discredited and shown to be false gods, mere "wind and confusion" (v. 29). Ironically, "wind" (rûaḥ) is the same word that often is translated "spirit," a description of the essential nature of God. Idols claim to have spiritual power, but they are filled only with air.

THE SERVANT OF THE LORD (42:1–25)

There is another person in this section who plays an even more important role than Cyrus, and He is called the Servant of the Lord. In chapter 48 the Persian king is alluded to for the last time. The Servant of the Lord is the central figure in chapters 49–53. Cyrus was called for the specific purpose of releasing Israel from exile, and the Servant was chosen to redeem the world from the dark prison of sin. Both are called "messiahs," or "anointed ones" (Cyrus in 45:1 and the Messiah in Dan. 9:26), but the work of the Servant would extend far beyond that of Cyrus. If "calling him in righteousness" is the correct translation for the calling of Cyrus (41:2), it parallels the calling of the Servant (42:6). The Lord took hold of the hands of both leaders (42:6; 45:1). At the approach of Cyrus, the nations trembled, but the coming of the Servant would bring justice to the world.

These comparisons strengthen the view that the Servant is

an individual, an interpretation that also is supported by the other three Servant Songs in chapters 49–53. If this is true, why is the servant called "Israel" in 41:8 and 9? Delitzsch is probably correct to understand Isaiah's concept of the servant in terms of the figure of a pyramid.[2] At the base of the pyramid is the nation of Israel. In several passages (e.g., 42:19) the servant represents Israel as a people who were chosen by God to be a kingdom of priests (cf. Exod. 19:6) but who were miserable failures in fulfilling their calling. The center portion of the pyramid represents those who were spiritual in Israel, the righteous remnant that remained faithful in the face of general apostasy (cf. 37:4). This group may be identical with "my servants" who receive the Lord's blessing (65:13–15). The apex of the pyramid represents the Messiah, the One who fulfilled all that Israel was meant to be. He became the High Priest who atoned for the sins of Israel and for those of the whole world. Through this narrowing of the concept of Israel, one can understand the latitude in the term "servant."

The Description of the Servant of the Lord (42:1–9)

The description of the Servant (42:1–7) has important links with the Davidic Messiah whom Isaiah previously alluded to. The Spirit would rest on the Messiah (v. 1), as it did on the Branch from the stump of Jesse (11:2). Chapter 11 also emphasizes the justice and righteousness that would characterize the Messiah's rule (11:3–5), and "justice" is mentioned three times in 42:1–4 (cf. 9:7). The poor and the downtrodden would not be crushed or "snuffed out" by Him (cf. 11:4; 42:3). It is no wonder that the distant coastlands will "put their hope" in His law (v. 4; cf. 2:2–4).

Verse 5 portrays the power of the Creator who guarantees that the Servant would be able to complete His glorious task. Strengthened by the almighty God, the Messiah (v. 6) would "be a covenant for the people and a light for the Gentiles" (v. 6). "People" refers to Jews (cf. 49:8; Acts 26:17–18). The

[2]Franz Delitzsch, *Biblical Commentary on the Prophecies of Isaiah,* trans. James Martin, 3d ed., 2 vols. (1877; reprint, Grand Rapids: Eerdmans, 1967), 2:174.

Messiah would be a "covenant" for them because He would be the everlasting ruler who was promised in the Davidic covenant. First, however, He would die on Calvary to institute the New Covenant. Moses was the mediator of the covenant at Sinai, but in a far more comprehensive manner, Christ would be the mediator of the New Covenant.

The phrase "light for the Gentiles" (v. 6) also appears in 49:6, a passage that shows that "light" is a synonym for "salvation." Christ's use of Isaiah 61:1 in Luke 4:18–19 also links recovery of sight and freedom from confinement with the salvation of souls. Earlier in Isaiah the opening of blind eyes occurred in passages that deal with the messianic age (29:18; 32:3; 35:5). Therefore the release from the "prison" (v. 7) of Babylon was only a forerunner of a greater restoration in the future. The coming of Cyrus was good news for Israel (41:27), but the coming of the Messiah would be even better news.

God's ability to predict the rise of Cyrus demonstrated His superiority to idols (ch. 41), and the great prophecies concerning the Servant confirm that supremacy (42:8–9). When the exiles saw the fulfillment of the predictions regarding Cyrus, they knew that some day the ones about the Messiah also would come true.

Praise for the Deliverance of Captive Israel (42:10–25)

The prospect of a world full of justice and freedom calls for a song of praise, and so the whole world rejoices over the destruction of wickedness (vv. 10–13). The news resounds through the desert and is carried across the seas; the Lord has won a great victory. The warlike activity of God (v. 13) is quite unlike the opening part of the chapter. To establish justice on earth, God must defeat the wicked who oppress His people (cf. 63:1–6).

In verses 14–17 Isaiah focused on the Lord's action on behalf of His captive people. The Lord suffered when His people suffered, and He had to restrain Himself until the time of punishment was over. The same verb is used of Joseph who struggled to control himself while sending his brothers through the ordeal they deserved for selling him into slavery (Gen.

43:31; 45:1). When the seventy years had passed, the Lord would remove all obstacles and clear the way for the return of His people. Verse 15 seems to contradict 41:18, but both descriptions are positive ones. Rivers and swamps could prove to be formidable barriers for travelers, but where drinking water was needed, it would be available. Making "rough places smooth" and leveling mountains (vv. 15–16) recalls 40:4.

Moving one step backward, the Lord explains why Israel found herself in this pitiful position (vv. 18–25). Although Israel was God's "servant," she was a different servant from the One described in verses 1–7! Israel was blind and deaf to the things of God. She had been entrusted with His great and glorious law (v. 21), but she had refused to obey that law in which the nations one day will "put their hope" (v. 4). Consequently Israel had been plundered and looted and had suffered a fate worse than that which her ancestors had suffered at the hands of the Midianites (Judg. 6:2–4). The "prison" (v. 7) turned out to be Babylon, and there was no early release.

All these troubles came on Israel because the Lord fought against her, not because He was weaker than the gods of Babylon. In His anger God had punished His people as a warning, but they had refused to change their sinful ways (cf. 5:25; 9:19). A future generation, perhaps, would listen to the prophet's message and react differently (v. 23).

THE REDEMPTION OF ISRAEL FROM BABYLON
(43:1–44:5)

With characteristic speed Isaiah abruptly returned to the happy subject of restoration (43:1). This rapid interchange between the topics of salvation and judgment also was common in chapters 28–33. The last seven verses of chapter 43 again portray the sin of Israel, and in chapter 44 Isaiah returned to the joyful theme of God's blessing. Both chapters 43 and 44 begin with the words "but now" and offer the assurance that Israel no longer needed to fear. The Lord calls Israel by name (43:1), and by calling themselves "Jacob" or "Israel" (44:5), the people acknowledged that they belonged to the Lord. Cyrus, too, is called by name (45:4).

Israel's Restoration Through the Power of God (43:1–13)

The description of the restoration (vv. 1–8) employs the imagery of chapter 42. This time the rivers are not dried up (42:15), but the Lord promises that the floodwaters will not sweep His people away (43:2). Although Israel had felt the burning anger of God (42:25), the flames of oppressors would not harm them (43:2). The experience of Daniel's three friends in Nebuchadnezzar's furnace is a remarkable fulfillment of this verse (Dan. 3:25, 27). Natural forces would not stop the return of God's people to Israel, and great distances would not halt them, either. The geography in verses 5 and 6 compares with the account of the regathering in 11:10–12. The vast dispersion implied may indicate that Isaiah's prophecy embraces the great return prior to Christ's second coming as well as the restoration from Babylon.

This chapter gives a prominent place to the theme of redemption. God promised to reclaim the people that He sold into captivity. The word "redeem," or "ransom," occurs in verses 1, 3, and 14, and "redeemed" or "Redeemer" is mentioned in 44:6, 22, 23, and 24. To prove His love for His people, God was willing to give Egypt, Cush, and Seba as a ransom for Israel (vv. 3–5). These three nations may symbolize Israel's great worth, or they may have been named in anticipation of the subsequent Persian conquests. Under the leadership of Cambyses, the Persians were able to conquer these lands, and this may be viewed as their reward for giving Israel its freedom (cf. Ezek. 29:18–19). The same three nations are described in 45:14 as willingly submitting to Israel in the last days.

Verse 7 contains three of the verbs that appeared in verse 1 that emphasize God's work as Creator. The phrase "for my glory" is added to show the purpose for which God created Israel. Verses 8–13 resume using the legal language that was so prominent in chapter 41. The Lord summons the Jews (v. 8) and the Gentiles (v. 9) to court to prove once again His tremendous power. As in 42:17, Israel is called "blind" and "deaf," but it is the Lord's desire that the eyes of her spiritual understanding be opened wide (v. 10). The nations are again challenged to produce evidence that they and their idols have been able to predict the future (cf. 41:22–23), but they are unable to find witnesses. The Lord, however, can point to Israel as His witness (vv. 10, 12; 44:8). The very existence of Israel as a nation was living proof of God's power. He had redeemed her from the bondage of Egypt, and He was about to rescue her from the captivity of Babylon.

Several parts of verses 1–13 reflect the Song of Moses in Deuteronomy 32:39. The assertion of God's uniqueness (vv. 10–11) is clearly drawn from that passage. The words "No one can deliver out of my hand" (v. 13) are taken from the same verse in Deuteronomy. Chapter 45 repeats the essential thrust of verse 11 six more times, and the same teaching also is given in 46:9. How important for Israel to understand that there is only one God and that His name is "the LORD"!

God's Outpouring of Blessing on the Chosen Nation (43:14–44:5)

According to 43:14 (the first mention of Babylon since chapter 39), God would intervene in Babylon on Israel's behalf. The Chaldeans—the conquerors of Jerusalem— would become fugitives. Perhaps Isaiah mentioned ships (v. 14) because of Babylon's extensive use of the Persian Gulf and the Tigris and Euphrates rivers for trading purposes. The Lord had promised judgment on the commercial vessels of arrogant nations (2:16), and His power is emphasized by the series of titles in verses 14 and 15. Four times the pronoun "your" is used because the Lord was the God of Israel. Lest anyone doubt God's ability to defeat Babylon, Isaiah referred to God's victory over Egypt at the Red Sea (vv. 16–17). Pharaoh's mighty chariots thundered after hapless Israel, but the waters of the sea closed over them. Horses and riders perished together; they were destroyed as easily as one snuffs out a wick.

As great as that victory may have been, Israel was encouraged to look to the future (vv. 18–21). During the Exodus, Israel learned that God could supply all the water His people needed to wander in the wilderness (Exod. 15:22–25). The same God who miraculously made a road through the sea (v. 16) would now make a road through the desert (v. 19). As

God promised in 35:6, there would be "streams in the wasteland" (vv. 19–20) because He would provide for His people during the journey from Babylon. Even the jackals and owls (34:13) would be thankful for the transformed desert.

In verse 7 Isaiah noted that Israel was created for God's glory. Verse 21 states that the nation was formed to recount the Lord's praise. Any people so marvelously blessed by God could be expected to acknowledge His goodness. Throughout her history, however, Israel had failed to serve the Lord, and verses 22 through 28 discuss this negligence. God loved His people and did not burden or weary them with excessive demands (vv. 22–23), but Israel did not respond to His gracious love. Instead, she "burdened" or "wearied" the Lord with all her sins (v. 24). The charge that Israel was lax in bringing sacrifices to the Lord seems to contradict 1:10–13. Perhaps the Israelites were insincere in their worship. When they did bring offerings, they simply went through the motions of worship, and so God did not consider their empty sacrifices to be true sacrifices at all.

In spite of Israel's sin, God promised that He would forgive her (v. 25). Using the same style as in verse 11, the Lord declared that "I, even I, am he who blots out your transgressions" (cf. 44:22). Before this redemption from Babylon, however, Israel had to be punished, and verses 26–28 recount the unhappy details. God had a solid case against the nation because the people had persistently sinned against Him. "First father" (v. 27) may be a reference to Abraham (cf. 51:2), though the more sinful Jacob is favored by some commentators. The "spokesmen" were probably the priests and prophets, the intermediaries between God and the nation, whose spiritual collapse Isaiah had referred to earlier (28:7).

So serious was Israel's sin that the Lord had "to consign Jacob to destruction"—to place Israel under the ban (v. 28)— the technical term that is frequently used to refer to the total destruction of the cities of Canaan (cf. comments on 34:2). Israel had become a pagan nation, and her cities and temple were demolished by foreign armies.

Anxious to leave this somber theme, Isaiah quickly returned to the promise of blessing. Isaiah 44:1–5 is best understood as the conclusion of chapter 43. The first two verses of chapter 44 closely follow the style of 43:1, though verse 2 adds the idea that Israel was "formed in the womb." This tender phrase is also used of the prophet Jeremiah (Jer. 1:5) and of the Servant (49:1, 5). In verses 1 and 2 "my servant" and "chosen" are put in parallel, and the same association occurs elsewhere (43:10; 41:8, 9; 42:1). In the later Servant Songs this explicit parallel is not used.

Like the previous section (43:10–13), chapter 44 makes several allusions to the Song of Moses. The name "Jeshurun" (v. 2), which may mean "righteous" or "forthright," is elsewhere applied to Israel only in Deuteronomy 32:15 and in 33:5 and 26. The divine title "Rock" was used a number of times by Moses in chapter 32 (vv. 4, 15, 30). The symbolism of water and streams (v. 4) goes beyond that in 43:19–20, particularly in comparing water to the pouring out of God's Spirit. A similar reference to the Spirit is found in 32:15 in a description of the messianic age, and the "springing up" of plants and trees is also associated with the coming of the Messiah (cf. 4:2; 11:1). Verses 3 and 4 need not be restricted to a future age, however, for they depict both the material and spiritual blessings that God wants all His people to enjoy. The picture in verse 5 contrasts with that in 43:22–28. In 44:5 people are proud to be called Israelites (because of Israel's identification with the Lord) and are not reluctant to bring honor to the God of Jacob by displaying His name (cf. 43:1, 7, 21).

GOD'S SUPERIORITY TO IDOLS (44:6–23)

The Lord's case against the worship of idols (which began in chapter 41) is brought to a climax in chapter 44. Every chapter from 40–48 contains some reference to idols, images, or pagan worship, but chapter 44 presents the strongest attack against them. Verses 6–8 follow the style of 41:4, 21–23, which describe God's uniqueness. The idols are challenged to produce witnesses to prove that they can foretell the future, but Israel is brought forward as God's witness (cf. 43:10), and the Lord concludes that He alone is God. He is the solid "Rock" (v. 8) who can be trusted, unlike the lifeless idols of stone, wood, or metal that were worshiped by the nations and that had become attractive to the exiles who lived in the midst of Babylon's splendor. In the Chaldean capital, beautifully decorated idols were carried in procession and given credit for bringing victory to the Babylonian armies.

Verses 9–20 expose the sheer folly of idolatry by describing the process used in making an idol. This effective satire is handled by some translations as prose and by others as poetry. A good case can be made for either position. The parallelism is not as clear as in most of the poetic sections of Isaiah.

The first paragraph (vv. 9–11) introduces the subject by making two basic observations: idols are man-made, and they are worthless. The word translated "make" (v. 9) or "shape" (v. 10—yāṣar) is rendered "formed" when it describes God as the Creator of Israel (43:1; 44:2). God has created man, but how can a man create God (v. 10)? The very suggestion reveals the impossibility of such an undertaking. A man has to be blind and ignorant to attempt it. The term in verse 10 that expresses the worthlessness of idols was used to emphasize Egypt's failure to do anything beneficial for Judah (30:5).

In verses 12–17 Isaiah mockingly described the steps that are involved in making an idol. He discussed two different craftsmen: the blacksmith (v. 12) and the carpenter (vv. 13–17). The two types of images they represent—metal and wooden— were mentioned in 40:18–20. There the wooden idol was made for a poor man, and since wooden idols were more common than metal ones, Isaiah concentrated on them. Verse 12 dramatizes the frailty of the craftsman. A blacksmith may be strong and healthy, but after working on the idol for some time, he soon becomes hungry and thirsty. Although the divine Creator never grows weary or tired (40:28), the idol's existence depends on a weak human being.

Carpenters used the best wood available to make idols. Cedar, cypress, and oak were hard, durable, and valuable as building materials (9:10). But these stately trees depend on rain to make them grow, and if God withholds the rains, there would be no material for an idol. Isaiah's sarcasm reaches its climax in verses 15–19 where he describes how the same wood that is used to make an idol is also used for cooking and heating. The idolater, however, bows down to this block of wood and calls it his god (vv. 15, 17, 19). Such gods are helpless (v. 17), blind, and ignorant, much like Israel's condition (cf. 6:9–10). No wonder God detests idols (Deut. 27:15) and calls them a fraud (Jer. 10:14). Not even devoted worship can help the idolater.

In contrast to idols, God is a powerful Redeemer who forgives His people. They had paid for their sins by going into exile, and God would bring them back home to Israel. This joyful news elicits praise even from the mountains and trees (v. 23; cf. 49:13).

THE RESTORATION OF ISRAEL THROUGH CYRUS
(44:24–45:25)

In 41:2 Isaiah had first alluded to the king who would bring about Israel's release, but now in successive verses he mentions him by name (44:28; 45:1). The ability to name Cyrus 150 years before his time underscores God's power as Creator (v. 24); He thwarts false religious leaders (v. 25), fulfills His prophets' words (v. 26), and dried up the Red Sea (v. 27; cf. 43:16–17). This mighty God promises that Jerusalem and the towns of Judah would be rebuilt (vv. 26, 28). Although Cyrus's decree permitted only the rebuilding of the temple (Ezra 1:1–3), a restored temple would surely lead to a rebuilt Jerusalem.

Cyrus is called God's "shepherd" (44:28) and His "anointed" (45:1). "Shepherd" is often applied to rulers (Jer. 23:2), and "anointed" can refer to kings (2 Sam. 5:3). "Anointed" is the word from which "Messiah" comes, and in Daniel 9:26 Christ is called "the Anointed One" (cf. 61:1). Apparently Cyrus was not a believer in Israel's God (vv. 4, 5), but God raised him up to accomplish His purposes. The Lord would "go before" him (v. 2) like the angel that led Israel through the wilderness (Exod. 23:20). Even if the wooden gates of a city turned out to be bronze (v. 2), they would not stop Cyrus. The treasures of many nations would be his (cf. 41:2f.).

God called Cyrus "by name" (vv. 3–4), i.e., He chose him to carry out a special mission. As a result of Cyrus's work, the whole world would understand God's power and uniqueness. The opening lines of verse 5 are repeated in verses 6, 18, 21, and

22 (cf. 43:11). Through Cyrus, God would make things right for His people (v. 8; cf. 41:2; 45:13). Israel would be delivered, but Babylon and other wicked nations would face "disaster" (v. 7; cf. 31:2).

Verses 9–13 describe those who object to God's plans. As in 29:15–16, the Lord pronounced woe on those who complain about His sovereign work, and Paul used 29:16 and 45:9 in Romans 9:20. God is the potter, and His children are the clay. No one can question His actions. Just as God controls the parade of the stars across the heavens (v. 12), so He would raise up Cyrus to release the exiles (v. 13), though Cyrus would not receive any immediate payment (cf. 43:3–4).

Israel's release would be a harbinger of happier times. Nations such as Egypt and Cush would bring gifts to Israel and be submissive to her (cf. 11:14; 14:1–2; 18:7). The nations will bring their wealth to Israel during the Millennium (60:5). Isaiah's description of their acknowledgment of Israel's God is parallel to the account in 2:3 and in Zechariah 8:20–23. The Lord had been "hidden" or "inactive" during the Exile, but His deliverance of Israel would end her disgrace and prove His superiority over the idols (vv. 15–17). It would be Babylon's turn to endure shame (46:1–2).

The reference to God as creator (v. 18) emphasizes that the world was not made to be empty. The land of Israel was empty during the Exile, but soon it would be inhabited. God's promise was not made "in a land of darkness" (v. 19)—perhaps an allusion to the shady world of mediums and spiritists (8:19)—for the Lord had spoken "the truth" and declared "what is right" (v. 19).

In verses 20–25 (as in 43:9), the nations and their idols are summoned to court and challenged to acknowledge the greatness of God that is evidenced by His ability to predict the future. Because He alone is God, the whole world is invited to turn to Him. Eventually all people will have to bow before Him (v. 23)—a concept that Paul used in Romans 14:11 and in Philippians 2:10–11. Verse 24 brings to a climax the refrain first mentioned in verse 5. The Lord alone has the power to vindicate His people and to judge His enemies.

THE FALL OF BABYLON AND HER GODS
(46:1–47:15)

The Contrast Between God and the Idols of Babylon
(46:1–13)

The return of the exiles depended on the defeat of Babylon, and in these two chapters Isaiah described the collapse of the mighty Chaldean kingdom. Babylon's fall is seen in the disgrace of its gods (vv. 1–2). "Bel" was probably another name for "Marduk," the most prominent deity. "Bel" itself means "lord" and is equal to the Canaanite "Baal." "Nebo," the son of Bel, was the god of learning and writing. When Babylon fell these idols were powerless and were taken captive along with the people (cf. Jer. 48:7; 49:3). Their helplessness proves the truth of Isaiah's ongoing critique of idols.

Unlike the idols God was able to sustain His people and even to rescue them from calamity (vv. 3–4). Idols could not respond when men cried out for help (v. 7). They had to be carried around and carefully set in place. Even though they were made of silver and gold, they were of no value whatever (cf. 40:18–20). None of the gods was like the Lord (v. 9), a fact that rebellious Israel was slow to learn.

The final verses of chapter 46 emphasize God's power. His plans regarding Israel and Babylon would be carried out, and Babylon would be conquered by "a bird of prey" (v. 11), a reference to the swiftness and strength of Cyrus's conquest (cf. 41:2; Jer. 49:22). The defeat of Babylon would mean salvation for Israel because Cyrus would bring about her release. "Righteousness" (v. 13) is almost a synonym for "salvation" or "deliverance" (cf. 45:8; 59:11). Through Cyrus, God was carrying out His righteous purposes (cf. 41:2) and would bring glory to His name (cf. 35:2). Isaiah's description of Cyrus's rise to power marks the climax of the prophet's teaching about God's sovereignty over the nations, a theme that goes back to 8:9–10 where the Lord declared that the plans of the nations would not succeed. Neither Assyria, Babylon, nor Persia acted independently. God controls and superintends the affairs of nations (cf. 40:15–17).

The Collapse and Humiliation of the Queen of Kingdoms (47:1–15)

Chapter 47 graphically describes the fall of Babylon. Verses 1–3 portray the shame and humiliation the city would suffer. Babylon is called a "Virgin Daughter" (v. 1) because no enemy had been able to breach her walls. Although she had not been destroyed, or raped (cf. 23:12; 37:22), under Cyrus the Medes and Persians would humble her and bring her down in mourning. The Babylonians would be subjected to the menial task of grinding flour (cf. Exod. 11:5), and they would wade through streams on their way to exile. Babylon's virginity would be gone when she faced the vengeance of the "LORD Almighty," "the Holy One of Israel" (cf. 13:4; 41:14).

In verses 5 and 7 Isaiah referred to Babylon as the "queen" who will lament her fate in silence. Babylon possessed a wealthy empire, and the city itself was very beautiful (cf. 13:19). Part of her wealth resulted from God's using her to destroy and plunder Israel (42:24), and, like Assyria (10:12–13), Babylon was filled with pride over her accomplishments. Her boasting (v. 7) is reminiscent of the words of Nebuchadnezzar in Daniel 4:30.

Verses 8–11 contrast Babylon's lofty opinion of herself with the lowly position assigned to her by God. Twice (vv. 8, 10) Babylon boasts "I am, and there is none besides me," a claim similar to that which the Lord Himself made (43:11; 45:5–6). Babylon's security was a false one (cf. 32:9, 11) because the queen would become a widow and lose all her children (cf. 13:16, 18). This double calamity is also applied to the exiled Israel in 54:1 and 4. Babylon would face disaster in spite of her sorceries and spells (vv. 9, 12), which used magic to avoid danger and to bring harm to the enemy. Daniel 2:2 mentions the "magicians, enchanters, sorcerers, and astrologers" that Nebuchadnezzar depended on. None of these individuals or their dubious methods would be able to prevent disaster, and no payment of ransom would convince the enemy to spare Babylon (cf. 13:17).

Verses 13 and 14 focus on the astrologers and stargazers because Babylon relied on them more than did any other nation (cf. Dan. 2:2, 10). The Babylonians' ability to read the skies would not delay the judgment that was coming on the astrologers and on the nation. The Babylonians would be destroyed as rapidly as stubble (v. 14; cf. Mal. 4:1). All of Babylon's resources—sorcerers, astrologers, and the like—would be as helpless as their idols (46:1–2); no one would be able to rescue her.

THE RELEASE OF REBELLIOUS ISRAEL (48:1–22)

The final chapter in this section (chs. 40–48) summarizes the major themes that Isaiah had emphasized. God is superior to idols because He is able to predict the future and to accomplish "new things" (v. 6), such as raising up Cyrus to deliver Israel from Babylon. In verses 1–5 Isaiah reminded Israel of her privileged position and of her incorrigible stubbornness. Only Israel belonged to God and possessed the holy city, Jerusalem, where the temple was located. Although Israel prayed to God and appeared to rely on Him, the nation did so hypocritically. All too frequently she failed to worship God and worshiped the idols that Isaiah so forcefully condemned. Even at Mount Sinai the stubborn Israelites bowed before the golden calf (Exod. 32:8–9). All of God's former predictions and accomplishments failed to impress His people (cf. 41:22; 42:9).

God was about to perform new things (v. 6; 42:9). He would restore Israel, and the messianic age would come (cf. 65:17). God would restore Israel, though Israel did not deserve it. She had been rebellious and treacherous (v. 8), and God had punished her in the furnace of affliction. Her experience in Egypt had been like being in an "iron-smelting furnace" (Deut. 4:20), and her experience in Babylon was similar. As Israel's collapse had dishonored God's name (v. 11), so her restoration would cause it to be praised (cf. 42:8). In spite of Israel's sin, God would be faithful to His covenant (cf. 55:3) and would act for His own sake.

In verse 12 (as in 41:4) God is called "the first and the last." He is the great Creator (cf. 40:21–22) who continues to work in the present (cf. v. 7). Just as all creation responds to His commands (40:26), so Cyrus would carry out God's mission

203

against Babylon (vv. 14–15), a mission first announced to the world by God Himself (v. 16; 41:25–27).

The phrase "the Sovereign LORD has sent me, with his Spirit" either means that God sent Isaiah to speak these words through the power of the Holy Spirit or that God would send the Servant as another of the "new things" He would perform (v. 6). The Spirit is said to come upon the Servant (42:1; 61:1), though in the latter verse this could refer in a limited sense to Isaiah.

Verses 17–19 lament Israel's condition. If Israel had listened to the commands God gave through His prophets, the nation could have enjoyed abundant peace under just rulers (cf. 66:12; Amos 5:24). Her population would have been like the sand on the seashore, as God promised Abraham in Genesis 22:17. Instead judgment was necessary, and thousands would be cut off (cf. 10:22). Only the remnant would be spared. In the light of the suffering God's people would experience, the promise that the remnant would return was good news. Once again God would redeem His people. The command to flee from Babylon recalls Israel's rapid flight from Egypt. Although Israel did not have to flee from Babylon (cf. 52:12), the Israelites were urged to leave quickly because God was going to judge the Babylonians (cf. Jer. 51:6). When Israel left Egypt, God miraculously provided water in the desert. Moses struck the rock and water poured out (Exod. 17:6; Num. 20:11). On the way home from Babylon, the Israelites would again have sufficient water, God promised (cf. 35:6; 43:19–20).

For the wicked, however, there would be no peace or rest. Those who rebel against God, whether Jew or Gentile, will experience judgment. Verse 22 is a refrain that occurs again in 57:21, and both times it comes at the end of a nine-chapter section (see *Structure*).

12

THE MINISTRY OF
THE SERVANT OF THE LORD
49:1–57:21

After chapter 48 there are no further references to Cyrus, the Persian king who delivered Israel from Babylon. Instead chapters 49–57 focus on the greater Deliverer, the messianic Servant of the Lord who would bring salvation to the world (cf. ch. 42). Chapters 49–53 contain three more Servant Songs that describe the Servant's work. The climax of the third song is a description of the Servant's death as an atonement for sin that makes salvation available to the whole world (53:11–12; cf. 55:1; 56:6–7).

THE SERVANT OF THE LORD AND THE EXALTATION OF ISRAEL (49:1–26)

The Work of the Servant (49:1–7)

Although there are significant parallels between this song and the song in 42:1–7, this song introduces the theme of opposition to the Servant (49:4, 7). In the opening verse (v. 1) the Servant addresses the nations because in Him "the islands will put their hope" (42:4). The Servant tells of being called before birth, much like the prophet Jeremiah (Jer. 1:5) and the apostle Paul (Gal. 1:15). God mentioned His name because He had chosen the Servant for a special task (cf. 43:1; 45:3–4) that eventually would make Him a ruler. The Servant's words would have the power of a sharp sword (v. 2), a figure similar to the "rod of his mouth" (11:4). In Revelation 1:16 the one "like a son of man" had a sharp sword in His mouth to represent His authority. The "polished arrow" (v. 2) is linked with the ability to judge in Deuteronomy 32:23, 42.

Because the Servant's work would bring redemption to mankind, God's glory would be displayed through Him (v. 3). The nations would see God's glory when Israel was redeemed from Babylon (35:2; 40:5; 44:23), but a greater redemption would come through Christ. The Messiah's task would not be easy, however, for He would face strong opposition. Yet God would give Him a "reward" (v. 4), a term that probably refers to the people who would believe in Christ (cf. 40:10), the "offspring" mentioned in 53:10.

Verses 5 and 6 describe the Servant's work in greater detail. He whom God so tenderly led (cf. 44:2) would restore Israel and give the Gentiles an opportunity to come to the light of salvation. Israel's restoration would include release from the Babylonian captivity and redemption from sin. The "servant" who would bring release from Babylon may include the faithful remnant in Israel (cf. v. 8). Ultimately, however, the light of the world is Christ, and salvation in a final sense comes only through Him (cf. 42:6 and comments).

The servant who was "despised and abhorred" (v. 7) could be Israel. Zion was despised by the nations (60:14), though one day the kings who oppressed her would bow down at her feet (cf. 49:23) and acknowledge her exaltation. But the suffering Servant was "despised and rejected by men" (53:3), and kings would be astonished at His suffering and subsequent glory (52:15). Since "nation" is singular, it seems to refer to opposition from within Israel. The chosen nation persecuted her prophets and put to death the Son of God Himself.

The Return Home and the Growing Population (49:8–26)

Verses 8–12 emphasize the return of Israel to her homeland. The background of verse 8 is probably the Year of Jubilee, the time when all land was to revert to its original owners (Lev. 25:10). The Year of Jubilee is compared to "the year of the LORD's favor" (61:2). Just as the Year of Jubilee was to be a time of freedom and rejoicing, so the release from captivity would return the people to their beloved land. Paul understood verse 8 to refer to a greater deliverance, salvation through Christ (2 Cor. 6:2).

The mention of a "covenant" (v. 8) ties in well with Paul's use of verse 8 because the Servant was called "a covenant for the people" (42:6). But since Isaiah closely related "covenant" and the restoration of the land (v. 8), it may be best not to restrict "covenant" to a Christological interpretation. As with "servant" (v. 5), "covenant" may include the faithful in Israel, those who deserved to repossess the land that God promised Abraham when He made His covenant with him (Gen. 15:18). The land had lain desolate for decades; but after 539 B.C., tribes and families would again live in their allotted portions. Those who had been captives in Babylon would at last be free.

On their homeward journey, God would wonderfully meet Israel's needs. Israel would find pasture, even on hills that were usually barren, and God would provide sufficient water in the hot deserts (cf. 35:6–7; 41:18). In His great compassion the Lord would lead Israel like a shepherd, and by leveling the mountains and building highways, God would remove the obstacles that separated Israel from her homeland (cf. 35:8; 40:3–4). The exiles would return from every direction, though the east is not explicitly mentioned. Isaiah also describes Israel's regathering in 11:11–12 and in 43:5–6. "Sinim" (v. 12) is probably Aswan, near the southern border of Egypt.★ As in 44:23, the description of Israel's restoration elicited a burst of praise from all of nature. The Lord would comfort His people as He redeemed them from captivity. In 2 Corinthians 1:3–6 Paul wrote about the God who comforts believers in their sufferings. God is still the Father of compassion.

Amidst the description of joy and restoration, Zion objects and claims that the Lord has forsaken her (v. 14). Jerusalem has fallen, and her people are in exile. How can there be such jubilation? The Lord responds by stating that His love for Israel

---

★This assumes that "Sinim" is derived from $s^e w \bar{e} n \hat{i} m$ ("Syene" or "Aswan," Ezek. 29:10; 30:6). If the Masoretic Text is correct, a long-standing interpretation connects Sinim with China.

surpasses that of a mother for her baby. Some mothers might abandon their children (Ps. 27:10), but God will never abandon His. The name of Jerusalem was engraved on His palms, just as the names of the tribes of Israel were engraved on stones and attached to the ephod of the high priest to continually remind God of His people (Exod. 28:9–12). Jerusalem's walls and the former splendor of her towers will not be forgotten. Proof of God's love is seen in the description of the return of Jerusalem's inhabitants. The sons of Israel would soon be regathered and would be like the beautiful jewels worn by a bride. Although Assyria and Babylon devastated the entire land and deported its inhabitants, soon the land would be filled with people called "children born during your bereavement" (v. 20) because during the Exile Israel was viewed as a widow who had lost her children (cf. 54:1). The size of the population suggests that more is involved than the return from Babylon. Perhaps the regathering associated with Christ's second coming is in view, and some commentators believe that spiritual offspring—including Gentiles and Jews—are referred to (cf. 54:3, 17).

Because the nations were to assist the exiles on their way home, in verse 22 Isaiah returned to the familiar theme of raising a banner to summon the Gentiles (cf. 11:10–12). This description probably looks beyond the help that Cyrus gave Israel to the day when the Gentiles would be a part of Christ's kingdom (cf. 60:9; 66:20). Verse 23 also looks ahead to the Millennium for its final fulfillment. During the Millennium nations and kings will submit to Christ's rule, and Israel's exaltation will demonstrate the power of her God (cf. 60:16).

The splendid picture drawn in verses 19–23 is interrupted by a disturbing question. Who would rescue the Israelites from the mighty armies of Babylon (v. 24)? The harsh realities were that Israel was to be a captive nation, but her God would intervene at last. He would take up the cause of His people and turn the tables on the enemy. During the siege of Jerusalem some parents actually ate their children (Lam. 4:10), but soon the oppressors would "eat their own flesh" (v. 26). The drinking of blood may be a metaphorical way to describe the numerous casualties Israel's enemies would incur (cf. 51:17). The overthrow of Babylon and of all Israel's oppressors would show the world who God is. He is the Lord, the "Mighty One" (v. 26; cf. 1:24; 60:16).

THE SUFFERING SERVANT (50:1–11)

The third Servant Song is found in 50:4–11. In this section Isaiah showed the difference between the responsiveness of the Servant and the sin of the nation as a whole. The opening three verses explain why Israel was taken captive. It was not because God was too weak to prevent it. He is the One who dried up the Red Sea and at whose command the rivers run dry (42:15). When He sent plagues on Egypt, the fish died (Exod. 7:18), and darkness blotted out the sun (Exod. 10:21). The reason for the Exile was Israel's sin and rebellion. No one listened to what God said (v. 2) because the nation was strangely deaf (6:10).

Although Israel's exile was like a divorce, chapter 50 begins with a question that implies that no certificate of divorce existed. Normally a husband gave such a certificate to a wife he was divorcing (cf. Deut. 24:1, 3). Jeremiah 3:8 says that God gave the northern kingdom a "certificate of divorce." Judah was in line to receive one, too. Perhaps the rhetorical question in verse 1 is a way of putting the blame for the divorce on Judah. She broke the relationship by sinning against God; He did not initiate the divorce. Another possibility is that God considered the Exile a period of separation, not divorce.

Verse one draws a second analogy. If a man did not pay his debts, his children could be sold as slaves (2 Kings 4:1). But God does not have any creditors, and He received nothing when He sold His people (52:3). The idiom of selling Israel into the hands of the enemy occurs several times in the Book of Judges (3:8; 4:2; 10:7).

Israel's sin and rebellion contrast with the description of the Servant's obedience and submission. His ears are open to the Lord, and every day He is eager to be taught by Him so that He might speak words of encouragement to the weary (cf. 42:3). The Servant Himself has to undergo suffering and humiliation. He would be beaten as if He were a criminal or fool (Prov. 19:29; 26:3), and His beard would be pulled out to demonstrate the people's deep contempt for Him (2 Sam. 10:4–5). The mocking and spitting were also intended to insult and disgrace Him. This entire description is a preview of the flogging and mocking that Christ endured prior to His death on Calvary (cf. Matt. 27:26, 30–31).

The beating and mocking of the Servant, however, did not put Him to shame (v. 7). Like the prophets He stood firm and prevailed against His opponents. Christ "resolutely set out for Jerusalem" (Luke 9:51) to die for the sins of the world, and the final result of His death was great honor and glory (cf. 52:13). The Servant had done nothing to deserve such punishment, and so God defended His righteousness. God assures those who accept the divine Servant as their Savior that no charges can be leveled against them; the Servant has endured their punishment (vv. 8–9; cf. Rom. 8:33–34). None of the Servant's opponents will last long, and those who bring false charges against the righteous will be devoured by moths (v. 9; cf. 51:8).

"Sovereign LORD" is used four times in verses 4 through 9. This particular title is composed of the two words that are normally translated "Lord" (*Adonay*) and "LORD" (*Yahweh*). When they occur together, these two names for God emphasize His sovereign control over the nations and His covenantal relationship with Israel. Although the title "Sovereign LORD" is used sparingly in Isaiah (7:7; 30:15; 49:22; etc.), it appears dozens of times in Ezekiel.

Verses 10 and 11 challenge the entire nation to follow the lead of the Servant who testified of His close relationship with the Lord. If Israel would truly trust in the Lord, she would find comfort and be restored. The dark days of distress and unbelief would give way to salvation. Those who "light fires" (v. 11) refers to men who had their own schemes and their own gods. Because they had rejected the light of God's Word, they would face terrible punishment.

GOD'S PROMISE TO RESTORE HIS PEOPLE
(51:1–16)

A series of imperatives mark the paragraphs that lead up to the final Servant Song. Several times the people are told to "listen" to the Lord (51:1, 4, 7, 21). Isaiah 51:9 contains the first of four double imperatives, a plea for the arm of the Lord to awake from its inactivity. This is followed by two commands that urge Jerusalem to awake from her drunkenness and from the stupor that was induced by her captivity (51:17; 52:1). The final "Depart, depart" is the long-awaited order to leave Babylon (v. 11).

The opening paragraphs of this section (vv. 1–8) are mainly addressed to the believing remnant, those Israelites who, like the Servant in chapter 50, were obedient to the Lord. They pursued righteousness (v. 1) and had the law in their hearts (v. 7). These were the descendants of Abraham, the "rock" (v. 1) who believed God even when he had no children. Because of God's blessing, Abraham had a son in his old age; and from this son, Isaac, came the mighty nation of Israel. Israel was then in exile, but soon God would restore her to the land. Jerusalem would become an Edenlike paradise, full of joy and singing (v. 3), and justice would prevail (vv. 3–5). God's justice would be "a light to the nations" (v. 4), a phrase that is applied to the Servant (42:6; 49:6).

The description in verses 3–8 has several other links with previous Isaianic descriptions of the messianic age. The law will go forth from the Lord and be dispersed from Jerusalem (v. 4). The nations will look to the Lord (v. 5) as they looked to the temple (2:2–3) and to His law (42:4). The Day of the Lord includes judgment, and verse 6 speaks of the heavens vanishing like smoke and the earth wearing out like a garment. These figures are similar to other descriptions of the last days (24:4; 34:4). In verses 3–8 Isaiah seems to have looked beyond the return from Babylon to the second coming of Christ and His millennial rule.

"Righteousness" and "salvation" are mentioned in parallel constructions in verses 5, 6, and 8. These terms refer to the deliverance from Babylon that God brought about through Cyrus (cf. 46:13) and to that far richer salvation that would be accomplished through Christ. The righteousness that lasts forever (vv. 6, 8) is reminiscent of the eternal rule of the Messiah "with justice and righteousness" (9:7).

God's people were told not to fear the insults of men (51:7). Their experience was like that of the Servant in 50:6, and this supports the idea that the believing remnant was the "servant" during Isaiah's day and during the period of captivity. Those who opposed the Servant and God's people would be devoured by moths (50:9; 51:8).

This glowing description (vv. 3–8) stirred Isaiah and the people to call God into action (v. 9). The arm of the Lord that had dried up the Red Sea (50:2) would bring justice to the nations (v. 5). God made a road through that sea so that His people could be "freed," or "redeemed," from Egypt (v. 10). "Redeemed" may refer back to the use of this word in 35:9, and it may have prompted Isaiah to repeat 35:10 in its entirety in verse 11. As in 30:7, Egypt is called "Rahab" (v. 9), perhaps a name for the crocodile. Although Israel feared Egypt, the mighty Egyptian armies were no match for the power of God, and chariots and charioteers together sank to the bottom of "the great deep" (v. 10; cf. Exod. 15:5).

The Lord's response is a heartening one (vv. 12–16). All men are as weak and temporary as grass, and Babylon was no stronger than Egypt had been. Compared with the wrath of God, the wrath of Babylon (v. 13) was insignificant. After all, God was the mighty Creator of the heavens and earth (vv. 13, 16). If the waves of the sea move at God's command, the nations will do His bidding also. Therefore the exiles in Babylon would soon be set free (v. 14). Although "dungeon" (v. 14) may mean "confinement," the years in Babylon were hard and unpleasant for many. God, however, would protect His people and restore them to their homeland. ★

GOOD NEWS FOR CAPTIVE JERUSALEM
(51:17–52:12)

The Lord had been urged to awake (v. 9), but now Jerusalem must be roused (v. 17; 52:1). Because she had drunk the strong wine of God's judgment, verses 17–23 describe Jerusalem as a drunkard. God's "cup . . . of wrath" (v. 22) was normally reserved for wicked nations (Jer. 25:15–26; cf. Isa.

★On the idiom "shadow of my hand" (v. 16) compare 49:2.

63:6). When parents are old or inebriated, it is the responsibility of children to steady them and to keep them from injury.[1] Because God had punished the Israelites who lay helpless in the streets, Jerusalem had no sons to help her. Starvation and war had decimated the population. The combination of "ruin and destruction" (v. 19) is alliterative (šôḏand šeḇer) and is found again in 60:18 and in Jeremiah 48:3.

Jerusalem had been afflicted (v. 21; cf. 54:11) for many years, but the Lord would reverse her fortunes. When God brought judgment on them, her Babylonian tormentors would have to drink the cup of wrath (cf. Jer. 25:26). The Lord's people had been humiliated and, perhaps, literally trampled (v. 23), but all of this would soon end.★

The second "Awake, awake" (52:1) is addressed to a captive city languishing in the dust. Jerusalem is told to don her "garments of splendor" (perhaps a reference to the beautiful garments of a priest) because she was "the holy city" (cf. 48:2). A new set of clothes was a symbol of strength and joy, just as sackcloth was a symbol of mourning. The "arm of the LORD" was asked to clothe itself with strength (51:9).

The "uncircumcised and defiled" refers to foreign invaders. The Philistines were the chief example of an uncircumcised nation (cf. Judg. 14:3), but all foreigners were considered ceremonially unclean.

Jerusalem would be free because the Lord would redeem His people. No price would be paid to obtain her freedom (45:13) because the Lord had given her up for nothing (50:1). Israel had suffered at the hands of Egypt and Assyria (v. 4), and now Babylon had taken them captive. Because the god of a defeated nation was considered weak (cf. Ezek. 36:20–23), the enemy had ridiculed Israel and blasphemed God's name. But the Lord would soon free Israel, and this would demonstrate His power to the people. God predicted their release (v. 6), and He would bring it about.

---

[1]Cyrus H. Gordon, *The Ancient Near East*, 3d ed. rev. (New York: W. W. Norton & Co., 1965), p. 95.

★The feet of victors were sometimes placed on the necks of the vanquished (cf. Josh. 10:24).

The news that Israel would be released is good news indeed, and verses 7–12 celebrate this great event. As in 40:9, the picture of a messenger who runs from a battle to bring back word of the outcome to an anxious people is the background of this section (cf. 1 Sam. 4:17; 2 Sam. 18:26). The defeat of Babylon and the return of the Jews leads to the announcement "Your God reigns" (v. 7). God is still the sovereign ruler, and all the world must acknowledge it (cf. Pss. 97:1; 99:1). The Lord will return to Zion (v. 8) in that His people are returning (cf. 40:9–11). In the person of the incarnate Son of God, the Lord came to Zion, and so Paul correctly applied Isaiah's message of good news to the work of Christ on behalf of sinners (Rom. 10:15). The reign of Christ awaits His second coming and His direct rule over the nations (Rev. 20:6).

The watchmen who see this happy return (v. 8) are probably those in Jerusalem who had long awaited the messengers. According to Ezekiel, the prophets were the leading "watchmen" for the nation (Ezek. 3:17). Both the watchmen and the ruins of Jerusalem shout for joy and sing about the comfort and redemption Jerusalem receives (v. 9). The arm of the Lord has responded to Israel's plea and taken action against the enemy, and all mankind will hear about it (v. 10; cf. 51:9).

Verses 11 and 12 include instruction and information about the return. When they departed the people were not to touch anything that was unclean. This is probably a warning not to take with them any religious objects that could lead to idolatry. Not long after the Exodus, Israel had worshiped the golden calf, undoubtedly under the influence of Egyptian bull worship. Jacob's household had taken foreign gods with them when they left northern Mesopotamia (cf. Gen. 35:2). This time the nation was encouraged to be pure, especially the priests and Levites who carried the articles that Nebuchadnezzar had seized from the temple (cf. Ezra 1:7–11).

Although the people would not have to flee from Babylon, they were assured of the Lord's protection. He would superintend their journey as He did through the angel and the pillar of cloud and fire during the Exodus (cf. Exod. 13:21; 14:19–20).

SALVATION THROUGH THE DEATH OF THE SERVANT (52:13–53:12)

The suffering and salvation of the nation led Isaiah to his fullest disclosure of the suffering and exaltation of the Servant, who is "Israel" par excellence. The fourth Servant Song describes the meaning of the death of Christ and its significance for a sinful world. The song consists of five stanzas, each three verses long.

The Suffering and Exaltation of the Servant (52:13–15)

In the opening stanza (52:13–15), Isaiah graphically described both the suffering and the exaltation of the Servant. The Servant "will act wisely," or "prosper" (v. 13), because He would be obedient to God's Word (Josh. 1:8), and God's blessing would be on Him (cf. 1 Sam. 18:14). Ironically the term for acting wisely is used in Genesis 3:6 to describe Eve's perception of the fruit of the forbidden tree after Satan had tempted her. Eve thought that the fruit was "desirable for gaining wisdom." Unlike the first Adam and his wife, Eve, the Second Adam would take no shortcut as He carried out His work. In Jeremiah 23:5 the messianic king is said to "reign wisely."

The exaltation of the Servant is described in 53:12 and in the New Testament (Acts 2:33; Phil. 2:9–11). The last line of verse 13 also describes His exaltation. The words "raised and lifted up" were used in 6:1 to describe the mighty Lord of Isaiah's vision who was seated on His throne. John 12:41, a quotation from Isaiah 6:1, says that Isaiah saw *Jesus'* glory.

But before Christ was glorified, He suffered, and verse 14 highlights the depths of that suffering. When Christ died men were appalled at Him, just as the nations were appalled at the terrible fate of the city of Tyre (cf. Ezek. 27:35–36). Christ was disfigured by the beatings He received, and His form was "marred," a term used of a blemished animal that was unsuitable for sacrifice (Mal. 1:14). Yet the Servant was the perfect sacrifice. Through His death atonement was made for the nations because His blood was sprinkled, as it were, on the atonement cover in heaven's Holy of Holies (cf. Lev. 16:15; Heb. 9:12).

Kings would be astonished at the Servant's suffering and atonement. Apparently they would understand His mission, and one day they will bow in submission before Him (v. 15; cf. 49:7). Verse 15 may be an indictment of the Jews' spiritual blindness and deafness because it says that some of the Gentiles would understand and believe (cf. Rom. 15:21).

The Rejection of the Servant (53:1-3)

The second stanza (53:1-3) emphasizes the lowliness and rejection of the Servant. Verse one states that even the message about Him, the Good News of salvation that would be given to Israel and to the nations, was not accepted by many. And when He did come to earth, He had very humble beginnings. David's dynasty was like a dry stump (11:1) from which the Servant grew as a shoot. Apparently He did not have an attractive, striking appearance. The word "beauty" (v. 2—*tō'ar*) is used to describe David to Saul in 1 Samuel 16:18 ("fine-looking, handsome").

The reaction to the Servant (v. 3) is totally negative. Twice we read that He was "despised," a term used in Daniel 11:21 of Antiochus IV Epiphanes—the hated persecutor of the Jews and the one whose actions sparked the Maccabean revolt of 165 B.C. Hatred of the Servant is also described in 50:6, where mocking and beating are mentioned (cf. Ps. 22:6-7).

The "sorrows" endured by the Servant include both physical and mental distress. The word appears in Exodus 3:7 where it describes the suffering of Israel in Egypt (cf. Ps. 69:29). A summary of Christ's sufferings is given in Luke 18:32.

The Substitutionary Death of the Servant (53:4-6)

Verses 4-6 deal mainly with the substitutionary death of the Servant. The first person plural pronoun occurs ten times as Isaiah describes Christ's suffering *for us*. "Infirmities" is primarily a reference to sins, though this term may also refer to physical diseases. Matthew understood Jesus' healing ministry as the fulfillment of Isaiah 53:4, which he quoted in Matthew 8:17. The description of the Servant's work (v. 4) is similar to the description of Israel in Isaiah 1:5–6. There the moral and spiritual collapse of Israel is compared to wounds and illness. A number of terms found in 1:5–6 correspond to words in 53:4–5 (see *Authorship*). For example "smitten" (v. 4) is equivalent to "beaten" in 1:5. When Christ suffered, men thought that He was paying for His own sins, that God had struck Him down the way He had afflicted Pharaoh (Gen. 12:17).

The truth was that the Servant died for the sins of mankind. He was pierced, as a man would be run through with a sword or spear (cf. Ezek. 28:7; Num. 25:8). This happened when the Roman soldiers drove spikes through Christ's hands and feet and "pierced Jesus' side with a spear" as He hung on the cross (John 19:34). Other Old Testament references to the piercing of the Messiah are Psalm 22:16 and Zechariah 12:10. Verse 5 also states that our iniquities crushed Him. This "crushing" (vv. 5, 10) probably refers to the psychological and spiritual suffering that Jesus endured. All the sins of the world were placed on Him as in those awful hours He became sin for us. "Crushed" appears alongside "brokenhearted" in Psalm 34:18 and "lowly in spirit" in Isaiah 57:15. The punishment He endured brought peace and well-being to sinners. Mankind was desperately sick, but through His death the healing of forgiveness was possible. Healing and forgiveness are joined together in Psalm 103:3 and in 1 Peter 2:24.

In verses 6 and 7 men and the Servant are compared to sheep, but the comparisons are vastly different. Men are like sheep because they wander off so easily and stray into sin. Christ is like a lamb because He was the substitute who bore our sins (Lev. 1:4).

The Suffering and Death of the Servant (53:7–9)

The stanza found in verses 7–9 tells how the Servant suffered, died, and was buried. He was oppressed, just as Israel had suffered at the hands of her Egyptian slave drivers (Exod. 5:6). But the Servant did not resist His tormentors and went quietly to His death like a lamb, the "Lamb of God" spoken of by John the Baptist (John 1:29). The New Testament records Jesus' refusal to answer the chief priests, Pilate, and Herod (Matt. 27:12–14; Luke 23:9). He who was to reign forever in righteousness was unjustly tried and condemned to die.

Since Jesus never married, He had no descendants to carry on His name, a fate that was considered tragic by the Jews (cf. 2 Sam. 18:18). The Jews also placed great importance on a person's burial (cf. 22:16), and Jesus was originally assigned an ignominious grave with the two robbers who were crucified with Him (Matt. 27:38). Through the intervention of Joseph of Arimathea, however, Christ received an honorable burial. His body was laid in the tomb of that wealthy Jewish leader (Matt. 27:57–60).

Christ's suffering and death were undeserved. He neither acted violently nor spoke deceitfully. For this reason Peter quoted verse 9 to encourage believers who were suffering unjustly not to retaliate or threaten their persecutors (1 Peter 2:22).

The Triumph of the Servant 53:10–12

The concluding stanza (vv. 10–12) returns to the theme of exaltation that was begun in 52:13. Because of the Servant's death, many will be justified and He will have a place among the great. Verse 10 discusses the Servant's work with reference to the will of God. It was in accord with God's mysterious purposes that Christ died (cf. Acts 2:23) to make atonement for the guilt of the world. But it was also God's will that Christ would "see his offspring and prolong his days" (v. 10), probably an indirect reference to the resurrection.* Those who would believe in Him would constitute His spiritual offspring and make His ordeal on the cross eminently worthwhile.

"By his knowledge" (v. 11) could refer either to the knowledge possessed by the Servant or to knowledge *of* the Servant. The former interpretation fits the earlier reference to the Spirit of knowledge that rested on the Messiah (11:2), and

---

*If "the light of life" is an authentic part of the text, it too can refer to the resurrection.

the latter interpretation emphasizes man's need to know Him personally to be saved (cf. John 17:3). Verses 11 and 12 each refer to the "many" who would be made righteous by the Servant. This term includes those from the "many nations" of 52:15 and prepares the way for the many offspring of Zion (54:1) and the large numbers who are added to God's people in 56:8. The death of the Servant was not in vain.

In verse 12 the work of the Servant is explained as a great victory. When Christ prevailed in death, He triumphed over Satan and earned the spoils of a victor. What seemed like a pitiful display of weakness turned out to be a victory of massive proportions. The penalty for sin was paid, and transgressors could be at peace with God. The term "made intercession" is a translation of the same Hebrew word that is rendered "laid on him" in verse 6. The most effective way of interceding for sinners was to be their substitute. Because of His vicarious death, Christ always lives to intercede for believers (Heb. 7:25).

GROWTH AND PROSPERITY FOR JERUSALEM
(54:1–17)

As a result of the Servant's death, joy and blessing will come to all mankind. Chapters 54–56 sum up the dimensions of salvation. Chapter 54 deals mainly with Jerusalem and the Jews. During the Exile, Jerusalem would be like a barren woman or a woman with no husband. Her streets would be deserted and the surrounding hillsides would be devastated. Paul compared the land to Sarah (Gal. 4:26–27) because she too had endured the shame of being childless. But just as Sarah became the mother of a whole nation, so Israel would again be filled with people. Her borders would have to be enlarged because she would be like a woman whose tent cannot hold all her children (v. 2). The scope of this magnificent restoration seems to extend beyond Israel's return from Babylon to include spiritual descendants of the nation (see comments on 49:19–21). The dispossessing of the nations may look ahead to the Millennium (cf. 49:23).

The "disgrace" of verse 4 probably includes two major periods of time. "The shame of your youth" best fits the years of slavery in Egypt (cf. Ezek. 16:60), and "the reproach of your widowhood" relates to the Exile. God had entered into a covenant with Israel at Mount Sinai, thereby "marrying" her, but the Exile was a period of separation that made Israel feel like a widow. The Lord had "abandoned" her (v. 7) because the nation's sin demanded punishment (cf. 50:1). When the "brief moment" (v. 7) of exile ended (seventy years), God would again show His deep compassion for His people.

In verses 9 and 10 the Lord emphasized the depth of His commitment to Israel. Jerusalem would be spared further punishment, just as God promised Noah that there would never again be a flood to destroy the world. The "covenant of peace" (v. 10) probably refers to the Davidic covenant in which God promised David an unending dynasty. God's "unfailing love" (v. 10) closely resembles God's "faithful love promised to David" (55:3). Mountains were a symbol of stability and permanence, but even they would perish before God broke the terms of His covenant (cf. Ps. 46:2). A "covenant of peace" was also made with the tribe of Levi (cf. Num. 25:12; Mal. 2:5).

The beauty and invincibility of Jerusalem is described in verses 11–17. Although she had once been "afflicted" and laid low by God's judgment (51:21), Jerusalem would be rebuilt with precious stones. Some of these stones would be used in the foundations, walls, and gates of the New Jerusalem (Rev. 21:18–21). Isaiah's highly figurative description may be based on Solomon's splendid temple, which also contained turquoise and other precious stones (1 Chron. 29:2).

Unlike the Jerusalem of the seventh century B.C., the people would be eager to learn from the Lord, a characteristic of the Servant in 50:4. In John 6:45 Jesus quoted verse 13 and said that all who are truly taught by God would come to Him. At long last peace and righteousness would be a reality, and the fury of Israel's oppressors would be gone (cf. 33:17–18). Before the Exile, Assyria and Babylon had been sent against Israel, but the Lord would punish His people no more. These nations were the destroyers of verse 16, the rod of God's anger that struck down Israel and other countries.

Another characteristic of the Servant is applied to the nation in verse 17. Just as no accusation against the Servant could be proved, so no accusations against God's people could be proved (cf. 50:8–9). Those who would be vindicated in this manner are called "the servants of the LORD" (v. 17) for the first time, and from this point on in the Book of Isaiah the singular "servant" no longer appears. The plural occurs again in 63:17; 65:8, 9, 13–15; and in 66:14. It is a term that seems to include all true believers, whether Jews or Gentiles. The faithful remnant of Israel and the foreigners who love the Lord (56:6–8) would enjoy this heritage, but the rebels in the nation of Israel would be destroyed (cf. 65:11–15). The inclusion of Gentiles has already been suggested in verse 3 and in 49:19.

INVITATION TO TRUST THE LORD (55:1–13)

The note of joy in chapter 54 turns into a great invitation to a thirsty people in chapter 55. Men who crossed the desert often suffered from thirst (cf. 41:17–18), but those without God were spiritually thirsty. To them Christ offered the water of life so that streams of living water could flow within them (John 4:14; 7:37). In times of drought, water had to be purchased, but the waters of spiritual life are free because the death of the Servant (53:6) paid the price for sin (cf. Rev. 21:6; 22:17).

Wine and milk (v. 1) are symbols of abundance and enjoyment (Song of Sol. 5:1; Joel 3:18) and can be linked with "the richest of fare" (v. 2). God will lavish His blessings on believers as He invites them to a spiritual banquet (cf. 25:6). The wicked, meanwhile, feed on "what is not bread" (v. 2), perhaps a reference to the tasteless husks of pagan religions.

In verses 3–5, God's invitation is connected with the Davidic covenant. God had promised David that the covenant would last forever (2 Sam. 7:14–16), and God's unfailing kindnesses guaranteed that Israel would continue as a nation and that eventually the Messiah would reign on David's throne (cf. 9:6–7). Luke quoted verse 3 in Acts 13:34 to show that the resurrection of Christ was the fulfillment of God's promises to David. Jesus would rule forever.

It is difficult to know whether verse 4 refers to David or to Christ. David was a witness to the nations, exalting the Lord among the people he conquered (cf. Ps. 18:43, 49–50). Christ, the Servant of the Lord (42:6; 49:6), was a light to the nations. "Leader," or "ruler," is applied to David in 1 Samuel 13:14; 25:30; and to the Messiah in Daniel 9:25.

The picture of the nations coming to Israel (v. 5) is similar to Isaiah's earlier descriptions of the nations being attracted to Jerusalem and to the God of Israel (2:2–4; 45:14). During the Exile, Israel was sent to nations she did not know (cf. Deut. 28:36), but someday the reverse would be true. Like the Moabitess Ruth, Gentiles would become part of a people they "did not know before" (Ruth 2:11) because the Lord would restore Israel physically and spiritually.

A series of imperatives in verses 6 and 7 encouraged the people to repent of sin and turn back to the Lord. Verse 6 is similar to Jeremiah 29:13–14. There Jeremiah predicted that Israel would seek and find the Lord, who would bring her back from captivity. God's eagerness to forgive His people was emphasized earlier in Isaiah 43:25 and in 44:22.

Israel had acted wickedly, and in defeat she was discouraged. But God's thoughts and ways were different from her thoughts and ways! Verses 8 and 9 emphasize the greatness of God, and verses 10–13 reveal His marvelous purpose for His people. In 40:8 Isaiah said, "The word of our God stands forever," and verse 11 expands on this concept. God's plans and purposes will be accomplished as surely as the rain and snow water the earth and make it fruitful (cf. 30:23). God sends the rain, and He sends His word as a messenger (cf. 9:8; Ps. 107:20) to do His bidding. This significant use of "word" might have been in John's mind as he spoke about the incarnate Word (John 1:1, 14). The "word" in verse 11 probably incorporates the promises of verses 3 and 5, especially the assurance in verse 12 that Israel would leave Babylon in joy and peace. The Lord had promised in 46:10–11 that His plans for Cyrus would surely be fulfilled, and the Persian king did release Israel from captivity.

The joyous scene portrayed in verses 12 and 13 reflects the language of 44:23 and 52:8–9. There, too, the mountains and the trees burst into song as all nature joins in the praise of God. The sound of mountain streams and of the wind blowing through the branches of trees is poetically construed as the music of rejoicing (cf. Ps. 98:7–8). The thriving pine trees and the myrtle will reverse the desolation that overwhelmed Israel. Several times Isaiah had spoken of the thorns and briers that were to mark the destruction of the land (cf. 5:6; 32:13), but soon all would be changed. Trees symbolize fertility and beauty in 41:19 and in 60:13, too.

The release of Israel from captivity and her return to Jerusalem would bring great renown to the Lord, the same sort of fame He won when He brought the nation out of Egypt (cf. 63:12, 14). Israel's return from Babylon would be a New Exodus that would never be forgotten. Like the stones carried from the Jordan River and set up along its shores (Josh. 4:5–7), the end of the Babylonian captivity would be an everlasting memorial to the power of God.

THE WELCOMING OF FOREIGNERS INTO GOD'S FAMILY (56:1–8)

Previously Isaiah intimated that Gentiles would be part of God's people (49:19–21; 54:3, 17), but chapter 56 states this truth plainly. The "salvation," or restoration, of Israel from Babylon was soon to be a reality (v. 1) and so was the inclusion of foreigners in God's family.

When Israel was rescued from Egypt, God made a covenant with her at Mount Sinai and asked the people to obey Him in all things. Now that the nation was on the verge of being released from Babylon, the people could once again respond to the Lord wholeheartedly. Their obedience could be summed up as keeping "the Sabbath" (v. 2) because the Sabbath was a sign of the covenant (cf. Exod. 31:13; Ezek. 20:12, 20). Unhappily Israel did not keep the Sabbath with much enthusiasm before the Exile (cf. Jer. 17:22–23), and so God's warning is clear. Foreigners and eunuchs who love the Lord and keep the Sabbath will find greater acceptance than rebellious Israelites. According to the law, foreigners and eunuchs could not participate in the assembly of the Lord (cf. Deut. 23:1, 3, 7–8), but a new era was dawning.

The promise of verse 5 is a startling one because the hope of every Jew was to have many children and grandchildren to insure the continuation of one's family line. Sometimes those who had no surviving sons built a monument as a memorial (e.g., 2 Sam. 18:18). The best memorial of all, however, is a life of obedience, and the Lord promises that those who serve him faithfully will never be forgotten.* One is reminded of the salvation of the Ethiopian eunuch, whose conversion through reading Isaiah 53 and the witness of Philip is recorded in Acts 8:26–39.

Verses 6–8 summarize the devotion of foreigners to the Lord and their participation in worshiping Him. Because of their commitment to the covenant, they will be invited to the holy mountain of Zion where the temple was located. The pilgrimage of the Gentiles to God's holy mountain also is mentioned in 2:2–3 and in 66:20. It is an important theme in Isaiah. The acceptance of the offerings and sacrifices of the Gentiles is similar to Isaiah's description of worship during the messianic age (60:7). Earlier, Isaiah denounced the sacrifices brought by hypocritical Israelites (11:1–13).

The last two lines of verse 7 recall the words of Solomon as he dedicated the temple (1 Kings 8:41–43). In his prayer Solomon asked the Lord to respond to the prayers of foreigners so that all nations would know about the greatness of Israel's God. When Jesus cleansed the temple, which had become a "den of robbers" rather than a house of prayer, He quoted these two lines from verse 7 (Matt. 21:13; Mark 11:17). Jesus may also have had verse 8 in mind when He spoke of "other sheep that are not of this sheep pen" (John 10:16). The restored exiles would join with Gentiles who love and serve the Lord.

A SUMMARY OF ISRAEL'S SINS (56:9–57:21)

Isaiah was fond of sharp transitions (cf. 9:8), and in verse 9 he returned to the theme of judgment. In 52:1–56:8, Isaiah reveled in God's good news for Israel and the nations—good news that was based on the work of the Servant. But from 56:9–59:15 he concentrated once again on the sins of Israel. In

---

*An interesting application of this verse is the "Yad vaShem" (A Memorial and a Name), the building in Jerusalem to honor the Jews who died in the holocaust during World War II but whose names are recorded in perpetuity.

these chapters Isaiah's description could apply to Israel's condition both before and during the Exile.

A Condemnation of Injustice and Idolatry (56:9–57:13)

The invitation to "come and devour" (v. 9) contrasts with the "come, buy and eat" of 55:1. Here foreign invaders are the beasts who are summoned to devour Israel (cf. Jer. 12:9; Ezek. 34:5, 8). Israel's plight was partially due to her pathetic leaders. "Watchmen" (v. 10) refers to Israel's blind and ignorant prophets (cf. 52:8). Although they were supposed to be watchdogs who guarded the sheep and sounded a warning in times of danger, they were fast asleep. When they were awake, however, they devoured the sheep (v. 11; cf. Ezek. 34:3). As in Ezekiel 34:1–6, the shepherds of verse 11 could include rulers as well as prophets. The rulers were to lead and protect the sheep, but "they all turn to their own way" (v. 11) like the sheep of 53:6. Their thirst for wine and beer (v. 12) is similar to the description of unfaithful prophets and priests in 28:7. In the midst of their sinful indulgence, they looked forward to even happier times. The attitude of the leaders is similar to that of the rich fool who planned to "eat, drink and be merry" for many years to come (Luke 12:19; cf. Ps. 10:6).

Israel's sinful condition fostered the persecution of the righteous, and 57:1–2 reveals that some of them died. Isaiah described their death as entering into peace and finding rest— words that resemble Paul's statement that "to die is gain" (Phil. 1:21). In 2 Kings 22:20 the prophetess Huldah had predicted that Josiah, a godly king, would die and be spared the agony of seeing Judah crushed by invading armies. Yet Josiah's death and the death of the righteous mentioned here severely weakened the nation.

In 56:9 the enemy was invited to "come and devour" Israel; in 57:3 the sinners within Israel are told to "come here" and face God's charges against them. God calls them "sons of a sorceress" (v. 3) because of their involvement in soothsaying and black magic (cf. 3:2). The reference to adultery and prostitution is developed in verses 5, 7, and 8, which describe worship in the high places. It was common to commit "spiritual adultery" by worshiping Baal and other idols while engaging in sexual immorality. This deadly combination devastated the nation as early as Numbers 25:1–3. The "oaks" of verse 5 are the same as the "sacred oaks" mentioned in 1:29. Gardens and hill shrines were favorite areas for Israel's pagan sacrifices and immorality (cf. 65:3; 66:17).

Isaiah's strongest words in verses 3–13 are leveled against the sin of idolatry. Israel had rebelled against God and sneered at Him (v. 4) while having a love affair with other gods. The nation shamelessly offered herself to these deities and gave to them her sacrifices and offerings. Using perfumes and ointment, she sought to allure new lovers (cf. Ezek. 23:40). No stone was left unturned as Israel pursued her goals. Ironically the words "It is hopeless" (v. 10) are applied in Jeremiah 2:25 and in 18:12 to Israel's futile attempt to stop chasing foreign gods. Israel showed more determination during her times of rebellion than during her infrequent periods of repentance.

The worst aspect of idolatry was the sacrifice of children, a practice sometimes associated with the worship of Molech (v. 9) or Baal (Jer. 19:5). Molech was the leading deity of the Ammonites and was worshiped by Solomon in his later years (1 Kings 11:5). Child sacrifice took place in Topheth, in the Valley of Hinnom, south of Jerusalem. Perhaps the "ravines" (v. 5) include Topheth. According to 2 Chronicles 28:3, King Ahaz sacrificed his sons in the Valley of Ben Hinnom.

Israel feared men more than God, and this is a partial explanation of why she was unfaithful (51:12). Neither God's judgment nor His saving power had been seen in years, and so Israel easily forgot Him. All her "righteous" deeds turned out to be empty and useless (vv. 11–12). Because Israel worshiped idols, when trouble came those idols would have to save them (cf. Judg. 10:14). But as Isaiah had already shown (44:9), idols were utterly helpless. Israel's only hope was to return to the Lord in obedient trust and thereby be assured of a place in Mount Zion and the promised land.

The Healing and Restoration of Israel (57:14–21)

The mention of "the land" and "my holy mountain" (v. 13) led Isaiah to repeat the theme of preparing a highway to bring the exiles back to Israel. Nothing would stand in the way of God's people as they returned from Babylon (cf. 40:3–4). God had been angry with His sinful people and had hidden His face from them (vv. 16–17; cf. 54:8–9), but He would not be their adversary forever. Verses 18 and 19 summarize Israel's healing and restoration. The Lord had promised (30:26) that He would someday heal the wounds He had inflicted on His people. Repeatedly He had promised to comfort them as He redeemed and saved them (cf. 40:1; 49:13; 51:3, 12), and frequently He assured them of His guidance (40:11; 42:16; 49:10).

God is called "the high and lofty One" (v. 15). These words are used in 6:1 to describe the almighty and holy God whom Isaiah saw in His vision. But how can a holy and righteous God heal and comfort a sinful people? Verses 15 and 19 imply that at least part of the nation would repent of their sins. The "contrite" (v. 15) are those who are "crushed in spirit" (Ps. 34:18). Their hearts have been broken, humbled by the sin they have committed (Isa. 66:2), just like David who committed adultery and murder (Ps. 51:17). The "mourners" (v. 19) are those who lament the fall of Jerusalem and the sin that caused it (66:10). It is to this faithful remnant that God offers peace and healing. "Those far and near" (v. 19) may include Gentiles who truly love the Lord (cf. 56:1–8; Eph. 2:17).

The faithful will enjoy peace, and their lips will offer praise to the Lord, but the wicked will not find rest. Isaiah compared the state of the wicked to the churning sea because the wicked are forever dredging up evil thoughts and schemes. Verse 21 repeats 48:22 and concludes another nine-chapter section.

13

ULTIMATE BLESSING FOR GOD'S PEOPLE
58:1–66:24

The final nine chapters of the Book of Isaiah concentrate on restoration and the glories of the last days, but chapter 58 moves in that direction very gradually. Until 59:16 Isaiah continued the accusations against Israel that began in 56:9. Beginning with the last five verses of chapter 59, however, Isaiah emphasized the coming of the Lord to save His people and to endow Jerusalem with glory and splendor. Joy and praise will characterize the nation as the ancient ruins are rebuilt and the messianic age draws near. Contrasting with the brilliant light of God's kingdom and the creation of a new heaven and new earth is the awful darkness of judgment. God will take vengeance on His enemies and reveal His wrath to His foes. For God's servants there will be unending peace, but the wicked will endure everlasting punishment.

THE CHALLENGE TO TRUE RIGHTEOUSNESS
(58:1–14)

The subject of the first half of the chapter is the sin of hypocrisy, especially as it relates to fasting. During the Exile the number of days set aside for fasting increased (Zech. 7:5) as Israel mourned the collapse of Jerusalem and all Judah. Fasting was a time of self-denial and repentance, but it degenerated into an external display of piety. So serious was Israel's hypocrisy that the Lord called on Isaiah to raise his voice like a trumpet

(v. 1). The message was to be as loud and clear as the thundering voice of God at Mount Sinai, a sound that struck fear into the hearts of the people of Israel (Exod. 19:19; 20:18–19). The nation was still rebellious, in spite of the fact that the Israelites sought God daily (v. 2). Perhaps they mechanically offered sacrifices or prayers, a practice alluded to in 1:11–15. Israel wanted to impress people with her spirituality, but her behavior was nothing more than empty ritual. Therefore the nation was upset when God failed to notice her devotion. What was the use of fasting if God was unimpressed (cf. Mal. 3:14)?

The reason Israel's fasting was useless is given in verses 3–5. Employers were forcing their employees to work harder, perhaps to make sure that fasting did not hinder production. The lack of food made people temperamental and resulted in quarreling and fighting. How could this sort of behavior win the favor of the Lord? Outwardly the Israelites were bent over in prayer. They donned the usual sackcloth and ashes, but they did not exhibit genuine humility. A sincere humbling before the Lord would produce the kinds of visible results mentioned in verses 6–7. Injustice and oppression would give way to freedom as burdensome yokes were broken. One is reminded of the Hebrew slaves who were released by Zedekiah and his nobles during the siege of Jerusalem and then enslaved again by their greedy masters (cf. Jer. 34:8–11). The provision of food, clothing, and shelter was another practical way to demonstrate true righteousness. In Matthew 25:35–36 Jesus said that those who take care of the hungry and homeless are ministering to Him. In Isaiah's day some individuals were failing to care for their own relatives, turning away from their own "flesh and blood" (v. 7).

To those who respond wholeheartedly to Him, God promised a great reward (vv. 8–9a). "Light" and "healing" (v. 8) probably include the joy of salvation and prosperity. God would protect His people on all sides, as He did when Israel was released from Egypt (cf. 52:12). The "glory of the LORD" (v. 8) recalls the pillar of cloud and fire that shielded the nation during her dangerous travels (cf. Exod. 13:21; 14:20). God would be with His people, and He would be quick to answer Israel's prayers (cf. 30:19; 65:24).

Verses 9b–14 explain more fully the blessings that would come to the nation if the people obeyed the admonitions of verses 6 and 7. Again Israel was challenged to care for the needy and the oppressed. The "pointing finger" (v. 9) was a gesture of contempt and was also condemned in Proverbs 6:13. If the people did away with sin, their "light" would be "like the noonday" (v. 10); they would have a promising future. The Lord would guide them through a "sun-scorched land" (v. 11), a reference to the difficult journey back to Palestine (cf. 49:10). Israel would be a "well-watered garden" (v. 11), a figure similar to the fruitful vineyard mentioned in 27:3. In 1:30 a Jerusalem steeped in sin was called "a garden without water." The new, revived Jerusalem would be rebuilt, its walls and houses restored. When Cyrus issued the decree that allowed the Jews to return to Palestine, the first steps to rebuild the city were taken (44:26, 28). Under the leadership of Nehemiah, the walls of Jerusalem were restored about 445 B.C. (Neh. 2:17).

The final verses of the chapter (vv. 13–14) return to the issue of keeping the Sabbath, a subject that began Isaiah's lengthy survey of Israel's sin (56:2–6). The Sabbath was instituted as a day set apart to the Lord, a time when the people were to take delight in the Lord and in His Word (Exod. 20:8; Pss. 1:2; 37:4). Instead it had become a day for personal amusement and for pursuing business interests. Isaiah urged the people to restore the Sabbath to its rightful place, promising that if they did so the Lord would put joy in their hearts, that Israel would once more possess the Promised Land—a control probably symbolized by the figure of riding "on the heights of the land" (v. 14; cf. 33:16; Deut. 32:13)—and that the people would have plenty of food as they feasted in the land they had inherited from Jacob. These are great promises, spoken by the mouth of the Lord, and that mouth cannot lie (cf. 1:20; 40:5).

ISRAEL'S GREAT SIN AND THE REDEMPTION OF THOSE WHO REPENT (59:1–21)

The Results of Israel's Great Sin (59:1–15a)

The potential blessings described in chapter 58 whetted the appetites of the nation. Why had the Lord delayed this great deliverance? The problem was not with God. His arm was powerful, and He had heard His people's cries for help. But before God's arm achieved the salvation described in verse 16, Isaiah graphically described the sins that delayed His intervention. These sins separated Israel from God, causing a breach in the marriage covenant that bound them (cf. 50:1-2).

Verses 3-7 mention five parts of the body that are involved in sin. The hands (vv. 3, 6) and the feet (v. 7) of God's people participated in murder, a crime first mentioned in 1:15 and 21. Their tongues told lies and refused to defend the poor and the helpless (vv. 3-4). Their energy produced nothing except trouble and evil—symbolized by the viper's eggs and the spider's web (v. 5). Both figures represent death and destruction, and the spider's web also stands for what is weak and fragile (cf. Job 8:14-15). Verse 7 epitomizes the depravity of Israel's thoughts and actions, and Paul quoted part of verse 7 and the first line of 8 in his famous catalog of the sinfulness of man (Rom. 3:16-17). Both man's mind and his activities are thoroughly corrupt, and neither he nor his victims will know any peace or justice. The "crooked roads" (v. 8) are those that are unsafe and that lead to destruction. How different are the thoughts and ways of man from those of God! His thoughts are full of mercy and compassion (55:7-8), and His ways lead to joy and peace (55:12).

In verses 9-11 Isaiah recited the sad results of Israel's sin, and the use of the first person pronoun shows that he now identified himself with the people. He first bemoaned the absence of justice and righteousness, and it is significant that at least one of these terms occurs in verse 11 and in verses 14-17. Because Israel did not practice justice in personal or governmental matters, the nations that held her captive would not show any justice to her. Nor would "justice"—which sometimes means "deliverance" (v. 11)—come her way. In verses 9 and 14, justice and righteousness are personified, as they were in 1:21. The absence of justice is compared to darkness and deep shadows (v. 9). These terms and others were used to describe the distress caused by the Assyrian invasions (5:30; 8:21-22; 9:1-2). There is no trace of the light that was promised in 58:8 and 10. It is so dark that men stumble about at midday as if they were blind, a plight mentioned in Deuteronomy 28:29 as a curse for disobedience (cf. Job 5:14). "The strong" (v. 10) may refer to Israel's enemies or oppressors. Discouraged and frustrated, the people growl like bears, and the sound of their lamenting resembles the moaning of doves (38:14). They are a defeated people, held captive by their foes.

In verses 12 and 13, however, Isaiah confessed the sins of the nation, as did Ezra in the fifth century B.C. (Ezra 9:6–7). Isaiah acknowledged that Israel's offenses had been numerous, and chief among them was the sin of rebellion against God. It is a description reminiscent of the harsh words in 1:2–4. The state of the nation seemed hopeless. Justice and righteousness, which had seemed so close in 46:13, now stood at a distance, and truth* and honesty could not gain a hearing. The importance of truth is displayed in the fact that a restored Jerusalem is called "The City of Truth" in Zechariah 8:3.

The Lord's Intervention to Save His People (59:15b–21)

The picture painted by Isaiah is indeed a gloomy one, but suddenly the Lord bursts on the scene and all is changed (vv. 15b–21). Perhaps it was the repentance described in verse 12 that stirred the Lord to action because the repentant ones also are mentioned in verse 20. The Lord who "made intercession for the transgressors" (53:12) intercedes again to bring about the salvation of His people. This deliverance refers initially to the rescue of the nation from captivity, as it did in 52:10 where the mighty arm of the Lord also is described as going into action. Spiritual salvation is not to be excluded from the meaning of the words in verses 15b–21, however, for Paul quoted Isaiah 59:20 in connection with the salvation of "all Israel" by the second coming of Christ (Rom. 11:26).

As the Lord intervenes He is sustained by "his own righteousness" (v. 16). In 63:5, a verse almost identical to this one, "wrath" is substituted for "righteousness." It was God's righteousness and holiness that made Him angry and moved

*Compare the personification of wisdom developed in the Book of Proverbs (8:1; 9:1).

Him to judge the wicked. The vengeance and retribution mentioned in verses 17 and 18 recall 34:8, a passage that describes the Day of the Lord. God would repay the nations for their sins, and wicked Israelites would not escape punishment. They too would face judgment because of their rejection of the Lord (cf. 65:6–7). Only the remnant, the true servants of the Lord, would experience salvation (cf. 54:17; 65:9).

In verse 17 the Lord is portrayed as a warrior equipped for battle. The breastplate of righteousness and the helmet of salvation are mentioned in Ephesians 6:14 and 17. There Paul described the Christian's armor in the war against Satan, but neither the garments of vengeance nor the cloak of zeal have a place in Ephesians. The garments are similar to those spattered by blood in the parallel passage of 63:3. "Zeal" refers to God's jealous love that motivates Him to take action on behalf of His people (cf. 42:13).

God's intervention will bring Him the reverence and respect of all nations (v. 19). The same thought is found in 45:6, a passage linked with the raising up of Cyrus to deliver the Jews. Significantly, 45:6 uses the idiom "from the rising of the sun to the place of its setting," an expression very similar to the one in 59:19. Malachi 1:11 also refers to the recognition of God's great name from the east to the west. The display of His power and glory brings great honor to His name.

The last part of verse 19 describes the coming of the Lord as a rushing, irresistible torrent. In 30:27–28 similar imagery is used to depict the Lord's appearance as He overwhelms Assyria, whose invasion of Israel had been compared to "mighty flood waters" (8:7). If the alternate translation of verse 19b is followed, "flood" would again refer to the enemy and "breath" would refer to the Spirit of the Lord who drives back the foe. Both interpretations describe the mighty power of God.

When God puts on His armor and judges the wicked, He will rescue Israel from exile and bring them back to Jerusalem. "The Redeemer will come to Zion" (v. 20) means that God's people will return home and acknowledge that it was the Lord who delivered them and guided them. This picture is also found in 40:9–11 and in 52:7–9. Paul related 52:7 and 59:20 to the coming of Christ (Rom. 10:15; 11:26) because redemption in its fullest sense awaited His work on Calvary. Salvation through Christ is "good news" that surpasses the release from the Babylonian exile. Those who return to Jerusalem would be repentant and responsive to the Word of God.

The "covenant" of verse 21 recalls the "covenant for the people" that is associated with the work of the Servant of the Lord in 42:6 and in 49:8. It may also be related to the "new covenant" predicted in Jeremiah 31:31–34, a passage that emphasizes the wholehearted reception of the Word of God. Jeremiah mentioned the implanting of the law on the mind and heart, and Isaiah drew attention to the mouth that will never cease to speak God's Word. The reference to the Spirit of God is similar to another great passage about restoration, Ezekiel 36:26–27. There the Spirit provides the power to follow God's decrees and laws. Elsewhere in Isaiah the Spirit of God is linked with the Messiah or with the messianic age (11:2; 32:15; 44:3).

When God's words are lodged firmly in the mouths of His people, Israel would realize her true calling. Long ago Joshua had been challenged not to let the law of Moses depart from his mouth (Josh. 1:8). Unhappily his godly example was not followed by the majority of the nation, and the Mosaic covenant was often ignored.

THE BRILLIANCE OF GOD'S KINGDOM (60:1–22)

The Glory and Wealth of Zion (60:1–9)

The coming of the Redeemer to Zion (59:16–21) sets the stage for a chapter that describes unparalleled glory and splendor. The light promised in 58:8 and 10 now illuminates the scene with dazzling brilliance. As in 58:8, the "glory of the LORD" (v. 1) may allude to the pillar of cloud and fire that had guided Israel in the wilderness. From the imagery of the glory "rising" and from the parallels in verses 19 and 20, it is clear that Isaiah compared the Lord to the sun. Although the earth will be shrouded with the darkness of oppression and sin, Zion will bask in the light of the Lord, a light to which the nations will be attracted. The coming of the nations to Mount Zion was a theme first introduced in 2:2–4, and it reaches a climax here in chapter 60.

Verses 4–9 describe the restoration of Jerusalem in terms of a growing population and a great increase in wealth. Verse 4 begins with two lines that are almost identical to the start of 49:18, and it ends with a couplet found in 49:22. There the setting emphasized the return from the Babylonian captivity as sons and daughters were brought home from great distances. The picture in chapter 60 seems to refer to the more glorious era of the Millennium, though the return from exile represented a partial fulfillment of this prophecy (cf. 11:11–12).

The great joy mentioned in verse 5 is linked with the arrival of the wealth of the nations. Israel, a destitute and impoverished nation, would regain the prosperity she once enjoyed, especially under King Solomon. The herds of camels (v. 6) recall the caravans that brought valuable goods to Israel. It is ironic that camels of Midian are mentioned, however, since the camel-riding Midianites had devastated Israel before Gideon drove them off (Judg. 6:5; Isa. 9:4). "Gold and incense" from Sheba (v. 6) alludes to the visit of the queen of Sheba, who was overwhelmed by Solomon's riches and offered praise to the Lord (cf. 1 Kings 10:2, 9). The "ships of Tarshish" (v. 9) used to bring silver and gold to Solomon every three years (cf. 1 Kings 10:22). Now these large trading ships are depicted as transporting the scattered children of Israel. Another possible link to the former greatness of Israel may be the "flocks" and "rams" of verse 7. The king of Moab had to send a hundred thousand lambs to Ahab as a tribute payment each year (cf. Isa. 16:1). The main thrust of verse 7, however, is the acceptance of these animals as offerings to the Lord. In 56:7 sacrifices presented by foreigners are also viewed with favor.

Elsewhere in the Book of Isaiah the nations are also described as bringing riches to Jerusalem (18:7; 45:14; 61:6; 66:12), as they are in Haggai 2:7 and in Zechariah 14:14. While the primary reference of such verses has to do with conditions during Christ's reign in the Millennium, the assistance given to the returning exiles by the Persian government may have been an initial fulfillment. In 520 B.C. king Darius helped pay for the rebuilding of the temple and even supplied animals for sacrifices

(Ezra 6:8–10). With Darius's help Zerubbabel was able to complete the temple by 516 B.C. Significantly, the adorning of the temple is mentioned in verse 7 and again in verse 13. Isaiah mourned the destruction of the temple in 63:18 and in 64:11, but here he reflected on its glorious renewal. The restoration of the temple symbolizes the nation's physical and spiritual revival, which brings honor to the Lord, who "has endowed you with splendor" (v. 9; cf. 55:5).

Zion's Prosperity and Righteousness (60:10–22)

Verses 10–16 review Jerusalem's relationship with the nations, a position of dominance that is diametrically opposed to her pitiful condition that resulted from Babylon's invasion. Isaiah had spoken of Israel's exaltation in 14:2 and in 49:23, but not so elaborately. The nations would serve Israel (vv. 10, 12), and former oppressors would bow at her feet (v. 14). Even kings would submit to her rule (v. 11).

The sequence of events described in these verses resembles Isaiah's words in 54:7–15. After God's anger has been poured out on His people, He has compassion on them and rebuilds Jerusalem (cf. 54:7–8, 11; 60:10). Both passages mention the gates of the city. In 60:10 the rebuilding of the walls is the work of foreigners. After the Exile, King Artaxerxes issued a decree in 445 B.C. that authorized Nehemiah to rebuild the walls of Jerusalem (Neh. 2:8), an event, however, that did not produce the spectacular results described in verses 11–16. The open gates (v. 11) are like the gates of the New Jerusalem (Rev. 21:25–26).

Elsewhere in the Book of Isaiah trees beautify the desert (41:19; cf. 35:2), but here (v. 13) they adorn the sanctuary. The "glory of Lebanon" (v. 13) refers to the fabulous cedars that were used in abundance in Solomon's Jerusalem. Cedar and pine were the primary building materials in that temple (1 Kings 6:15). "The place of my feet" (v. 13) probably refers to the temple and the ark of the covenant, which is sometimes called God's "footstool" (cf. 1 Chron. 28:2; Ps. 132:7–8). Jerusalem lay desolate and empty during the Exile, but her restoration would bring pride and joy to her inhabitants. She will be known as "Zion of the Holy One of Israel" (v. 14), the same Holy One her people had spurned and mocked (1:4; 5:19). The "riches of the nations" (v. 5) will be hers, a situation poetically described as being "nursed at royal breasts" (v. 16). Jerusalem will enjoy excellent nourishment from the kingdoms that she served. Isaiah had said that Israel's rescue would result in all mankind knowing that God is the Savior (49:26). Using the same three names for God—Savior, Redeemer, and The Mighty One of Jacob—Isaiah now acknowledged that Israel herself would know who God really is (v. 16).

The transformation of Jerusalem is further described in verses 17–22. Once again gold, silver, bronze, and iron are described as being plentiful (v. 17; cf. v. 9; 1 Kings 10:21, 27). The peace and righteousness characteristic of the messianic age (9:7) will be present, and the terrors of violence will be gone (cf. 54:14). Ruin and destruction had leveled Jerusalem (cf. 51:19), but someday "Salvation" and "Praise" will be her protection (v. 18; cf. 26:1). According to verses 19 and 20, not even the light of the sun or moon would be needed. God would be His people's everlasting light (cf. vv. 1–2), and it would never get dark again. Such a glorious picture also is seen in the description of Jerusalem in Revelation 21:23 and 22:5. There God and the Lamb are described as the eternal light, the source of unending joy and salvation.

At last God's people will be righteous; only the redeemed will be present in Jerusalem (cf. 35:8–10). They will enjoy full blessing in the land (cf. 57:13) and be firmly planted like the vineyard described in 5:7. God will put them on display as proof of His redemptive work. In Genesis 12:2 the Lord had promised that He would make Abraham's descendants a great nation (cf. 51:2), and nowhere is that greatness described more clearly than in this chapter.

RESTORATION AND SALVATION (61:1–11)

The glorious themes of chapter 60 continue into chapter 61, though etched in more subdued terms. Verses 1 and 2 are famous because Jesus quoted them in the synagogue at Nazareth (Luke 4:18–19). The Good News that He preached and the freedom from sin that He offered were indeed a remarkable fulfillment of these verses. And the Spirit of God rested on Christ as the Spirit is described as resting on the Servant of the Lord in Isaiah 42:1. But just as the good news mentioned in 40:9 and in 52:7 referred first of all to Israel's release from captivity, so Isaiah himself could have claimed that the Spirit worked through his ministry (cf. 48:16). The people of Judah were poor and brokenhearted (cf. 1:5–6), and because of the Exile the land desperately needed healing and restoration. "Freedom" (d°rôr) is the technical word used of the restoration involved in the Year of Jubilee (Lev. 25:10; cf. Isa. 49:8) and probably applies to the end of the Babylonian captivity. This is called "the year of the LORD's favor" in verse 2, a time that corresponds to "the day of salvation" in 49:8 and "the year of my redemption" in 63:4. The last reference—like verse 2—also mentions "the day of vengeance" because the salvation of God's people entailed the simultaneous judgment of their enemies. In Luke 4:18–19 Christ quoted only the first line of verse 2 because His avenging work primarily will take place at His second coming.

The release of the captives would at last bring comfort to the mourners in Zion. Those who sat in ashes wearing their sackcloth would anoint themselves with olive oil and praise God for delivering them. The crown of beauty (v. 3) was either a turban or a headdress (cf. 3:20). As in 60:21 the people are planted by the Lord for the display of His splendor. This time, however, they are compared to sturdy oaks rather than a shoot (cf. Ps. 92:12–13).

Back in the land God's people would rebuild the ruined cities, a prominent theme in 58:12 and in 60:10. The foreigners who are described as serving Israel (60:10–12) shepherd the flocks and work the fields (61:5), and Israel "will feed on the wealth of the nations" (v. 6; cf. 60:5, 11). At Mount Sinai, God had said that Israel could be "a kingdom of priests" (Exod. 19:6), and verse 6 describes her fulfillment of that role among the nations. God's people had experienced shame and disgrace, receiving double punishment for their sins (40:2), but soon a double share of the inheritance would be theirs. According to the law, the firstborn son inherited a double portion of the estate (cf. Deut. 21:17). Israel's good fortune would bring them the "everlasting joy" spoken of in 35:10 and in 51:11.

Verses 8 and 9 expand on the theme of God's goodness to His people. In exile Israel had been mistreated and oppressed (cf. 42:24), but all these injustices would be righted. The Lord would confirm the "everlasting covenant" He had made with Abraham (v. 8; Gen. 12:1–3) and with David (cf. Isa. 55:3). This "everlasting covenant" should probably be associated with the covenant referred to in Jeremiah 32:40 (cf. Isa. 59:21). God's people will be "known among the nations" (v. 9), not despised and mocked by them. The blessings promised to Abraham will be theirs, and all the world will see their material and spiritual renewal (cf. 44:3).

Israel's joy is represented by symbols that are related to clothing and farming (vv. 10–11). Zion is probably the speaker in verse 10, and the picture there is similar to that in 52:1. Beautiful clothes befit a nation that has been restored to her husband. Zion wears the turban, or headband, of a priest (Exod. 39:28) and the jewels of a bride (cf. 49:18; Rev. 21:2). Her beauty symbolizes salvation and righteousness, terms that are also joined together in 45:8; 46:13; 56:1; 59:16. "Righteousness" is mentioned again in verse 11, this time in relation to the imagery about the growth of seeds and plants that was borrowed from 45:8. Just as surely as the rain makes the ground fertile, so God will cause "righteousness and praise" to "spring up" (v. 11). When He delivered His people from the bondage of exile, God would set things right.

JERUSALEM, THE PRAISE OF THE EARTH
(62:1–12)

The theme of Israel's restoration introduced so grandly in chapter 40 is brought to a climax in chapter 62. Several motifs from chapter 40 are repeated and amplified. Compare verse 2 with 40:5, verse 10 with 40:3–4, and verse 11 with 40:9–10. The reference to keeping silent in verse 1 is close to the thoughts expressed in 42:14 and in 57:11. In those two passages the long period of exile is described as the time when God was silent. In view of the reference in 62:6 to the watchmen who are never silent, it is also possible to understand Isaiah as the speaker in verses 1 and 6, though it could be the Lord Himself who speaks. If Isaiah is the speaker, then he, like the watchmen, will never stop praying for God to restore Jerusalem.

As in 61:10, in 62:1 Isaiah joins "righteousness" with "salvation"; but in 62:2 "righteousness" is joined with "glory," much as in 58:8. The deliverance from Babylon would be a demonstration of God's glory to the world (cf. 40:5; 44:23), and it would signal the dawn of a new day for His people. Because of Jerusalem's change in status, the city would receive a new name. Several are suggested in verses 4 and 12 (cf. Rev. 3:12). In 61:3, Zion was to wear a crown of beauty; in 62:3 she will *be* a crown of splendor in the Lord's hand. God Himself is said to be "a glorious crown . . . for the remnant of his people" (28:5).

Verses 4 and 5 return to the marriage metaphor, using terms similar to those used in 54:5–8. The Lord will again rejoice over the land "as a bridegroom rejoices over his bride," and the land will be called "Beulah," that is, "married." Israel's covenant relationship with the Lord will be restored. The figure is also extended to the sons of Israel. They will "marry" the land by taking possession of the long-deserted country (cf. 54:1–2).

Encouraged by the prospect of Jerusalem's glory and splendor, the watchmen of the city eagerly await the news of the end of the Exile (v. 6). These watchmen are probably the prophets (cf. 56:10) who once had the responsibility of warning the nation about impending judgment but who now announce the restoration of the land. Their persistent prayer is similar to David's vow that he would not rest until he found a home for the ark of the covenant (Ps. 132:1–5). When Jerusalem is restored, all the nations will praise God for abundantly blessing His people (v. 7; cf. Jer. 33:9).

In 54:9 the Lord had sworn that He would never again be angry with His people. In verses 8 and 9 this oath is applied to the harvest of the land. Through Moses, God had warned that Israel's produce would be handed over to her enemies if she disobeyed Him (Lev. 26:16; Deut. 28:33), but that awful curse would not be repeated. Instead the people will eat and drink as they used to do during a festival or when they brought their tithes to the house of the Lord (cf. Lev. 23:39; Deut. 14:23).

Overjoyed by God's promises, Isaiah intensified his plea (v. 10). This is the only time we find two double imperatives in one verse in Isaiah. As the exiles begin their homeward journey, they will pass through the gates of Babylon (cf. 48:20; Mic. 2:12–13). The commands to "prepare the way" and "build up the highway" were discussed in the comments on 40:3 and 57:14 (cf. 49:11). The raising of a banner for the nations is linked with the return of the exiles in 11:12 and in 49:22.

Both 11:12 and 48:20 describe the regathering of the exiles and an announcement to the ends of the earth, and Isaiah again picked up this theme in 62:11. In doing so he alluded clearly to 40:9–10, a similar announcement to Jerusalem and the towns of Judah. The last two lines of verse 11 are identical to 40:10, and both passages indicate that the "reward" refers to the people God is bringing back to Jerusalem. The Lord is called "Savior" (v. 11) because He had delivered His people from captivity (cf. 52:7–8). The apostle John alluded to this verse in his description of the second coming of Christ (Rev. 22:12).

Verse 12 contains two names for God's people and two for Jerusalem. "Holy People" is closely associated with the designation "priests of the LORD" in 61:6, and both terms are derived from Exodus 19:6, God's blueprint for the nation of Israel. The title "Redeemed" alludes to God's rescue of Israel from Egypt (cf. 35:9–10; 51:10–11), but it is now applied to the release of those who had been sold into exile to Babylon (cf. 50:1–2). The two names for Jerusalem are the reverse of "Deserted" and "Desolate" (v. 4) and emphasize how much the city will be loved.

THE JUDGMENT OF THE NATIONS (63:1–6)

Chapters 60–62 spoke eloquently about the restoration and glory of Jerusalem and her people. In chapter 63, a passage closely related to 59:16–20, Isaiah returned to the theme of the judgment of the ungodly that must precede the redemption of God's people. The scene of the judgment is Edom, the same nation that was used to symbolize God's enemies in 34:5. As in

34:6, the important city of Bozrah is singled out because its name means "grape-gathering," and Isaiah developed a detailed comparison between treading grapes and pouring out blood. The garments of the One who takes vengeance are stained with blood, like the robe of Christ that is dipped in blood as He battles the enemy at His second coming (Rev. 19:13). This avenging Lord strides forward with great strength, the same awesome power that was described earlier in 40:26. As He saves, He does so "in righteousness" (v. 1), and these two concepts—salvation and God's righteousness—are joined together in 41:2; 46:13; and in 59:16. God will set things right as He delivers His people.

In verse 2 Isaiah asked the Lord another question and introduced the theme of "treading the winepress." God's answer (vv. 3–6) shows that this is no joyful trampling of grapes (cf. 16:10) but that it is a trampling of the nations in judgment. This graphic figure is used in Lamentations 1:15; Joel 3:13; and in Revelation 14:20 and 19:15. The blood-spattered garments—mentioned in each of the first three verses—correspond to the "garments of vengeance" (59:17).

God's "anger" and "wrath" (vv. 3–6) are linked with the Day of the Lord in 13:3 and in 34:2. Although He is a God of great patience, eventually the sins of the nations stir up His righteous indignation. The "day of vengeance" (v. 4) is also mentioned in 34:8, where it is parallel to "a year of retribution." Judgment on the nations resulted in redemption for God's people. Isaiah 61:1–2 also discusses the interrelationship between salvation and judgment.

Verse 5 repeats 59:16 almost word for word, a fact that helps us interpret the overall meaning of 63:1–6. Even though one is tempted to see the fulfillment of these verses only in the second coming of Christ, the initial reference is to Israel's deliverance from captivity. Words like "salvation" and "redemption" point unmistakably in that direction, as they do in 59:15–20.

In verse 6 Isaiah related the metaphor of the winepress to two other metaphors. Drunkenness is a metaphor for judgment. Enduring God's vengeance will be like drinking wine and getting drunk. In 51:17 Jerusalem had to drink "the cup of his wrath," but usually it is the nations who suffer (cf. Zech. 12:2; Rev. 14:10; 16:19). Sacrifice is a second metaphor for judgment. Just as the blood of animals was poured out at the base of the altar (Lev. 8:15), so the blood of soldiers will be shed on the battlefield (cf. 34:6).

A PRAYER FOR GOD TO INTERVENE (63:7–64:12)

Isaiah said many things about redemption, victory, and salvation for Israel, but he portrayed the land of Israel as lying in ruins. It was difficult to find a ray of hope anywhere. On the basis of God's great promises, however, Isaiah earnestly prayed that the promised restoration would become a reality. His prayer is in the form of a lament, a type of hymn similar to Psalms 44 and 74.

God's Tenderness and Compassion (63:7–19)

The passage begins with a review of God's past relationship with Israel, especially during the Exodus and the wilderness wanderings. In the Hebrew text, verse 7 begins and ends with the word "kindnesses," a term often used of God's faithfulness to His covenant with Israel (cf. 54:10; 55:3). "Not one of all the LORD's good promises to the house of Israel failed" (Josh. 21:45). They were God's special people, and when they suffered under Egyptian oppression, He too was distressed (v. 9). They cried out and the Lord sent "the angel of his presence" (v. 9; cf. Exod. 33:14, 15) to secure their release from bondage. This "redemption" lies at the heart of Isaiah's message (cf. 35:9; 41:14; 43:1–3). During their travels God "lifted them up and carried them" (v. 9) as a father carries his little children (cf. Deut. 1:31).

In response to God's love, the Israelites rebelled against Him in the wilderness (cf. Num. 20:10). Their repeated grumblings grieved Him deeply (cf. Ps. 106:32–33) and proba-bly provide the background for Paul's admonition to believers not to grieve the Holy Spirit (Eph. 4:30). Israel's sin angered the Lord, who handed her over to her foes (Ps. 106:40–41), eventually consigning even Jerusalem to destruction (Isa. 43:28).

When disaster struck, the humbled Israelites reflected on God's mighty deeds on their behalf. Once more they recalled the crossing of the Red Sea. There God "divided the waters before them" (v. 12) to the amazement of the pursuing Egyptians.* The "shepherd" who led them (v. 11) was Moses, whose right hand held the staff that was extended over the sea (cf. Exod. 14:16). The miracle at the Red Sea demonstrated how powerful God's arm really was (v. 12; cf. 51:9) and won for Him everlasting renown (cf. 55:13).

Verses 11 and 14 mention the ministry of the Spirit of the Lord. It was He who enabled Moses and the seventy elders to govern the complaining Israelites and to lead them to the Promised Land. "Rest" (v. 14) probably refers to the Israelites' long-awaited arrival in Canaan (Deut. 12:9; Josh. 1:13) where they found pastures and abundant water.

In the light of this reminder from history, Isaiah pleaded Israel's case (vv. 15–19). He petitioned the Lord to see Israel's plight and to return to His struggling people. Repeatedly, in an attempt to motivate the Lord to respond, Isaiah stressed the former close relationship between God and Israel.[1] Verse 15 uses the verb that in 42:14 is used to describe the difficulty Joseph had in withholding his love from his brothers (cf. Gen. 45:1). This same verb is used in 64:12, the last verse in the prayer. It seems as though Isaiah knew how difficult it was for God to keep punishing His beloved people. Not even Abraham or Jacob loved Israel as much as God, and so Isaiah referred to God as Israel's "Father" (v. 16; 64:8), and in 49:15 and in 66:13 he compared God's love for Israel to the love of a mother for her child.

When Israel went into exile, however, it appeared that God had forgotten all about His people. They had gone astray like sheep (cf. 53:6), and the Lord had let them wander into distant lands as captives. Their hearts had been hard and unresponsive (cf. 6:9–10), so the Lord confirmed them in that condition as He had done to Pharaoh long ago (cf. Exod. 7:3, 14). But the

---

*Compare Exodus 14:21 and Isaiah 11:15; 43:16–17; 44:27; 50:2; and 51:10.

[1] Claus Westermann, *The Praise of God in the Psalms,* trans. Keith R. Crim (Richmond, Vir.: John Knox, 1965), p. 55.

tribes of Israel were God's inheritance, and the people were His servants (v. 17). How could the Lord continue to ignore them? "Servants" is the title introduced in 54:17, and it implies that many of the people were now true believers. Out of all the nations, Israel alone bore God's name because she belonged exclusively to Him (v. 19; cf. 43:7). The Lord's dwelling place, the temple built by Solomon, had been savagely trampled by the enemy (cf. Ps. 74:3–7). This destruction was a challenge to God's honor, and Isaiah pleaded for God to notice and to take action.

A Plea for Help in Spite of Israel's Sin (64:1–12)

In chapter 64 Isaiah's prayer increased in intensity and in emotional fervor. Verse 1 requested a mighty revelation from God, one similar to His appearance on Mount Sinai. Isaiah portrayed the heavens as a tent curtain that would be torn by the Lord's coming (cf. 40:22). On Mount Sinai the thunder and earthquakes overwhelmed the Israelites (cf. Exod. 19:16–18). Nations also tremble before Him. When God makes His name known (v. 2), His power and glory are displayed (cf. 30:27). Never has there been a God like this, Isaiah argued, who comes to the aid of His people, rescuing Deborah and Barak from the Canaanites (Judg. 4:15) and Gideon from the Midianites (Judg. 7:20–21). Those who trust in this God are marvelously strengthened (cf. 40:31).

But Isaiah had to admit that Israel had turned her back on the Lord and had forfeited the blessings He had promised her. Therefore, in verses 5b–7, Isaiah lamented the sins of the nation, as he had done in 59:2–8. By using the first person pronoun, Isaiah identified with sinful Israel (cf. 59:12–13). All Israel had become ceremonially unclean, defiled by sins that Isaiah compared to having a terrible disease (cf. Lev. 13:45). The "righteous acts" (v. 6) of the people were no more genuine than those of the scribes and Pharisees (cf. Matt. 5:20). Isaiah called such deeds "filthy rags," probably a reference to the menstrual cloths used by a woman during her period, a time when she was ceremonially unclean, according to the law (cf. Ezek. 36:17).

In spite of the distress caused by sin, the nation refused to come to God in prayer. Instead Israel's sins overwhelmed her the way the wind blows away chaff. Israel suffered the same fate as the wicked nations; she was driven away by the Lord's rebuke (cf. 17:13; 40:24). God became angry with His people and turned His face away from them (cf. 59:2).

Although the situation seemed hopeless, Isaiah pressed his plea on Israel's behalf (vv. 8–12). After all, God was Israel's Father (cf. 63:16) and Creator, the One who fashioned a people to do His bidding.★ The petitions of verse 9 find support in passages such as 43:25 and 54:8. God had promised that His anger would soon end and that the day would come when He would not remember the sins of His people.

Isaiah's great prayer reaches a climax in 64:10–11 where he returned to the subject of the destruction of Jerusalem and the temple. Jerusalem and the cities of Judah were considered sacred because Israel was the "holy land" (Ps. 78:54) that had been set apart as God's special country, and so special honor was given to Jerusalem, the site of the temple (cf. 48:2). Now these cities lay desolate, overrun by the enemy, and even the temple had been burned to the ground (2 Kings 25:9). The Lord was thus deprived of the praises that once ascended to His throne from that glorious sanctuary. Isaiah concluded his powerful appeal with two questions that are similar to the two with which he began his petition in 63:15. How could the Lord fail to respond to the cries of His suffering people? Would He ignore them forever?

BLESSING FOR GOD'S SERVANTS (65:1–25)

Isaiah's earnest prayer did not go unanswered. In chapter 65 the Lord promised to break His silence and to take action (cf. v. 6). This action, however, involved a mixture of judgment and salvation as God distinguished between the rebellious and obedient segments of the nation of Israel. Once again the Lord recounted the terrible sins of Israel that had brought about the

★God is described both as "father" and "creator" in 45:9–10.

Exile, and He explained why sinners who refused to repent would continue to face judgment. Those who seek Him would receive the fulfillment of the promise that Isaiah sought—a return to joy and prosperity in the Promised Land.

The Destiny of God's Servants and of Unbelieving Israel (65:1–16)

In verses 1 and 2 God rehearsed His overtures to Israel. He had made Himself available to the nations and had held out His hands to them in love. But Israel was not interested enough to call on His name (cf. 64:7) or to seek Him earnestly. Whatever seeking Israel did was only superficial (cf. 58:2). The people were set in their ways, and those ways were evil ones. Paul quoted verses 1 and 2 in Romans 10:20–21 and, significantly, related verse 1 to the Gentiles, who neither asked for nor sought God. Although in the context of the Book of Isaiah both verses probably refer to Israel, it is true that in 56:6–8 Isaiah had already spoken of God's acceptance of Gentiles (cf. 54:17).

Israel's sins are specified in verses 3–7. Israel defied the Lord by worshiping idols, a practice that usually involved sexual immorality and that took place "in gardens" (v. 3; cf. 1:29; 66:17) or "among the oaks" (cf. 57:5). Verse 7 links such worship with the sacrifices offered to Baal on the high places. "Burning incense on altars of brick" (v. 3) may allude to the worship of the "Queen of Heaven" that is described in Jeremiah 44:17. Some people sat among the graves (v. 4), perhaps to consult the dead. That practice was condemned in 8:19. Some Israelites ate the flesh of pigs, deliberately flouting Moses' prohibition (66:3, 17; Lev. 11:7–8). Yet those who enjoyed such pagan rituals had the nerve to claim they were better than other people, a claim also made by the Pharisees of Jesus' day (cf. Luke 7:39; 18:9–12). Their air of superiority was as irritating to God as smoke in one's nostrils (v. 5), and He would repay them for their sins. Twice Isaiah mentioned that this payment would be measured "into their laps" (vv. 6–7). Sinners would receive what they deserved (cf. 59:18).

Not all the people had to face judgment, however. Verses 8–10 introduce the believing segment of the nation, who are called God's "servants." This plural term was used earlier in 54:17 and in 63:17, but its significance is developed most fully here in chapter 65. "Servants" probably denotes the remnant, that part of the nation that would survive God's judgment and return to the Holy Land. God promised not to destroy His people (Jer. 31:36), and verse 9 speaks of descendants from the northern kingdom (Jacob) and the southern kingdom (Judah). These descendants will "possess my mountains" (v. 9), probably a reference to the whole land and its many hills and ravines. The plain of Sharon (v. 10) lay along the Mediterranean coast north of Joppa (part of Tel Aviv), but the Valley of Achor was located near Jericho (cf. Josh. 7:24, 26). From its western to its eastern edge, Israel will once again be inhabited.

But those Israelites who had forsaken the Lord were doomed to destruction. They were presenting offerings to the gods "Fortune"★ and "Destiny," so their destiny would be the sword (vv. 11–12). God's mighty sword was aimed against enemies such as Edom (cf. 34:5–6), but rebellious Israelites also would feel its relentless blows (cf. 1:20). The Lord repeatedly called the nation through the prophets, only to have the people turn a deaf ear (cf. 50:2; Jer. 25:4). Israel chose what displeased God, unlike the often-despised eunuchs of 56:4.

The contrast between God's servants and unbelieving Israel reaches its peak in verses 13–16. The "servants"—mentioned five times—enjoy God's gracious provision of food and drink and, like the description in 54:1 of the once-barren city of Jerusalem, burst into songs of joy. They are given another name, perhaps the "new name" of "Hephzibah" ("my delight is in her") referred to in 62:2 and 4. This is strongly suggested by the emphasis on God's "delight" in 65:18–19. Those who reject the Lord, however, will face starvation, and their cries of anguish will parallel the agony of the nation when it suffered during the Assyrian invasions (cf. 8:21–22). Their names will be used as examples when men pronounce curses (v. 15). When men take oaths, however, they will "swear by the God of

★The god "Fortune" (Heb. "Gad") may be part of the name "Baal Gad" in Joshua 11:17.

truth" (v. 16, Heb. "Amen"; cf. Rev. 3:14), not by a false god such as Baal.

The Creation of New Heavens and a New Earth
(65:17–25)

The emphasis in verses 9–14 on the joy and restoration of God's "chosen people," His "servants," led Isaiah into a description of ultimate happiness and peace (vv. 17–25). The section begins with God's announcement that He will "create new heavens and a new earth" (v. 17), and the "former things" will be forgotten. Since 42:9 Isaiah contrasted the "former things" with "new things" (43:18–19; 48:3, 6–7). The "new things" include the return of the exiles to Jerusalem and the work of the Servant of the Lord. In 48:7 the Lord said, "They are created now." "Now" suggests that the reference to creating Jerusalem (v. 18) could be related to a restored Jerusalem after the Exile. Just as chapter 54 began with a description of the repopulation of Jerusalem after the Exile and then went on to describe the new Jerusalem (vv. 11–14), so the context of 65:17–19 may begin with the present before leading far into the future.★ The apostle John spoke about the new heaven and new earth in connection with the "new Jerusalem, coming down out of heaven" (Rev. 21:2). Like Isaiah (65:19), John, who drew heavily on Isaiah 25:8, noted that crying and mourning will be gone because "the old order of things★ has passed away" (Rev. 21:4).

Verses 20–25 depict the physical and material conditions of the new age. As in the days of Adam and his descendants (cf. Gen. 5), men will once again live for hundreds of years. Their life spans are compared to the age of trees (cf. Pss. 1:3; 92:12–14). These "chosen ones" (v. 22) will enjoy fine houses and the fruit of their vineyards, a picture that contrasts sharply with the fate of the disobedient, whose houses and vineyards will be

---

★E. J. Young feels that Isaiah did not distinguish sharply between time and eternity, between the New Testament era and the eternal state (*The Book of Isaiah*, 3 vols. [Grand Rapids: Eerdmans, 1965–72], 3:514).

†The terminology is very close to the "former things" of 65:17.

taken from them when they sin (Deut. 28:30). God will bless both the righteous and their children, and neither death nor captivity will overtake them. When they pray God will hear and be quick to respond (cf. 30:19; 58:9). How different from the days when the sins of the people made it impossible for God to hear them (cf. 59:1–2)!

Finally, verse 25 describes the peace that will exist in the animal world, once more recalling the conditions of Paradise. Lines one and two are very similar to Isaiah 11:6–7, and the last sentence is identical to the first part of 11:9. Only the reference to dust as the serpent's food is different, though the harmlessness of the cobra and viper is mentioned in 11:8. Eating dust was the curse that God placed on the serpent in Genesis 3:14, after Adam and Eve had succumbed to his wiles.

The description of the messianic age in verses 17–25 in many respects could find its fulfillment during the Millennium, but some of the features of Isaiah's description of the messianic age seem to look ahead to the eternal state.

SUMMARY AND CONCLUSIONS (66:1-24)

The final chapter of the Book of Isaiah summarizes many of the key themes of this magnificent prophecy. Once again Isaiah emphasized the greatness of God the Creator and called on man to repent of his sin and hypocrisy. The Lord would comfort His people and bring rejoicing to Jerusalem. But at the same time the Lord would come with fire to judge sinners. These twin themes of salvation and judgment reach a climax in verses 22–24 where many bow before the Lord in worship while rebels perish in everlasting fire.

The Judgment and Restoration of Jerusalem (66:1-13)

Fittingly, the chapter begins with a glimpse of the mighty God enthroned in heaven far above the earth (cf. 40:22). Here the earth is called God's "footstool" (v. 1), a term normally applied to the ark of the covenant in the Holy of Holies (1 Chron. 28:2). But how could a man-made building contain the God of the universe (cf. 1 Kings 8:27)? Stephen quoted verses 1 and 2 in Acts 7:49–50, agreeing with Solomon and Isaiah about the greatness of God the Creator.

One would expect that all who knew about this God would "tremble at his word" (vv. 2, 5), but verses 3–6 paint a far different picture. As in 1:11–15 Isaiah bemoaned the hypocritical worship of the people. He compared the sacrifice of a bull to murder and the sacrifice of a lamb to breaking a dog's neck. A dog was ceremonially unclean and could not be used in offerings. Pigs, mentioned in verses 3 and 17, were also unacceptable as sacrifices (Lev. 11:7–8). Verse 4 announces that because these sinners chose what displeases God, God "will choose harsh treatment for them." The last four lines of this verse are almost identical to the words in 65:12.

There were some, however, who did tremble at God's word (v. 5), and they were hated by their fellow Israelites. These false brothers cast them aside and then sarcastically asked them to rejoice in the Lord (cf. 5:19). In response to such an attitude the Lord declares that He will repay them what they deserve (cf. 65:6–7). Jerusalem and its magnificent temple will be destroyed.

No sooner were these words of judgment uttered than Isaiah turned to the subject of restoration (vv. 7–13). In words reminiscent of 54:1, Isaiah spoke of Zion painlessly giving birth to children. A country is born in a day as the Lord gives delivery. How different was Hezekiah's reference to "the point of birth" (v. 37:3) when the Assyrians seemed on the verge of wiping out Jerusalem! Hezekiah's agony is contrasted with the great joy of a renewed Jerusalem. This rejoicing began with the return from the Babylonian captivity and it may include the joy of those who by faith become Abraham's spiritual descendants (cf. Gal. 4:26–27).

So abundant are the resources of Jerusalem that she is spoken of as a nursing mother (v. 11). All who mourn over her will now be satisfied at her breasts. In 60:16 Jerusalem was drinking the milk of the nations (cf. 49:23) as the riches of the nations became hers (60:5). Again these riches are referred to in 66:12. They are described as coming to Jerusalem like a flowing stream—not at all like the destructive flood of Assyria's armies (8:7–8). Along with wealth God "will extend peace to her like a river" (v. 12), a comparison drawn from 48:18. "Peace" sometimes connotes prosperity, and it is also linked with the righteous rule of the Messiah (9:7). This section concludes with a verse that repeats the word "comfort" three times (v. 13). The last half of the Book of Isaiah had begun with the twofold command, "Comfort, comfort my people" (40:1). That comfort is now complete.

The Wrath and Glory of God (66:14–24)

Lest the reader be carried away with thoughts of exultation, Isaiah returned to the theme of judgment (vv. 14–16). Only God's servants* can rejoice under His protecting hand because His enemies must endure His wrath. In 5:28 God's anger was unleashed through the armies of Assyria, whose chariots were also like a whirlwind. Fire has been associated with God's judgment since 1:31. The breath of the Lord was like a stream of burning sulfur that destroyed Assyria (30:33) and Edom (34:9). Babylon also felt the wrath of the Lord as He mustered an army against her (13:3–4). Judgment of this magnitude is associated with the Day of the Lord, the final judgment on the nations (cf. 13:9–13; Ezek. 38:21–22).

Some of the reasons for God's judgment against wicked Israelites are given in verses 17 and 18. The people were worshiping idols in sacred gardens, purifying themselves with special rituals (cf. 1:29; 65:3). They ate the forbidden meat of pigs and rats to demonstrate their firm opposition to God's laws (cf. 65:4). Because of their sinful actions, these Israelites would face God's wrath when He gathers the nations for judgment. All who see this judgment will acknowledge God's power and glory (cf. 59:19).

Those who survive the judgment will return home to spread the news about the great power of Israel's God. They will go to Tarshish (perhaps in Spain or North Africa) and Libya, to Asia Minor and Greece, and to the other coastlands of the Mediterranean. From there these Gentiles will bring back

*This is the last occurrence of the plural "servants," discussed most fully in 65:8–15.

the Jewish remnant to Jerusalem. This theme is also developed in 11:12; 14:2; and in 49:22. Jerusalem was first called "my holy mountain" in 11:9, and throughout the Book of Isaiah there are a number of references to the coming of both Jews and Gentiles to Mount Zion, the temple mount (cf. 2:2–3; 27:13; 56:7; 60:3–4). When the Gentiles return, bringing the Israelites as a kind of "offering," the Lord will reward them by appointing some of them as priests and Levites. Based on 61:6, other interpreters understand the "priests and Levites" as a reference to believing Jews.

The consequences of belief and rebellion are clearly explained in verses 22–24. Those who believe—whether Jew or Gentile—will have a name and a posterity that will never be cut off (contrast 48:19). Weekly and monthly they will worship the Lord, keeping the Sabbath and observing His festivals (cf. Zech. 14:16; Isa. 56:2–5). Those who rebel will die and suffer everlasting torment. The Valley of Ben Hinnom, the New Testament Gehenna, was prepared for their arrival (cf. 30:33; Jer. 7:32).

Part III

THEOLOGICAL EMPHASES

14

CHRISTOLOGY

The Book of Isaiah contains some of the richest and most extensive references to the person and work of Christ found anywhere in the Old Testament. Almost every facet of Christ's life, death, and second coming are dealt with in this remarkable prophecy. For this reason some scholars have called Isaiah "the Gospel of Isaiah,"[1] so splendid is its picture of the Savior and the Good News He brings. The New Testament makes full use of the passages in Isaiah that refer to Christ, and in this chapter a large number of quotations and allusions will be examined.

I. THE INCARNATION

A. The Virgin Birth

One of the most famous passages about the Messiah is also the most controversial, the reference to the Virgin Birth (7:14). Commentators have long struggled to maintain the meaning "virgin," as opposed to "young woman," while at the same time relating this maiden to the historical context of Isaiah's day. Along with Dr. Gleason Archer[2] and others, I believe that "virgin" refers to Isaiah's fiancée who, after marrying Isaiah,

---

[1] See Allan A. MacRae, *The Gospel of Isaiah* (Chicago: Moody Press, 1977).

[2] See *The Wycliffe Bible Commentary,* ed. Charles F. Pfeiffer and Everett F. Harrison (Chicago: Moody Press, 1962), p. 618 and Gleason L. Archer, Jr., *Encyclopedia of Bible Difficulties* (Grand Rapids: Zondervan, 1982), pp. 266–68.

gave birth to Maher-Shalal-Hash-Baz (8:1–3). The description of the boy in 8:4 corresponds closely to the words about Immanuel in 7:16: "Before the boy knows how to say 'My father' or 'My mother'" is equal to "before the boy knows enough to reject the wrong and choose the right." The "two kings" of 7:16 represent Damascus and Samaria in 8:4.

Isaiah used ʿalmâ, not bᵉtûlâ, the more common word for "virgin," because the former word means "a virgin about to be married," whereas the latter word can refer to a virgin at any stage of life. There is one example in the Old Testament where a married virgin (bᵉtûlâ) was "grieving for the husband of her youth" (Joel 1:8). This probably means that the couple was legally betrothed, but the marriage had not been consummated prior to the tragic death of her fiancé.

One might well ask why Matthew 1:23 quoted Isaiah 7:14 if the verse in Isaiah did not exclusively refer to Jesus and Mary. A helpful parallel is found in Matthew 2:15 where Hosea 11:1 is cited: "Out of Egypt I called my son." In its Old Testament context the verse refers to the Exodus of Israel from Egypt. In Matthew it is applied to the flight of Jesus to Egypt "where he stayed until the death of Herod" (v. 15). No one reading Hosea would have suspected that the verse would refer to the Messiah. Likewise, no one reading Isaiah 7:14 would have anticipated a miracle because of its reference to the virgin. The reader would have understood the verse as a blessing on an upcoming marriage in which a woman who was a virgin when the blessing was pronounced bore a child naturally. Matthew clearly explains the difference in the case of Mary when he says "before they came together, she was found to be with child through the Holy Spirit" (1:18). Isaiah 7:14 was beautifully suited for the incarnation because the name "Immanuel" means "God with us." Never before had God been with His people the way He was present with them as the incarnate Son of God.

The question remains as to whether Isaiah understood that he was prophesying the Virgin Birth of the Messiah. Did he know that the verse would ultimately refer to Jesus and Mary? I believe that it is quite likely that Isaiah understood the fuller meaning of the text. His great titles for the Messiah in 9:6 immediately follow the two chapters that emphasize the title

"Immanuel" (cf. 8:8, 10). Isaiah possessed such extensive knowledge of the details of Christ's life and death that this most mysterious detail, the Virgin Birth, was probably revealed to him by the Holy Spirit as well.

B. Christ's Deity

The divine nature of Christ is best illustrated by the title "Mighty God" (9:6). With great accuracy Isaiah tells us that "to us a child is born, to us a son is given." The son was "given" in that the child was the preexistent Son of God who was alive from eternity past. For that reason He can be called "Mighty God" (*'ēl gibbôr*), a term applied to the Holy One of Israel in 10:20–21. The "son" who will one day rule on David's throne (cf. 9:7) is thus equal to God Himself.

The close proximity to this passage of the occurrences of "Immanuel" (7:14; 8:8, 10) underscores the full significance of this name. Linguistically speaking, "Immanuel" is a name like "Ezekiel" ("God is with us" and "God strengthens"), but the symbolic significance of "Immanuel" indicates that He was a child who would be "God with us" in a unique sense. His power and ministry are explained in the first seven verses of chapter nine.

Christ's deity is also evident from a comparison of 6:1 and 52:13. In chapter six Isaiah saw a vision of the Lord Almighty "seated on a throne, high and exalted." The same two terms occur in 52:13 where it is said of the Servant of the Lord: "He will be raised and lifted up and highly exalted." This exaltation would follow the suffering endured on the cross, the subject of chapter fifty-three.

One could also argue for Christ's deity on the grounds that a number of titles used for Christ in the New Testament are used of God in Isaiah. Terms such as "Redeemer" (41:14), "Savior" (43:3), and "the first and. . .the last" (Alpha and Omega, Rev. 1:8) are regularly applied to the Almighty Creator in Isaiah.

II. CHRIST'S CHARACTER

A. His Lowly Beginning

A number of passages use the word "shoot," or "branch," to refer to the Messiah, implying that His beginnings would be humble. In 11:1 Isaiah mentions that a "shoot will come up from the stump of Jesse." One day David's dynasty would collapse, but eventually God would restore it. Chapter fifty-three describes the Suffering Servant as one who grew "like a tender shoot, and like a root out of dry ground" (53:2). The same verse indicates that the Messiah was not striking in appearance like David and other kings, though this description of His appearance may refer to Christ's disfigurement before the crucifixion as He wore the crown of thorns and purple robe (John 19:1–5). But from the shoot came "the Branch," and this term is twice associated with fruitfulness (4:2; 11:1). Eventually beauty and glory would characterize the Messiah and His rule.

B. His Royal Lineage

The "plant" imagery used to describe Christ's humble beginning is also linked with His royal lineage. The "shoot" of 11:1 comes from "the stump of Jesse," the father of King David. In 11:10 the same "Shoot," or "Branch," is called "the Root of Jesse," the One who "will stand as a banner for the peoples." Paul quoted this verse when he wrote about the salvation of the Gentiles through Christ (Rom. 15:12). In Revelation 5:5 John describes the triumph of the "Root of David," the "Lion of the tribe of Judah." Later, in Revelation 22:16, Jesus said, "I am the Root and Offspring of David." The addition of the word "Offspring" helps to clarify the meaning of "root." Isaiah used "root" to describe the descendant of an Assyrian king who would spring up as a viper "from the root of that snake" (Isa. 14:29).

Christ's tie with the royal family is also made explicit in 9:6, and according to 16:5, He will reign on David's throne. This remarkable child will one day rule as a legitimate heir to the throne of "Israel's singer of songs" (2 Sam. 23:1).

C. His Wisdom

The first of the four great titles in 9:6 is "Wonderful Counselor." A literal translation of this title would be "a wonder of a counselor." Christ would not have to depend on the advice of others before making decisions. The counsel that He gave and the wisdom that He possessed would be nothing short of miraculous. According to 11:2, the Spirit of the Lord that was to rest on the Messiah was "the Spirit of wisdom" and "the Spirit of counsel." Therefore the Messiah would not have to govern by hearsay; He would render decisions in full accordance with justice. In his magnificent chapter on the greatness of God, Isaiah asked if anyone had ever served as the Lord's counselor (40:13). Who had ever been His teacher or advisor? Paul quoted this passage in 1 Corinthians 2:16 but added that Christians "have the mind of Christ."

D. His Eternity

The title "Everlasting Father" is the most difficult one to interpret in 9:6. Why is the Father mentioned in a passage that speaks about God the Son? Some interpreters prefer the translation "father of eternity," understanding the phrase to refer to the "possessor" or "author of eternity," to the One who gives eternal life. Walter Kaiser states that this name represents "the fatherly rule of Messiah and His divine attribute of eternity."[3]

Another title that closely links the Father and the Son is "Alpha and Omega." It is taken from the expression "I am the first and I am the last" (Isa. 44:6; 48:12; cf. 41:4). God is the Creator and Redeemer, the everlasting and only God. He is the beginning and the end. In Revelation 1:8 the title is applied to God the Father, but in Revelation 1:17 and in 22:13 it clearly refers to the Son, the One who was dead but is alive for ever and ever.

[3] Walter C. Kaiser, Jr., *Toward an Old Testament Theology* (Grand Rapids: Zondervan, 1978), p. 210.

E. His Peacefulness

A prominent theme in Isaiah is peace on earth (cf. 2:2–4; 11:6–9; 19:23–25; 65:25), and so it is fitting that Isaiah called the Messiah the "Prince of Peace" (9:6). His rule will be characterized by unending peace and by wholeness and prosperity in every area of society (9:7).

The first Servant Song emphasizes the gentleness of this "peaceful Prince" who "will not shout or cry out, or raise his voice in the streets" (42:2). How different from the kings who boasted and threatened and cruelly oppressed those they ruled! Christ would be a commander who genuinely cared for His subjects and who inspired their hope (42:4). Above all He endured "the punishment that brought us peace" (53:5).

F. His Truthfulness

In the final Servant Song (52:13–53:12) Isaiah depicted the suffering and death of the Servant. He was cut off and "assigned a grave with the wicked. . .though he had done no violence, nor was any deceit in his mouth" (53:9). The Messiah did not deceive people or try to achieve His goals by treacherous means. He spoke the truth and could be trusted implicitly. When Peter quoted this passage to encourage believers, he noted that Christ did not retaliate when He was insulted, and He made no threats during His suffering (1 Peter 2:22–23).

The New Testament alludes to another Isaianic passage when it describes Christ as "the Amen, the faithful and true witness" (Rev. 3:14). Twice in Isaiah 65:16 the Lord is called "the God of truth," and the Hebrew word translated "truth" is the word "amen" (*'āmēn*). When the Lord promised to fulfill the oath He swore to Abraham and the patriarchs, Jeremiah responded with "Amen, LORD" (Jer. 11:5), affirming what God had said. Jesus said in John 14:6, "I am the way and *the truth* and the life."

III. CHRIST'S MINISTRY

A. John, the Preparer of the Way

Each of the synoptic Gospels includes a quotation of Isaiah 40:3, a verse that refers to the "voice of one calling," the one who says, "Prepare the way for the LORD" (Matt. 3:3; Mark 1:3; Luke 3:4–6). The "voice" is identified with John the Baptist, who preached in the Desert of Judea and who prepared the way for the ministry of Christ. John called the nation of Israel to repentance and warned the people of the judgment that would come if they refused to respond to his message.

In Isaiah 40:3 "preparing the way" has to do primarily with making a smooth highway to enable the exiles to return to Jerusalem. After the seventy years of exile were over, obstacles would be removed from the road, and the people would return home (57:14; 62:10). This was the good news that Isaiah proclaimed to a nation longing for comfort. Of course John the Baptist had even better news when he announced the coming of Christ, "one who is more powerful than I," who "will baptize you with the Holy Spirit and with fire" (Matt. 3:11). Deliverance from Babylon was not as great as salvation from sin.

B. The Proclamation of the Gospel

The Greek word for "gospel," *euaggelion,* is cognate to the verb that in the Septuagint translates the Hebrew verb "to bring good news, good tidings" (*biśśēr*). This is a verb that occurs several times in Isaiah and that provides an important background for the New Testament concept of proclaiming the gospel. Since the "good news" is associated with the preaching of John the Baptist, it is significant that it appears in Isaiah 40:9, a passage that is in close proximity to 40:3 and its description of John. Normally *biśśēr* is used of a messenger who runs from a battlefield to bring the news about what everyone hopes is a victory or of a messenger who informs a man that his wife has given birth to a son (Jer. 20:15). A Cushite brought David the news about Absalom's defeat (2 Sam. 18:31). Unfortunately the aged priest Eli was given news about Israel's terrible defeat at the hands of the Philistines, who captured the ark of the covenant (1 Sam. 4:17). The role of the messenger helps to explain the reference to the beautiful feet of those who bring good news to Jerusalem (Isa. 52:7). Paul cited this verse when he commented about those sent to preach the gospel, and he quoted Isaiah 53:1 as proof that not all will believe the Good News (Rom. 10:15f.). Ephesians 6:15 also mentions "feet" in conjunction with "the gospel of peace."

In 40:9 Isaiah mentioned the good news while a messenger announced to Judah and Jerusalem, "Here is your God!" God would return to Jerusalem in that He would gain the release of the Babylonian exiles (cf. 52:7–12). He would go before them and protect them as He did when the nation fled from Egypt. John the Baptist said "Look, the Lamb of God," not "Here is your God" (John 1:29), but the two descriptions are closely related (cf. Luke 3:18).

The other occurrence of preaching good news in the Book of Isaiah comes in 61:1, a passage quoted by Christ in the synagogue at Nazareth (Luke 4:18f.). When Christ applied the verse to Himself and then mentioned God's concern for the Gentiles, the people were infuriated and tried to throw Him off a cliff (Luke 4:28–30). Isaiah 61:1 does not specifically speak of Gentiles, but they, like the Jews, needed freedom from the captivity of sin. "The year of the LORD's favor" (61:2) is parallel to "the day of salvation" in 49:8.

C. The Anointed One

Isaiah 61:1 is the only place in the Book of Isaiah where "Messiah," or "the Anointed One," is linked with Christ. Only the verbal form appears (māšaḥ), and the anointing consists of the coming of the Spirit of the Lord on Him. Ordinarily prophets, priests, and kings were anointed with olive oil, though in David's case God's Spirit came on him when he was anointed (1 Sam. 16:13). The noun "messiah" (mᵉšîaḥ) occurs in Isaiah 45:1 where Cyrus is called the Lord's anointed. That great Persian monarch was used of God to bring about Judah's release from captivity.

D. The Empowering by the Spirit

In addition to 61:1, two other key passages emphasize the coming of the Spirit upon Christ. In 11:2 the Spirit comes to rest on the "Branch," a messianic title. Seven terms in this verse are associated with the Spirit; this number may be the basis for the "seven spirits," or the "sevenfold Spirit," mentioned several times in Revelation (1:4; 3:1; 4:5).[4] Enabled by the Spirit, Christ will rule the world with perfect justice, defending the poor and needy and slaying the wicked (11:3–4).

The other important verse is 42:1, the very first description of the Servant of the Lord. The Servant is God's chosen one on whom He will put His Spirit. As in 11:2–4, the presence of the Spirit is linked with just rule. Many interpreters find a clear allusion to 42:1 in the New Testament's descriptions of Jesus' baptism. When John baptized Jesus at the beginning of His ministry, heaven was opened and the Spirit of God descended on Him like a dove. A voice from heaven identified Jesus as "my Son, whom I love; with him I am well pleased" (Matt. 3:17; cf. Luke 3:22). This description closely resembles "my chosen one in whom I delight" (Isa. 42:1).

E. The Ministry of Service

Four important passages emphasize the ministry of the Servant of the Lord (42:1–7; 49:1–7; 50:4–11; 52:13–53:12). These so-called Servant Songs provide many insights into the life and death of Christ and are cited frequently in this chapter on Christology. The word "servant" ('ebed) is applied to Isaiah himself (20:3), to a high government official named Eliakim (22:20), and to the entire nation of Israel (41:8; 42:19).

As we saw in the previous section, the first Servant Song was alluded to at the beginning of Christ's ministry. There the apostle Matthew also quoted Isaiah 42:1–4 in connection with the healing of many who were sick (Matt. 12:18–21). Serving lay at the heart of Christ's life; He "did not come to be served,

---

[4] Merrill C. Tenney, *Interpreting Revelation* (Grand Rapids: Eerdmans, 1957), p. 46.

but to serve, and to give his life as a ransom for many" (Matt. 20:28). Christ took "the very nature of a servant . . . and became obedient to death" (Phil. 2:7f.), but God "glorified his servant Jesus" by raising Him from the dead (Acts 3:13–15). In life, as well as in death, Christ was preeminently a servant.

F. A Light for the Gentiles

The first two Servant Songs state that Christ will be "a light for the Gentiles" (42:6; 49:6). These are two of the greatest missionary texts in the Old Testament. When the aged Simeon saw the baby Jesus in the temple courts, he acknowledged that he had seen God's salvation, "a light for revelation to the Gentiles" (Luke 2:32). The apostle Paul quoted Isaiah 49:6 when he and Barnabas turned to the Gentiles after the Jews at Pisidian Antioch rejected the gospel (Acts 13:47). Later, in his defense before King Agrippa, Paul also spoke of Christ as a light to the Gentiles (Acts 26:23), and Jesus Himself declared "I am the light of the world" (John 8:12).

Almost all of these passages also contain some reference to Christ's ministry to the Jews because they were the primary recipients of His message. The Servant was "to restore the tribes of Jacob" (Isa. 49:6) and He "would proclaim light to his own people" (Acts 26:23). Isaiah 9:2–3 describes the Messiah as a great light who would shine on a people who walked in darkness. Israel would be enlarged amid great joy.

A different meaning of "light" is evident in 60:19–20. There the Lord is the "everlasting light," and the sun and moon are no longer needed. This description of the age to come parallels the description of the New Jerusalem in Revelation 21:23, a city that receives its light from the glory of God, "and the Lamb is its lamp."

G. Christ's Ministry in Capernaum

The reference to "light" in Isaiah 9:2 is related to the northern part of Israel, "Galilee of the Gentiles, by the way of the sea" (v. 1). According to Matthew 4:13–16, this prophecy was fulfilled when Jesus moved from Nazareth to Capernaum, on the shore of the Sea of Galilee. Capernaum lay on a highway called by the Romans the *Via Maris,* "the way of the sea," and this was the main road between Egypt to the south and Syria and Mesopotamia to the north. Therefore when Christ moved to Capernaum, not only did He minister to the Jews who lived there, but news about Him was carried far and wide by the Gentiles who traveled along that important highway.

H. Christ's Healing Ministry

Wherever Christ went the blind received sight, the lame walked, and the deaf could hear. People flocked to see Him, hoping to get near enough to touch Him and benefit from His healing power. Above all our Lord wanted to heal men of the dread disease of sin, but He did not ignore the cries of the physically ill. On one occasion He clearly alluded to Isaiah as He combined preaching Good News to the poor (Isa. 61:1) with healing the blind and the deaf (Matt. 11:5; cf. Isa. 35:5f.). Several times Isaiah spoke of such miracles in connection with the messianic age (cf. 29:18).

It is interesting that Matthew quoted four verses of a Servant Song (Isa. 42:1–4) just after Jesus healed many people (Matt. 12:18–21), but those verses do not directly mention healing. Isaiah 42:7 does refer to opening eyes that are blind, though this verse primarily refers to spiritual blindness. Physical and spiritual healing are also combined in a quotation from the final Servant Song, Isaiah 53:4. That whole chapter emphasizes spiritual healing. After Jesus healed many sick people in Capernaum, however, Matthew 8:17 says, "He took up our infirmities and carried our diseases."

Even after Christ's ascension the apostles healed people in the power of Jesus' name. A man crippled from birth was able to walk and jump as Peter called on the Lord to heal him (Acts 3:8). The messianic age had truly come (Isa. 35:6)!

I. The Everlasting Covenant

Isaiah lived in an era that witnessed the collapse of the northern kingdom and anticipated the destruction of Judah. In spite of the passing of the old world, Isaiah spoke about an everlasting covenant that the Lord would make with His people. This may refer to the confirmation of the Abrahamic and Davidic covenants—both of which were eternal—or to the new covenant that was yet to be instituted. The Davidic covenant is called an "everlasting covenant" in 55:3, and Christ will fulfill that covenant by ruling over David's kingdom forever (cf. 9:7 and Acts 13:34). The other reference to an everlasting covenant in 61:8–9 recalls the wording of the Abrahamic covenant and its emphasis on descendants and blessing. It is through Christ that "all peoples on earth will be blessed" (Gen. 12:3).

The Servant of the Lord is called "a covenant for the people" in 42:6 (cf. 49:8). By His death Christ became the mediator of a new covenant to free men from sin (Heb. 9:15). The new covenant may also be in view in Isaiah 59:21, a verse that emphasizes the presence of the Spirit and the implanting of the Word of God firmly in the minds of the people (cf. Jer. 31:33). Under the old covenant, God's Word was too often forgotten or ignored.

J. The Stone of Stumbling: The Cornerstone

Two verses that deal with the word "stone" are given christological import in the New Testament. The first is Isaiah 8:14, which speaks of the Lord as "a stone that causes men to stumble." The other is Isaiah 28:16, with its mention of "a precious cornerstone for a sure foundation." Romans 9:33 puts the two verses together as it delineates how Israel stumbled over the matter of works, refusing to pursue righteousness by means of faith. Meanwhile the long-despised Gentiles have come to God by faith and have been declared righteous.

According to 1 Peter 2:4–8, Christ is the "living Stone," the cornerstone of God's spiritual house and precious to God and believers. But those who refuse to believe have rejected that stone; they have stumbled over it and fallen.

K. The Parables of the Sower and the Tenants

Two of Jesus' parables relate in important ways to passages in Isaiah. The parable of the sower is given in each of the synoptic Gospels. Before Jesus' explanation of the parable, each Gospel account contains a quotation from Isaiah 6:9 or 6:9–10 (Matt. 13:14–15; Mark 4:12; Luke 8:10). In answer to the disciples' question about the reason for parables, Jesus cited Isaiah's prophecy that the people would keep on hearing but never understand, they would keep on seeing but never perceive. Their hard hearts were like the hard ground on which the seed fell; the Word of God does not penetrate, and the evil one snatches it away.

The parable of the tenants (Matt. 21:33–46; Mark 12:1–12; Luke 20:9–19) is a modification of the Song of the Vineyard (5:1–7). Both vineyards have a wall, a winepress, and a watchtower, and God is the owner. The stories diverge when it comes to the harvest. In Isaiah 5, the grapes produced are worthless; in Matthew 21, it is the tenants—those who work the vineyard—who are evil. In Isaiah the "loved one" is God, the owner of the vineyard. In Luke 20:13 the loved one is the Son, sent by God to collect the fruit, only to die at the hands of the tenants. The mistreatment of the Son meant the destruction of the vineyard—Israel.

L. Passages Quoted by Christ

During His ministry our Lord quoted several verses from Isaiah. The only one where Isaiah's name is mentioned is Matthew 15:8–9, a quotation of Isaiah 29:13. Jesus was responding to a question from the Pharisees and teachers of the law, and He condemned them for their hypocrisy. Like Israel of old, these leaders honored God with their lips but not their hearts, and their teachings were only man-made rules.

In the extended pericope in John 6 about the bread of life, Jesus quoted part of Isaiah 54:13 (John 6:45). Because they were convinced He was Joseph's son, the Jews were grumbling about Jesus' claim to be "the bread that came down from heaven" (v. 41). Christ replied that no one could come to Him unless the

Father drew him. "They will all be taught by God" (v. 45), and those who learn will come to Christ and live forever.

The only verse cited in each of the synoptic Gospels is the final part of Isaiah 56:7, "My house will be called a house of prayer for all nations" (cf. Matt. 21:13; Mark 11:17; Luke 19:46). Jesus quoted this verse when He was in the process of cleansing the temple, "driving out those who were buying and selling there" (Mark 11:15). The commercial attitude was not at all consonant with heartfelt worship. Each Gospel contrasts Isaiah 56:7 with Jeremiah 7:11 where the temple is called a "den of robbers."

The theme of judgment is introduced when Jesus quoted from the last verse in the prophecy, Isaiah 66:24. Jesus told the disciples that it is better to cut off a hand or a foot or to pluck out an eye that caused one to sin than to be thrown into hell, "where 'their worm does not die, and the fire is not quenched'" (Mark 9:48). In Isaiah this is the fate of those who have rebelled against God.

The final quotation comes from the Olivet Discourse where Jesus cited part of Isaiah 13:10 and 34:4. The Lord was explaining some of the details related to His second coming, and He noted that after the Tribulation the sun and moon would be darkened and "the stars will fall from the sky" (Matt. 24:29; Mark 13:25). At that time the Son of Man will come with power and great glory. In Isaiah these heavenly phenomena are associated with judgment and the Day of the Lord.

IV. CHRIST'S SUFFERING AND DEATH

Much of the material about Christ's atoning death is concentrated in the last Servant Song, Isaiah 52:13–53:12. Other details are introduced in the second and third Servant Songs (49:1–7; 50:4–11) as Isaiah moved firmly toward the climactic fifty-third chapter. Surprisingly, however, only one verse from Isaiah 53 is quoted in the Gospel accounts of Christ's death (v. 12 in Luke 22:37; cf. Mark 15:27). Nonetheless the fulfillment of numerous details is seen plainly in these accounts. Since the Servant Songs contain most of the references to the opposition Christ faced, it is easy to see why the term "Suffering Servant" developed.

A. Opposed

The first hint of opposition to the Servant appears in 49:4 where He seems to be laboring for no purpose. The verb "labor" is the same one translated "grow weary" in 40:28. God never grows tired or weary, but the Servant experienced a sense of fruitlessness and frustration. The incarnate Son of God felt what He had never known before. During His lifetime Christ encountered strong opposition among the very Jews He was trying to bring back to God (Isa. 42:5). The Pharisees, chief priests, and teachers of the law felt threatened by Christ's teaching and vigorously opposed Him. As His ministry grew in popularity, these leaders plotted to kill Him (Matt. 12:14). Some of His own townspeople were equally upset with His messianic claims and tried to throw Him down a cliff (Luke 4:28–30).

B. Despised and Rejected

Twice in the same verse we are told that the Servant was despised, so great was the hatred for Him (53:3). Men rejected Him; they gave up on Him completely and turned their backs on Him. The infinitely precious Son of God was considered to be worthless, struck down by God Himself (53:4). Isaiah 49:7 says that the Servant "was despised and abhorred by the nation." He was considered repulsive, like Job, whose close friends detested him when they saw his awful sickness, which they attributed to the hand of God (Job 19:19). Ironically, Christ was hated by the Jews with the same unreasoning passion that the Jews were hated by other nations (cf. Isa. 60:14).

C. Mocked and Spit Upon

The Servant lamented that He had been beaten and mocked (Isa. 50:6). Men added insult to injury by pulling out His beard and by spitting in His face. David went to war when the Ammonites shaved off the beards of his messengers and "cut off their garments in the middle at the buttocks" (2 Sam. 10:4). To David, someone who was despised and insulted was "a worm and not a man" (Ps. 22:6–7).

As the crucifixion drew near, Christ suffered these indignities at the hands of the Jewish Sanhedrin and the Roman soldiers. The Jewish leaders "spit in his face and struck him with their fists" (Matt. 26:67). The soldiers put a staff in His hand, then struck Him with it and spit on Him (Matt. 27:30; cf. Luke 18:32). The Servant "was crushed for our iniquities" (Isa. 53:5), and that could include the psychological distress brought on by this humiliation.

D. Beaten and Disfigured

The beatings Christ endured were the kind reserved for a criminal or a fool (Prov. 19:29; 26:3), though Pilate could not establish what that crime might be. Christ was struck repeatedly on the head (Mark 15:19) and the back (Isa. 50:6) as the soldiers carried out the command to flog Him (Matt. 27:26; John 19:1–3). "Wounds" (KJV "stripes") in Isaiah 53:5 may refer to these blows Jesus suffered. So severe was the beating administered that Isaiah tells us "his appearance was . . . disfigured beyond that of any man" (52:14). He did not look like a human being at all.[5] This was the way He went to the cross to die for all mankind.

E. Pierced for Our Transgressions

To be pierced by the sword was to die a violent death (Ezek. 28:7–8). Although Christ did not die in battle, His death on the cross was a different sort of violence. It was like the death of Zimri, leader of the tribe of Simeon, who was killed with the sword of Phinehas the priest because of his involvement in terrible immorality with Moabite and Midianite

[5] E. J. Young, The Book of Isaiah, 3 vols. (Grand Rapids: Eerdmans, 1965–72), 3:337–38.

women (Num. 25:6–15). So Christ died like a criminal, hanging there between two thieves, "numbered with the transgressors" (Isa. 53:12). Yet Christ did not die for His own sin; "He was pierced for our transgressions" (Isa. 53:5). He bore the punishment that all mankind deserved.

As Christ hung on the cross, His body was pierced with the spear of a Roman soldier (John 19:34). The soldiers broke the legs of the two men crucified with Christ, but when they saw that Jesus was already dead, they pierced His side instead. In his great prophecy of the crucifixion, the psalmist declared that evil men pierced Christ's hands and feet (Ps. 22:16).

F. Called the Lamb of God

When John the Baptist saw Jesus coming toward him he said, "Look, the Lamb of God, who takes away the sin of the world!" (John 1:29). According to the Mosaic Law, lambs, bulls, and goats were presented to the Lord on behalf of individuals or the nation as a whole. The individual normally placed his hand on the head of the offering as an indication that the animal was his substitute (Lev. 1:4). The Passover lamb was slaughtered and its blood sprinkled on the doorframe so that the life of the firstborn son might be spared (Exod. 12:21–23). Like the lamb, Christ died so that "the iniquity of us all" might be laid on him (Isa. 53:6).

Christ was "led like a lamb to the slaughter" (Isa. 53:7); that is, He was willing to die and He did not complain about the fate that awaited Him. Pilate was amazed when Jesus refused to answer any of the charges against Him (Matt. 27:12–14; Mark 15:5). King Herod asked Him many questions, but Jesus said nothing (Luke 23:9). In spite of vehement accusations and cruel insults, "he did not retaliate" (1 Peter 2:23).

G. Offered for the Guilty

The death of Christ is compared directly only to the sin offering (cf. Heb. 13:11–12) and the guilt offering (Isa. 53:10) because these were the only two offerings that dealt with specific sins. The guilt offering was brought when another person had been wronged, perhaps by stealing or extortion (cf. Lev. 6:1–4). The guilty party brought a ram as the offering and made restitution to the offended person (Lev. 6:5–7).

The sins of mankind constituted a terrible affront to the justice of God. Ultimately, sin is against God (Ps. 51:4), even when individuals are deeply hurt. But God was not pleased with the blood of great numbers of rams and bulls and lambs and goats, especially if hypocrites presented the offerings (cf. Isa. 1:11). Only one thing could satisfy His wrath and atone for the guilt of mankind, and that was the death of the sinless Lamb of God.

H. Crucified to Cleanse Others

One of the best-loved verses in all of Isaiah is 1:18:

"Come now, let us reason together,"
   says the LORD.
"Though your sins are like scarlet,
   they shall be as white as snow;
though they are red as crimson,
   they shall be like wool."

No verse better explains the transforming power of the blood of Christ that is able to purify the worst of sinners. Israel's sin was red like "scarlet" and "crimson" because the people were murderers with blood-stained hands (1:15). Snow is a beautiful symbol of the purity of one whose sins are forgiven. David, after his affair with Bathsheba, and though guilty of adultery and murder, prayed that he might be cleansed and made "whiter than snow" (Ps. 51:7). In Revelation 7:14 we read about believers who have come out of the Great Tribulation and who "have washed their robes and made them white in the blood of the Lamb."

I. Killed to Fulfill God's Purpose

On the Day of Pentecost, Peter declared to the Jews that Jesus had been handed over to them "by God's set purpose and foreknowledge" (Acts 2:23). This may be an allusion to Isaiah

53:10 where we are told "it was the LORD's will to crush him." The word translated "will" often has the idea of "pleasure," or "delight," such as the pleasure God feels when the Sabbath is faithfully kept (Isa. 56:4). The Lord did not take pleasure in inflicting pain on the Servant but in accomplishing His redemptive purposes. In Isaiah 46:10–11 God speaks of fulfilling His purposes through King Cyrus and doing "all that I please." Just as Cyrus would release the Jews from the Babylonian captivity (cf. Isa. 44:28), so Christ would bring freedom from sin and death.

J. Buried With the Rich

When Jesus died, a wealthy man named Joseph of Arimathea received permission from Pilate to bury the body in his own tomb (Matt. 27:57–60). His courageous action fulfilled the prophecy that Jesus would be buried with the rich, though "He was assigned a grave with the wicked" (Isa. 53:9). The word "wicked" is plural (which fits the two thieves who died with Christ), but the word "rich" is singular. This is an unexpected change in number because the words are in parallel lines. An interesting confirmation of the change from plural to singular is seen in the Saint Mark's Isaiah Scroll, one of the Dead Sea Scrolls. The scribe started to write the plural form of the word "rich," 'ašîrîm, realized that he made a mistake, and scratched out the last two letters, leaving the singular 'ašîr.[6]

V. THE RESURRECTION

A. The Light of Life

There are no explicit references to the resurrection of Christ in Isaiah, but a number of statements strongly hint that the Servant of the Lord would live again. According to Isaiah 53:10, the Servant would see His offspring and prolong His

[6]Millar Burrows, *The Dead Sea Scrolls of the St. Mark's Monastery,* 2 vols. (New Haven, Conn.: The American Schools of Oriental Research, 1950), 1, plate XLIV.

days. How could He see the spiritual offspring redeemed through His blood unless He rises from the dead? This interpretation also fits in with the assertion of verse 11 that "he will see the light [of life]."* This assumes that "light" was part of the original text. "Light" does not occur in the Masoretic Text, but it is found in the two large Isaiah Dead Sea Scrolls (1Q Isa a, 1Q Isa b) and in the Septuagint. This trio of texts provides rather convincing evidence that "light" is a genuine reading and not an insertion to smooth over a difficult grammatical construction.†

If "light" is the genuine reading, it probably means "the light of life." Psalm 49:19 describes the plight of the rich man who dies and takes nothing with him; he will be gone and will never see the light. The entire phrase, "the light of life," occurs in both Psalm 56:13 and in Job 33:30, and it clearly refers to being delivered from physical death. Since the Servant did die, however, "see the light" must mean "rise from the dead" in victory over the grave.

B. Exaltation and Victory

The final Servant Song begins and ends on a note of exaltation and victory (Isa. 52:13; 53:10–12). The Servant who suffers and dies is the One who is "raised and lifted up and highly exalted" (52:13). Peter may have alluded to this verse when he described the risen Christ as "exalted to the right hand of God" (Acts 2:33). Similarly, Paul contrasted the humbling of Christ as He endured death on the cross with His exaltation to the highest place as God "gave him the name that is above every name" and commanded every knee to bow before Him (Phil. 2:8–11). Christ took "the very nature of a servant" (Phil. 2:7) so that He might die for mankind.

The last verse of Isaiah 53 depicts the Servant's exaltation as a great victory. Like soldiers who "rejoice when dividing the

---

*The brackets enclose words supplied by the translators.

†Millar Burrows is still not persuaded that "light" is original. He argues that it is too facile a suggestion. *More Light on the Dead Sea Scrolls* (New York: Viking, 1958), p. 153.

plunder" (Isa. 9:3), the Servant "will divide the spoils with the strong" (53:12). John 12:31 indicates that by His death "the prince of this world will be driven out." When Christ died and then rose from the dead, Satan was dealt a crushing blow. Through the redemption accomplished by Christ, mankind could be transferred from the kingdom of darkness to the kingdom of light. Christ's resurrection also meant that "death has been swallowed up in victory" (1 Cor. 15:54; cf. Isa. 25:8). The final enemy, "the shroud that enfolds all peoples" (Isa. 25:7), has been vanquished.

C. The Fulfillment of the Promises to David

In Acts 13:34 the apostle Paul somewhat surprisingly links the resurrection of Christ with Isaiah 55:3, a verse that mentions "an everlasting covenant" and God's "faithful love promised to David." Paul's argument seems to be based on the promise to David that his throne and kingdom would be established forever (2 Sam. 7:16). Since Christ was the descendant of David who would reign on the Davidic throne forever (Isa. 9:7) and since Christ died and was buried, the only way He could rule over David's kingdom would be through His resurrection from the dead. Because of His faithfulness to the Davidic covenant, God did not let Jesus' body decay (cf. Acts 13:35).

VI. CHRIST'S SECOND COMING

Christ's first coming had a humble beginning and a seemingly tragic end. He came to His own, and His own did not receive Him. Isaiah described His ministry mainly in terms of a servant, the "Servant of the Lord" who would suffer and die. Through His death He paid for the sins of the world, bringing salvation to all mankind. The note of triumph associated with Christ's death and resurrection prepares the way for the glory and victory of His second coming. Our Savior will return in awesome power to save His people and to judge the wicked. He will sit on David's throne and rule the nations with a rod of iron.

It is often difficult to sort out verses that deal with the first coming from those that pertain to the second coming of Christ. In a number of passages, such as 40:1–11 and 61:1–2, the two events are closely intertwined. The Second Coming—like the First—is often described in terms that apply to the deliverance of Israel from Babylon. The return from Exile remains the basic starting point for Isaiah's promise of redemption.

Understanding the details surrounding the second coming of Christ poses many problems, partly because that event has not yet happened. Moreover, New Testament quotations and allusions from Isaiah that refer to Christ's return are not numerous, and they occur in apocalyptic material such as Matthew 24 and Revelation.

A. The Coming of the Redeemer to Zion

Isaiah 59:20, a verse with a strong futuristic flavor, is quoted by Paul in Romans 11:26. The Redeemer, dressed like a warrior, will come to Zion to repay His enemies and to intervene on behalf of His people. "Redeemer," or "Defender" as it is rendered in Proverbs 23:11, is a title for God that recalls the great deliverance of Israel from Egypt (cf. Exod. 15:13), and it also refers to Israel's rescue from Babylon (Isa. 52:9). In the New Testament, redemption is more closely associated with the person of Christ, and it looks ahead to the day when the believer will be perfected (cf. Eph. 1:14; 4:30). Paul cited Isaiah 59:20 in the context of the salvation of both Jews and Gentiles. He followed a text—probably influenced by the Septuagint—that has the deliverer coming *from* Zion rather than *to* Zion. Although this is also a possible translation of the Hebrew, it is not the easiest translation to support. Nevertheless the time when the people of Israel repent of their sins will be at the second coming of Christ (cf. Rev. 1:7). From that time on the Spirit of the Lord will enable them to obey the Word of God forever (Isa. 59:21).

B. Christ as Judge

Isaiah 63:1–6 is an important parallel passage to Isaiah 59:16–21. These verses vividly describe God's "day of vengeance," which He also calls "the year of my redemption" (v. 4). His coming will bring redemption to His people but awesome judgment (referred to as the wrath of God) to the enemy. The judging process is compared to treading the winepress, to the grape-gatherer who steps on the grapes, making the juice flow down into the wine vat (cf. 16:10). The nations are the grapes, and their blood is likened to the juice. Jeremiah employs the same powerful symbolism to describe the crushing of Judah at the fall of Jerusalem (Lam. 1:15).

The book of Revelation uses the figure of treading the winepress to depict God's future wrath. One "like a son of man" swings a sharp sickle to harvest the grapes of the earth and throw them "into the great winepress of God's wrath" (Rev. 14:14–20). The "Word of God," wearing "a robe dipped in blood," rides out at the head of the armies of heaven to strike down the nations (Rev. 19:13). As He judges, He "treads the winepress of the fury of the wrath of God Almighty" (Rev. 19:15). The allusion to Isaiah 63 is unmistakable.

Revelation 19 also refers to a sharp sword that comes out of Christ's mouth (v. 15). This imagery is at least partially derived from Isaiah 11:4, which states that the messianic figure known as the "Branch" (v. 1) "will strike the earth with the rod of his mouth" as He comes to rule with justice. John was certainly familiar with this chapter because he used another title, "the Root of Jesse" (Isa. 11:10), on two occasions (Rev. 5:5; 22:16). The "Branch of the LORD" is also associated with the cleansing of Jerusalem in Isaiah 4:2–6. The filth of the city will be removed "by a spirit of judgment and a spirit of fire" (v. 4).

C. His Reward

One of the joyous aspects of the Second Coming is the reward Christ will give to those who have faithfully served Him. This reward is mentioned in Revelation 22:12, a verse heavily influenced by Isaiah 40:10 and 62:11. Both of the Isaianic passages refer to the announcement that God is coming back to Jerusalem, leading His people home from captivity. The Babylonian exile is over, and the remnant, the Lord's "reward" or "recompense," is returning to Jerusalem. A highway is prepared in the desert to make that journey possible.

Our analysis of chapter 40 and the discussion above on "preparing the way" have shown that a number of these verses are used in the Gospels to refer to Christ's first coming. Now we notice how the Second Coming fits into the very same passages. Isaiah 40:5 mentions the revelation of the Lord's glory, and some New Testament verses refer to Christ's glorious return (Matt. 16:27; Titus 2:13). He will come, with His angels, in great power and glory. Matthew 16:27 mentions the glory of Christ's return and the reward He will bring, joining two ideas found in Isaiah 40 (vv. 5, 10).

"Reward" is the key term in Revelation 22:12, and it is the idea that differs most from the original context of Isaiah. In both Isaiah 40 and 62, the reward is apparently *God's* reward that He deserves because He redeemed His people from Babylon. It consists of the people that God, like a shepherd, leads home (cf. Isa. 40:11; 62:12). In Revelation the reward is clearly something given by the Savior to His people in accordance with what each has done. This is also true in Matthew 16:27 and is consistent with other passages (cf. 1 Cor. 3:14; Col. 3:24). This shift in the meaning of "reward" shows again how the New Testament gives a new twist to an Old Testament verse. The passages are fully appropriate to Christ's return, but they are applied differently.

D. Wonders in the Skies

In the Olivet Discourse, Jesus quoted from Isaiah 13:10 and 34:4 (Matt. 24:29; Mark 13:24). When the Son of Man returns after the Tribulation, darkness will envelop the sun and moon and the stars will fall from the sky. Revelation 6:12–13 connects these ominous signs with the opening of the sixth seal. There the apostle John added from Isaiah 34:4 the reference to the sky rolling up like a scroll, and he also mentioned a great earthquake (Rev. 6:14). This is defined as the great Day of the Wrath of God and the Lamb (6:16–17). The verses in Isaiah also refer to a cruel day of judgment and destruction as the Lord's wrath is poured out on His enemies.

In Old Testament times, when God appeared there was thunder and lightning, and the earth was shaken. At the great theophany on Mount Sinai, the people trembled as the Lord came down to give them the law (Exod. 19:16–19). Thick darkness covered the place where God was (Exod. 20:21).

E. The Gathering of the Elect

The Olivet Discourse's description of the gathering of the elect uses terminology similar to that used to describe the regathering of the exiles to Jerusalem. Angels gather the elect from the four winds as the sign of the Son of Man appears in the sky (Matt. 24:31). In Isaiah 11:10–12 the Root of Jesse (a messianic title) stands as a banner for the peoples, and the exiles of Israel will be gathered from the four quarters (literally, "wings") of the earth. A banner was often a signal pole raised on a mountain to serve as a rallying point (cf. Isa. 18:3), and perhaps the "sign" of Isaiah 66:19 was a banner.

Another term that is sometimes associated with a banner and that also occurs in Matthew 24:31 is the word "trumpet." A loud trumpet call signals the angels to gather the elect at the Second Coming. In the Old Testament the trumpet is blown and the banner raised to summon troops into battle (cf. Jer. 51:27).[7] In Isaiah 27:13, however, "a great trumpet will sound" when the Israelites are gathered from exile (cf. v. 12). The phrase "in that day," as well as the geographical sweep from Assyria to Egypt, link 27:12–13 with 11:10–11.

F. The King on David's Throne

Isaiah longed for the day when a king like David would rule Israel and the nations, and when justice and righteousness would again prevail. The messianic King will reign on David's throne forever (9:7). He will begin as a shoot from the stump of Jesse, but will become a fruitful Branch (4:2; 11:1) who will rule in beauty and splendor (33:17). According to Revelation 3:7,

[7]R. Laird Harris, ed., *Theological Wordbook of the Old Testament,* 2 vols. (Chicago: Moody Press, 1980), 2:583.

Christ is also the One "who holds the key of David." This is an allusion to Isaiah 22:22 where, interestingly, this phrase is not applied to the Messiah but to a high official named Eliakim, who served in King Hezekiah's household. Eliakim was to bear "on his shoulder the key to the house of David." As the palace administrator (cf. 36:3), Eliakim would have carried out many of the functions the king delegated to him, and his actions would have been final. Since the Messiah would in a much more complete way bear the government on His shoulders (9:6), the figure was appropriately applied to Him in the Book of Revelation. The authority represented by "the keys of the kingdom of heaven" that were given to Peter employs the same symbolism (Matt. 16:19).

The power of the messianic King is clearly reflected in the metaphor-"the rod of his mouth" (Isa. 11:4). When Christ becomes King, His word will carry such a great and fearsome authority that even the breath of His lips will slay the wicked. The apostle John combined Psalm 2:9 and Isaiah 11:4 to describe Christ's ruling with an iron scepter while a sharp sword comes out of His mouth (Rev. 19:15). This picture is quite different from that of the gentle "Suffering Servant," but even the Servant's mouth was compared to a sharpened sword in Isaiah 49:2.

When Christ becomes King, it will be a time of great rejoicing. Isaiah speaks about the good news contained in the announcement that the exiles would return from Babylon (cf. 40:9–11; 52:7–9). Restoration calls for shouts of joy and songs of praise (cf. 12:6; 54:1). This same "good news" was attached to the report that Jesus Christ was born in Bethlehem (Luke 2:10–11) and to the message of salvation preached through His name (cf. Rom. 10:15). How fitting, then, that the coming of His kingdom be included in that proclamation of good news to Zion, "Your God reigns!" (Isa. 52:7). Many thought that at His first coming He "was the one who was going to redeem Israel" (Luke 24:21), but the full extent of that redemption awaits His glorious return.

15

ESCHATOLOGY

Isaiah's view of the future includes times of unparalleled judgment and times of tremendous joy and prosperity in a paradise regained. The wicked will endure tribulation and distress as the wrath of God is poured out on them. The righteous, however, will experience redemption and salvation as the Lord comes to rescue them from the clutches of the wicked. We are given contrasting pictures of victory and defeat, of everlasting punishment and eternal bliss. In all of this God is the Judge and Commander, the Redeemer and Savior. From time to time a messianic figure emerges, the "Branch," the "Root of Jesse" (11:1, 10), or the "Wonderful Counselor" and "Prince of Peace" (9:6). He will come from the house of David and sit on his throne. Often, however, it is God, the "LORD Almighty," who marches out to punish the guilty and to save the righteous.

Isaiah was primarily interested in the fate of Judah and Jerusalem—God's chosen people, the main recipients of Isaiah's message. But the Book of Isaiah contains large blocks of material that deal with the nations (cf. chs. 13–23), and Isaiah described God as sovereign over the nations and in full control of their affairs. In the Book of Isaiah God's judgment is largely directed against the nations, but the light of salvation also extends to the Gentiles (cf. 49:6), and they participate in God's kingdom along with believing Jews (cf. 2:2–4; 56:6–7). Thus, Isaiah demonstrated how the Jews received the full blessing of the Abrahamic covenant and how "all peoples on earth will be blessed" through Abraham and his greater descendant, Christ (Gen. 12:1–3).

According to Isaiah, the future has at least three focuses. Because of his historical point of reference, Isaiah concentrated on the return of Israel from the Babylonian exile in 538 B.C. Almost all of the major themes of the book—including the highway in the desert, redemption, and the proclamation of good news—have as their starting point the release of captive Israel. Jerusalem will be rebuilt and repopulated, and joy and gladness will return to its streets. All of this will be made possible by the destruction of Babylon and by the emergence of the Persian Empire led by King Cyrus.

A second focal point for Isaiah is the first coming of Christ. Like Cyrus, He would be a great deliverer. Whereas God raised up Cyrus to bring about political "salvation" from captivity, Christ entered the world to save mankind from the greater captivity of sin. He was Isaiah's Suffering Servant who bore the sins of the world on Calvary (Isa. 53). There was also a political dimension to Christ's first coming, however, because He was descended from David and had the right to rule on David's throne. Isaiah looked forward to the time when a king like David would rule the nation with justice and righteousness. There are many references in Isaiah to Christ's ministry on earth, and these have been discussed in the chapter on Christology. In spite of the clear demonstration of Christ's royal lineage in the Gospels, He did not attempt to claim the throne at that time.

The rule of Christ as the messianic King awaits His second coming, and this is the third focal point of Isaiah. The prophet anticipated a world-wide judgment followed by an era of peace and justice not unlike the golden age of Solomon. There will be a new Jerusalem, and "the earth will be full of the knowledge of the LORD" (11:9). Israel and the nations will look to the Lord as the law goes forth from Zion (2:3), and the Spirit will be poured out from on high (32:15).

These three portraits of the future are difficult to separate in Isaiah's prophecy because he uses similar terminology to refer to all of them. The highway built to prepare the way for the Lord has significance for all three focal points (cf. Isa. 40:1–11). Likewise, the good news about the coming of the Lord is linked with the return from exile and with the first and second comings of Christ (cf. 40:10). This interdependence of terms complicates the interpretation of a given passage, though we can utilize one portrait to understand another. Each portrait is like a window through which we can look to appreciate more fully the next portrait.

If all of this were not confusing enough, we must also contend with the Book of Revelation as we interpret the Book of Isaiah. In its descriptions of cataclysmic judgments and the glory of the new heaven and new earth, the Apocalypse contains a significant number of allusions to the Book of Isaiah. The figurative language that characterizes both books makes it necessary to proceed with extreme caution as we invade the mysterious realm of eschatology.

I. THE DAY OF THE LORD

A key term in understanding the future is "the day of the LORD." This precise form occurs only in Isaiah 13:6 and 9, but two other verses have the statement "the LORD Almighty has a day" (2:12; 22:5), which is probably an equivalent phrase. Far more common is the phrase "in that day," which is found about thirty-five times, mostly in the first twenty-seven chapters. In the last twenty-seven chapters, it occurs only in 52:6. One could debate whether or not "in that day" is always used in the same technical sense as an equivalent for "the day of the LORD." Another important term is the phrase "in the last days" (*bᵉʾaḥᵃrît hayyāmîm*), which introduces the remarkable verses in 2:2–4 about peace among the nations. This world-wide peace and concomitant godliness apparently follow or come at the end of the Day of the Lord.

There are two distinct emphases to the Day of the Lord in the Book of Isaiah. One emphasis is a decidedly negative one. The Day of the Lord is a day of distress and wailing in which God shakes heaven and earth and unleashes His wrath against mankind. The nations are judged by a God who is a consuming fire. The other emphasis portrays the Day of the Lord as a day of victory and redemption. The righteous will be rescued and allowed to return home to Jerusalem, and the nations will bring back the remnant and will be attracted to Zion. Israel will take root in the land and assume control of her beloved country. These diverse emphases appear to be contradictory, but they are probably two sides of the same coin. When God intervenes directly in human affairs, it is to punish the wicked and to rescue the righteous. One nation (or group of nations) is defeated, another is victorious. Israel endured God's wrath when Jerusalem fell (cf. 3:7, 18; 22:5), but she experienced redemption when Babylon was defeated (cf. 13:6, 9; 14:1–3). For purposes of clarity, however, we will study the negative side of the Day of the Lord and then turn to the positive side.

A. The Day of the Lord as Judgment

1. A Day of Distress

When King Hezekiah and the people of Jerusalem were besieged by the Assyrian army of Sennacherib in 701 B.C., Hezekiah called it "a day of distress and rebuke" and compared it to the intense pains of childbirth (Isa. 37:3). Isaiah had predicted that the sin of Israel would result in darkness and distress, and now that pessimism was vindicated (cf. 5:30; 8:22). Assyria had already taken the northern kingdom into exile in 721 B.C., and Judah seemed sure to follow. A siege meant starvation, illness, and epidemics, then finally death or captivity. The same word for "distress," ṣārâ, occurs in Daniel 12:1 where it refers to the Great Tribulation. Hezekiah and Jerusalem were mercifully spared when the Lord struck down 185,000 Assyrian soldiers. Defeat was turned to victory as the yoke of Assyria was broken (Isa. 10:27).

2. A Day of Uproar

The Day of the Lord will be filled with the tumult and confusion that are associated with war. The sound of armies assembling for battle will fill the air as men and their equipment prepare to march and destroy. In Isaiah 5:30 the army of Assyria moves forward with the roar of a lion, and in 13:4 the forces of

Media and Persia are compared to the noise of a great multitude. It is enough to strike terror into any heart and, in fact, in 22:5 the Day of the Lord is called "a day of tumult and trampling and terror." Those affected by the battles are called on to weep and wail (13:6; 22:12) as they mourn the death and destruction that accompany the conflict. According to Isaiah 2:10, 19, and 21, men will flee to caves and holes in the ground to escape the awesome splendor of God when He comes to judge the earth.

3. The Wrath of God

God is a God of compassion, "slow to anger, abounding in love and faithfulness" (Exod. 34:6), but He is also a God of justice and of wrath. Sin must eventually be punished as God pours out His wrath on the guilty. The Lord's wrath is associated with the Day of the Lord primarily in Isaiah 13 (cf. vv. 3, 5, 9, 13), though the concept occurs in other important passages as well. In Isaiah 10:4 God's anger falls on a sinful Israel in the form of the Assyrian army, "the rod of my anger . . . the club of my wrath" (10:5). As they prepared to attack Babylon, Isaiah called the Medes "the weapons of his wrath" (13:5). The Lord's lips will be "full of wrath" when in anger He shatters Assyria (30:27).

Another graphic image is the "cup of wrath" that will be given to wicked nations. God holds in His hand "a cup full of foaming wine mixed with spices . . . and all the wicked of the earth drink it down to its very dregs" (Ps. 75:8). This powerful drink was given to Jerusalem as she staggered in her drunkenness (Isa. 51:17, 22), but it would later be drunk by her tormentors (51:23). God would trample the nations in His anger and make them drunk in His wrath (63:6). The apostle John expanded the figure to "the cup filled with the wine of the fury of his wrath" (Rev. 16:19). "Babylon the Great" will be forced to drink this wine, as will those who worship the beast and have his mark on their foreheads or hands (Rev. 14:10).

4. A Day of Vengeance

Closely connected with the wrath of God is the Day of Vengeance, a day mentioned three times in Isaiah (34:8; 61:2;

63:4) and equivalent to the Day of the Lord. Each time it is parallel to a year—"a year of retribution" in 34:8, "the year of the LORD's favor" in 61:2, and "the year of my redemption" in 63:4. The first and last passages relate to Edom, the enemy against whom the Lord will take vengeance on behalf of Zion. Edom was typical of the enemies who rejoiced over Judah's fall.

The coming of the Lord with vengeance and retribution (cf. 35:4) has as its first focal point the rescue of the exiles from Babylon. This also applies to the "garments of vengeance" worn by the Lord as He repays "wrath to his enemies and retribution to his foes" (59:17–18). The "garments stained crimson" (63:1) are to be understood in the same way. They will be red because the blood of the enemy will spatter Christ's garments as He treads the winepress. Again, Revelation makes use of this symbolism when it describes the second coming of Christ. One named "the Word of God . . . treads the winepress of the fury of the wrath of God Almighty" (Rev. 19:13, 15; cf. 14:19–20). Significantly, Christ quoted Isaiah 61:1–2 but stopped just short of mentioning "the day of vengeance" (Luke 4:18–19). Christ's first coming was "the year of the LORD's favor" and "the day of salvation" (Isa. 49:8), not the Day of Vengeance.

5. Judgment by Fire

The Book of Isaiah begins and ends with a reference to unquenchable fire as a means of judgment (1:31; 66:24). Jerusalem will be cleansed "by a spirit of judgment and a spirit of fire" (4:4), but the burning anger of the Lord will destroy the wicked (cf. 13:13). God is called a "consuming fire" (33:14). "His tongue is a consuming fire" (30:27), and His breath is "like a stream of burning sulfur" that ignites the fire pit that was prepared for the king of Assyria in Topheth (30:33). Topheth was located near Jerusalem, in the Valley of Hinnom (gē' hinnōm), known in the New Testament as "Gehenna," or "Hell." Burning sulfur also appears in 34:9 to describe the complete destruction of Edom. This is an allusion to the overthrow of Sodom and Gomorrah, which the Lord destroyed by raining down burning sulfur (Gen. 19:24).

The fires of judgment against Assyria are also mentioned in

10:17 and in 33:10–12. So powerful would those fires be that the people of Jerusalem would tremble with fear, and so Isaiah urged them to live pure lives in the presence of a holy God (33:13–16). Yet any rebellious Israelite, like the godless Gentiles, will encounter the Lord "coming with fire" to "execute judgment upon all men" (66:15–16). Only "his servants" will escape the fury of a God of wrath (66:14).

6. The Shaking of Heaven and Earth

The Day of the Lord will be accompanied by wonders in the heavens and by earthquakes and storms. When the Lord pours out His anger on the earth, the stars and their constellations will not give their light (13:10). The stars "will be dissolved" (literally, "will rot") and "will fall like withered leaves from the vine" (34:4) because God will shake the heavens (13:13). The sun and moon will also be darkened on the Day of Judgment (13:1; Joel 2:31). Earthquakes and windstorms will add to the terror as men flee to caves "when he rises to shake the earth" (Isa. 2:19, 21; 13:13; 29:6). The very foundations of the earth will tremble (24:18).

Christ quoted from Isaiah 13:10 and 34:4 in describing His second coming (Matt. 24:29). Revelation 6:12–17, an account of the great day of God's wrath, alludes to those same two passages and to Isaiah 2:19 and 21. This event is called "the wrath of the Lamb" in Rev. 6:16 and refers to the shaking of heaven and earth at Christ's second coming. Both darkness and earthquakes were also present at the crucifixion when Christ endured the awful judgment for sin (Matt. 27:45, 51).

7. The Destruction of Babylon

The primary objects of God's wrath will be the nations, and in Isaiah this is best illustrated by the fall of Babylon and Edom (chs. 13 and 34). Both nations are typical of political and religious forces that are hostile to God, but Babylon is clearly the more important of the two. There are five chapters in Isaiah that are devoted to a description of the collapse of Babylon and her king (chs. 13, 14, 21, 46, 47), and the "ruined city" of 24:10 may also be Babylon. Her importance stems from her role as God's instrument of punishment against Judah in 586 B.C. and from the fact that her collapse in 539 B.C. signaled the return of the exiles to Jerusalem. This destruction represents the "day of the LORD" for the immediate future (Isa. 13:6, 9, 19).

Babylon will continue as the archenemy of God in the end times. She must drink the cup of God's wrath (Rev. 16:19), and the fall of her religious and political system is the subject of Revelation 17 and 18. The announcement of her fall, "Fallen! Fallen is Babylon the Great!" (Rev. 18:2; 14:8), is derived from the report of Babylon's fall (539 B.C.) that is recorded in Isaiah 21:9: "Babylon has fallen, has fallen!"

8. Desolation on the Earth

The Day of the Lord is characterized by destruction and desolation because the Lord will come "to lay waste the earth and devastate it" (Isa. 24:1). Both Babylon and Edom would suffer the same fate as Sodom and Gomorrah. They would be overthrown by the Lord and deserted generation after generation (13:19; 34:9–10). Babylon would become a home for jackals, hyenas, and owls. No Bedouin or shepherd would go near what had been "the jewel of kingdoms" because it would be reduced to the haunt of wild animals and birds (Isa. 13:19, 21–22; cf. Rev. 18:2).

Edom would also be overrun with desert creatures of various sorts. Thorns and brambles would take over her formerly magnificent citadels, and even the dust would be turned into burning sulfur. The smoke that would rise perpetually from her ruins (34:10) is compared to the smoke of Babylon that "goes up for ever and ever" (Rev. 19:3). Edom suffered total destruction (34:2, 5), a fate reserved for the most corrupt of societies (cf. Josh. 6:17).

The desolation brought about by an earlier Day of the Lord was experienced by Isaiah and the people of Judah during the Assyrian invasions (near the end of the eighth century B.C.). Beautiful vineyards and terraced farmlands were covered with briers and thorns after armies had ravaged the countryside (Isa. 7:23–25).

9. The Judgment on the Powers of Heaven

In Isaiah 24:21 Isaiah indicated that "the LORD will punish the powers in the heavens above." The word "powers," ṣābā', "host," refers to the angels around God's throne in 1 Kings 22:19. Here it could signify the fallen angels who assist Satan in his rebellion against God. Their imprisonment (v. 22) may coincide with the confinement of Satan described in Revelation 20:1–10.

Another verse that begins with "in that day" is Isaiah 27:1, a verse that announces the slaying of "Leviathan the gliding serpent . . . the monster of the sea." Although it is true that terms like Leviathan and Rahab can refer to wicked nations such as Egypt (cf. 51:9–10), ultimately Satan's power lies behind these kingdoms. In fact Revelation 12:9 and 20:2 may allude to Isaiah 27:1 when they describe Satan as "the great dragon" (*drakōn*), "that ancient serpent" who was defeated by Christ and His angels. The Septuagint translates "Leviathan" as "dragon" (*drakōn*).

B. The Day of the Lord as Victory

1. Deliverance From Assyria and Babylon

A number of passages describe the Day of the Lord as a day of joyous victory because God's wrath and judgment will fall on the enemy and destroy them. Israel would rejoice when the oppressive yoke of Assyria was removed from her neck (Isa. 10:27). The prediction of Assyria's collapse is compared to the defeat of the Egyptians and Midianites (10:26). The defeat of Midian is called "the day of Midian" (9:4) because it was the day of Midian's defeat. Like Assyria, Midian had served as an instrument God used to punish sinful Israel (Judg. 6:1–3); but when Midian's power seemed invincible, the burdensome yoke was shattered.

The other great Day of Victory in Isaiah is the fall of Babylon, an event that marked the end of the seventy years of exile (14:3; 52:6). This triumphant event occurred in "the year of the LORD's favor" (61:2), "the year of my redemption" (63:4). Just as Israel had been redeemed from slavery in Egypt, so the nation would gain its freedom from Babylon amid great rejoicing (52:9; 61:1).

2. The Return of the Remnant to Jerusalem

After the fires of judgment ended, God promised that the survivors of Israel would return home. Isaiah had named his first son Shear-Jashub, "a remnant will return" (7:3; 10:21), to keep that hope before the nation. The Lord would gather the exiles "from the four quarters of the earth" (11:12). From Mesopotamia or Egypt or the distant coastlands—wherever they might be scattered—God would reach out His hand and reclaim His people (11:11; 27:12–13; 49:12).

To facilitate the return, the Lord would build highways on which His people could travel. Mountains and hills would be leveled (cf. 40:3–4) and all obstacles taken out of the way (57:14). Travel would be restricted to the redeemed, and no wild animals would interfere (35:8–9). When Israel came out of Egypt, there was a highway across the Red Sea, and the Lord assured the remnant that if necessary the Euphrates River would be dried up (11:15–16). Those who journeyed across the desert would find springs of water to quench their thirst (49:10).

3. The Nations' Help in the Remnant's Return

Repeatedly, Isaiah informs us that the Gentiles will assist the Jews in their return to Jerusalem. A banner will be raised for the nations, and "they will bring your sons in their arms" (49:22). In Isaiah 11:10 the banner is equated with "the Root of Jesse," a title that refers to the Messiah. The King on David's throne will attract the nations to His righteous rule. Normally a banner was like a flag on a mountain—a signal to summon troops (cf. 5:26). Sometimes a banner was used in conjunction with the blowing of a trumpet (cf. 18:3). A great trumpet blast would signal the exiles to return home (27:12–13). Raising a banner for the nations is linked with building a highway for the exiles in 62:10.

One way the Gentiles can help is to supply different forms of transportation. In Isaiah 66:20 the exiles are brought on horses, mules, and camels, and some ride in chariots and wagons. Others come by sea, sailing in the renowned ships of

Tarshish that once were used by Solomon to carry vast stores of silver and gold (Isa. 60:9; 1 Kings 10:22). Their human cargo is deemed far more precious.

The return from exile would demonstrate God's great compassion for Israel. The Lord loved His people and wanted to end their years of hard service (40:2). After their return, Israel would rule those who formerly oppressed her and who participated in bringing her home (14:1–2).

When the Babylonian exile ended in 539 B.C., the Gentiles rendered valuable assistance to the Jews. King Cyrus of Persia made the initial return possible, and King Artaxerxes gave his blessing to Ezra and the group he led in 457 B.C., providing financial support as well (Ezra 7:6, 21–22). Artaxerxes also gave his cupbearer, Nehemiah, the resources to rebuild the walls of Jerusalem about twelve years later (Neh. 2:8).

4. The Remnant Taking Root in the Land

In the Song of the Vineyard in chapter 5, Isaiah described how the Lord will turn the vineyard of Israel into a wasteland. But in 27:2–6 Israel is pictured as a fruitful vineyard that is carefully guarded by the Lord. The nation will "take root," produce buds and blossoms, and "fill all the world with fruit" (27:6). This fruitfulness is linked with the Branch and the shoot from Jesse's stump who will be the pride and glory of the remnant (4:2; 11:1).

After the stunning defeat of Sennacherib's army in 701 B.C., king Hezekiah was the leader of the remnant in Jerusalem who survived that ordeal. Just as they were able to "take root below and bear fruit above," so the remnant that survived in exile would face a hopeful future (37:4, 31–32). When they returned home, the nation would be enlarged and able to extend its borders (54:2–3; 26:15). This was partially true of the remnant who came back to Jerusalem in 538 B.C. The final fulfillment of this prophecy awaits the second coming of Christ and the flourishing of Israel under His glorious rule.

C. Conclusion

The Day of the Lord is both a time of judgment and a time of salvation. For the wicked, this day brings God's wrath, resulting in distress and punishment. For the righteous, the Day of the Lord will bring victory over the forces of evil and a return to peace and prosperity. In the Book of Isaiah several different historical periods are linked with the Day of the Lord. The Assyrian oppression of Israel and Judah (734–701 B.C.) was ended by the destruction of Sennacherib's army in 701 B.C., a great day of victory for Judah. The rise of the Neo-Babylonian kingdom precipitated the fall of Jerusalem in 586 B.C. and ushered in the seventy years of captivity. The collapse of Babylon in 539 B.C. meant salvation and redemption for Judah; it allowed the remnant to return home to Jerusalem.

Beyond these three periods, however, looms the greater Day of the Lord that will occur at the second coming of Christ. At that time the nations of the world will feel the full force of God's judgment as Christ returns to save His people and to begin His righteous reign. The deliverance from Assyria and Babylon will seem insignificant compared to the scope of Christ's redemption when He comes in power and glory.

II. THE RULE OF THE MESSIAH

The triumphant return of Christ will climax the Day of the Lord and will usher in a period of unparalleled peace and prosperity. The nations will pay heed to the Word of God, and truth and righteousness will prevail. This period may very well be considered part of the Day of the Lord, though it is also closely tied to the new heaven and new earth. Under the leadership of the Davidic king, the world will be renewed and a Paradiselike environment restored.[1] The blessings promised to Israel and to all the nations in the Abrahamic covenant will be fully realized (Gen. 12:2–3).

A. The Prevalence of Justice

Throughout the Book of Isaiah the prophet lamented the lack of justice and righteousness in Judah. The very first chapter

---

[1] Walter C. Kaiser, Jr., *Toward an Old Testament Theology* (Grand Rapids: Zondervan, 1978), pp. 218–19.

presents a scathing indictment of the rulers of the land who ignore the cries of the widow and the fatherless and who regularly take bribes (vv. 17, 21, 23). The poor are deprived of their rights (10:1–2), and justice and truth are excluded from society (59:14–15).

But someday a king, one who "seeks justice and speeds the cause of righteousness," will reign on David's throne (16:5; cf. 9:7). This King, the "Branch" (11:2), will defend the poor and the needy with the wisdom of the Spirit of the Lord that rests upon Him (11:2–4). Justice will be so integral to His rule that He is said to wear a belt of righteousness (11:5; cf. Eph. 6:14). When wind and storm come, this king will provide shelter and refuge (32:1–2). At long last there will be peace and security for the people of the land (32:16–18).

B. The Authority of His Rule

Unlike the lowly beginning at Bethlehem, Christ's second coming will demonstrate tremendous power. Isaiah emphasized God's display of power in bringing the exiles home (cf. 40:10; 52:10). This was the same might that saved Israel at the Red Sea (cf. 51:9). The powerful arm of the Lord will be laid bare more dramatically as Christ returns on behalf of His own (cf. 59:16). His rule will be characterized by unchallenged authority. His word will be so powerful that it will be like a rod that comes out of His mouth (11:4). Revelation 19:15 heightens the imagery from "rod" to "sword," though it also mentions the iron scepter with which Christ will rule. He will slay the wicked "with the breath of his lips" (Isa. 11:4). The Messiah will reign as the "Mighty God," and His government will continue to increase (Isa. 9:6–7). As He rules, "the Spirit of counsel and of power" will rest on Him and strengthen Him (11:2).

C. The Splendor of His Kingdom

"Your eyes will see the king in his beauty
and view a land that stretches afar" (Isa. 33:17).

The coming King will rule with the splendor of Solomon, endowed with great riches and reigning over a vast domain. Once again cedar and cypress wood will be plentiful, and silver and gold will abound (Isa. 60:13, 17). "In that day the Branch of the LORD will be beautiful and glorious," and the whole land will be fruitful (4:2). All mankind will see the glory of the Lord at the Second Coming (cf. 40:5; 66:18), and God will reign "in Jerusalem . . . gloriously" (24:23). The majesty and splendor of this kingdom will be unsurpassed.

D. Peace on Earth

The messianic King will be called "Prince of Peace" because His subjects will experience safety and well-being in all areas of life (9:6–7). At the start of the prophecy, Isaiah had envisioned a time when the nations would "beat their swords into plowshares and their spears into pruning hooks" (2:4). Wars and their awful consequences will be eliminated. In chapter 19 Isaiah describes a day when the Assyrians and Egyptians will worship the Lord together and, along with Israel, will be a blessing on the earth (vv. 23–25). Egypt and Assyria were the two major military powers in the eighth century B.C., and the highway between them frequently conveyed hostile troops. If these two giants were at peace, it would be a symbol of a general peace among the nations.

Part of the reason for such calm and contentment is the righteous rule of the King. Several passages link the concepts of justice and peace; a just and honest government leads to peace and security (cf. 9:7; 32:16–17). Of equal importance is the people's responsiveness to God. The nations will be eager to listen to "the word of the LORD" (cf. 2:3), and "the earth will be full of the knowledge of the LORD" (11:9).

Peace between the nations is beautifully reflected by peace in the animal world. Isaiah 11:6–9 takes us back to the Garden of Eden, where wild animals do not kill and poisonous snakes are harmless. In the future the wolf will not attack the lamb, and. "the leopard will lie down with the goat"; neither will molest the child who leads them (v. 6).[2] The passage emphasizes the safety of infants and little children, helpless creatures who often suffer a horrible fate in war (cf. Isa. 13:16). Isaiah mentioned the absence of wild animals on the highway for the redeemed (35:9), and once again in his portrayal of the new heaven and new earth, he described the change in the nature of the lion and the wolf (65:25).

E. The Healing of the People

The messianic age will also be characterized by physical and spiritual healing. Isaiah knew that Israel could not see, that she was hard of hearing, and that her heart was calloused (cf. 6:9–10; 42:18–20). But there will come a day when the eyes of the blind will see, the ears of the deaf will hear, and the lame will jump for joy (cf. 35:5–6). Isaiah related that joyous day to a king who "will reign in righteousness" and who will foster security and well-being (cf. 32:1–4, 17). The Servant of the Lord will also "open eyes that are blind" (42:7).

Blindness and deafness in the Book of Isaiah primarily refer to a spiritual problem—the inability and unwillingness of the people to respond to God. The spiritual and the physical are closely intertwined, however, and even Moses talked about the diseases that would accompany disobedience (Deut. 28:21–22). When Christ ministered in Palestine, He healed the blind and the deaf, and He preached the Good News of salvation (Matt. 11:5). Spiritual wholeness is more essential than physical well-being, but the healing of physical infirmities heralded the coming of the messianic age.

F. A Time of Feasting

In the Old Testament, feasts were associated with joyous occasions such as weddings (Judg. 14:10) or coronations

---

[2]Compare the description of the land of Dilmun, a paradise where the lion and wolf do not kill and where sickness is absent. See "Enki and Ninhursag" in J. B. Pritchard, *Ancient Near Eastern Texts* (Princeton, N. J.: Princeton University Press, 1955), p. 38.

(1 Kings 1:19, 25). Great quantities of food were consumed by the assembled guests. According to Isaiah, the triumph of the God of justice will usher in an era in which food and drink will be abundant. Rains will be plentiful, bringing rich harvests enjoyed by both men and animals (30:23–24). This was the kind of prosperity Moses promised those who heeded God's commands (cf. Deut. 28:11–12).

Two passages in particular describe a banquet of rich food that the nations will enjoy. In Isaiah 25:6 the prophet spoke of a feast on Mount Zion "with the best of meats and the finest of wines." Similarly, in 55:1–2 an invitation is extended to the hungry and thirsty to "delight in the richest of fare." It is clear that such feasting symbolizes the enjoyment of vast spiritual blessings. A parallel idea is found in Matthew 8:11, which mentions the feast with the patriarchs in the kingdom of heaven. According to Revelation 19:9, many will be invited to the wedding supper of the Lamb, and there will be great rejoicing over the reign of the "Lord God Almighty" (v. 6).

G. The Submission of the Nations to Israel and to God

Several verses that refer to the submission of the nations to Israel and to her God are sprinkled throughout the Book of Isaiah. This description of Israel's future supremacy over the nations contrasts sharply with her actual situation from 750 B.C. to the present. It was the armies of Israel and Judah that were crushed in battle. Their cities were devastated, and their people became slaves of foreign powers. But all of this would be reversed in the future. Inveterate enemies such as the Philistines, Edom, and Moab will be subject to Israel (11:14). The nations who once held the Israelites captive will themselves become captives (14:2). The Gentiles will bow down before the Israelites (45:14) and lick the dust at their feet (49:23). Foreigners will tend their flocks (61:5) and rebuild their walls, and even kings will serve them (60:10; 49:23). Israel will expand her borders and take possession of foreign cities (14:2; 54:3).

A number of these passages also mention submission to Israel's God. The Egyptians and Sabeans will bow down before Israel because her God is the only God (45:14). Nations that do not know Israel will hasten to her "because of the LORD your God" (55:5), and in 2:2–4 the nations stream to Mount Zion to learn the ways of the God of Jacob. It is the Lord and His Word that will attract the nations to Jerusalem. Because of this important spiritual dimension, some interpreters explain the Gentiles' submission to Israel in terms of belief in her Messiah. Others anticipate both a political and spiritual submission during the Millennium.

H. The Flow of the Nations' Wealth to Israel

Another significant contrast with the actual condition of Israel during Isaiah's lifetime was the influx of the wealth of the nations to Jerusalem. Isaiah predicted that the Babylonians would carry off the treasures of Jerusalem, as they did between 605 B.C. and 586 B.C. (cf. 39:6). But when the Gentiles bring back the remnant and submit to Israel's God, the wealth will return to Jerusalem. The phrase "the wealth of the nations" (*ḥêl gôyîm*) occurs three times in Isaiah (60:5, 11; 61:6), and the closely related *kᵉḇôḏ gôyîm* (literally, "glory of the nations") is used in 66:12. Revelation 21:26 mentions "the glory and honor of the nations" (cf. v. 24) that will be brought into the New Jerusalem.

The language of Isaiah 60 is reminiscent of the age of Solomon when silver and gold poured into the capital and visitors such as the queen of Sheba (cf. v. 6) brought valuable gifts to the king. The nations that were part of Solomon's empire would send regular tribute payments to Jerusalem (cf. 1 Kings 4:21; Isa. 18:7). Therefore Isaiah meant that the rule of the Messiah will have all the splendor of Solomon's kingdom.

After the Exile, the Persian kings Darius the Great and Artaxerxes sent a measure of "wealth" to enable the Jews to rebuild the temple and the walls and buildings of Jerusalem (cf. Ezra 6:8; Neh. 2:8). But the submission of the nations to the Messiah will bring far greater honor and glory in the future.

I. The Outpouring of the Spirit

The righteous rule of the coming King is associated with the outpouring of the Spirit on high (32:15). Earlier, Isaiah spoke of the Spirit of the Lord resting on the Branch to give Him wisdom and power (cf. Isa. 11:2). Just as the Spirit came on David in power when he was anointed king (1 Sam. 16:13), so the rule of David's greater Son would be inaugurated by the Spirit's ministry.

Both Isaiah 32:15 and 44:3 compare the outpouring of the Spirit to the abundant rains that turn the desert into a fertile field. On the Day of Pentecost, Peter referred to the pouring out of the Spirit as the Church was instituted (Acts 2:17–18; cf. Joel 2:28–29). The last days began with the first coming of Christ, and before His ascension Jesus promised that He would send the Holy Spirit to guide the disciples into all truth (John 16:7–13). The Spirit who convicts and counsels will be present in even greater power at the consummation of the age when Christ returns.

III. THE NEW HEAVEN AND NEW EARTH; THE NEW JERUSALEM

It is somewhat artificial to distinguish the new heaven and new earth from the previous section, the rule of the Messiah. Isaiah understood all of them as the culmination of God's work of salvation, and it is difficult to divide them into separate categories. Chapter 11, which was frequently cited in the discussion of the Messiah's rule, has many parallels with 65:17–25, a section that deals with the creation of the new heaven and new earth as well as the new Jerusalem. I have arbitrarily included an examination of the great banquet of Isaiah 25:6 in the "Rule of the Messiah," but the next two verses (25:7–8)about swallowing up death are reserved for "the New Heaven and New Earth."

A. The Creation of New Things

The creation of "new heavens and a new earth" (65:17) climaxes a series of verses about "new things" that goes back to 42:9. Isaiah contrasted the "new things" with the "former things," God's previous accomplishments and predictions (41:22; 43:9, 18). The Lord promised that He would make a road in the desert for His people (43:18) and that He would create things "now, and not long ago" (48:7). The word "now" may be a clue that this new age and new Jerusalem (cf. 65:18) may refer initially to the restoration after the Exile. The return from exile was the first of Isaiah's three focal points, though it does not seem spectacular enough to compare with the "new Jerusalem" of Revelation 21:2. From the standpoint of the Book of Isaiah, however, it was absolutely essential that Israel be restored after the Exile to guarantee the fulfillment of even greater prophecies.

The destruction of the present heaven and earth in conjunction with Christ's second coming is described in Isaiah 24:19–23 and in 34:4. These are verses of judgment and wrath that relate to the Day of the Lord. Isaiah 51:6 asserts that "the heavens will vanish like smoke" and "the earth will wear out like a garment." In its place will be a new heaven and new earth that will endure (Isa. 66:22).

B. The Creation of the New Jerusalem

Isaiah's whole prophecy was entitled "the vision concerning Judah and Jerusalem" (1:1), and in that same first chapter the prophet lamented the corruption of the once faithful city that had "become a harlot" (1:21). After a thorough purging away of her impurities, however, Jerusalem will be called "The City of Righteousness, the Faithful City" (1:26). The sins of Jerusalem brought her suffering, invasion, and destruction; but Isaiah looked ahead to the day when Jerusalem will again be called "The City of the LORD, Zion of the Holy One of Israel" (60:14). According to 62:2, she will be given a new name, such as "Hephzibah" ("my delight is in her"—62:4) or "The City No Longer Deserted" (62:12). God promised that He will "create Jerusalem to be a delight" (65:18), and the first phase of this "new Jerusalem" may very well have been the city that was rebuilt after the Exile. Chapter 54 also combines features of the postexilic Jerusalem with those that are similar to the future "Holy City" that John saw coming down out of heaven. Like Isaiah, John mentioned the New Jerusalem one verse after mentioning a new heaven and new earth (cf. Isa. 65:17–18; Rev. 21:1–2).

C. The Splendor of the New Jerusalem

The beauty of the restored Jerusalem resembles the splendor of the city at the time of Solomon. The cedars of Lebanon, along with pines, firs, and cypresses, will "adorn the place of my sanctuary" (60:13). Silver and gold will again be present in abundance, supplemented by bronze and iron (60:17). Solomon's temple was decorated with onyx, turquoise, and other precious stones (1 Chron. 29:2), but Jerusalem will be built with turquoise and its foundations with sapphires (Isa. 54:11). The parapets on top of the walls will be adorned with rubies and the gates with sparkling jewels. The walls of the city will be made of precious stones (cf. 54:12).

It is likely that John's description of the New Jerusalem (Rev. 21:18–21) is based on Isaiah 54:11–12.[3] Precious stones abound in the construction of the city, and a few of the stones correspond to those in Isaiah. Sapphire was used to decorate the second of the twelve foundations of the city (Rev. 21:19). The wall and the first foundation were made of jasper (21:18–19), and the Greek word for jasper (*iaspis*) appears in the Septuagint as the translation of kadkōd, which is translated "rubies" in the NIV. The pearl gates of the New Jerusalem will never be shut (Rev. 21:25), and the prosperity and peace of Isaiah's city allows the gates to be open perpetually (Isa. 60:11, 18).

D. The Absence of Tears and Sorrow

Sin and rebellion brought on the nations the judgment of God and all of the weeping and wailing that went with it. Destroying armies left in their wake mourning and bitter sorrow, and joy and gladness seemed gone forever (cf. 16:9–10). Yet Isaiah looked forward to a glorious day when "the Sovereign LORD will wipe away the tears from all faces" (25:8).

---

[3] I. H. Marshall, "Jewels and Precious Stones," in *The New Bible Dictionary*, ed. by J. D. Douglas (Grand Rapids: Eerdmans, 1962), pp. 633–34.

The Lord will redeem His people and give them joy and gladness, but "sorrow and sighing will flee away" (35:10). The residents of Jerusalem "will weep no more" because the Lord will put an end to their affliction and will quickly answer their prayers (30:19–20).

Isaiah links this time of rejoicing with the creation of the new heaven and new earth and the creation of a Jerusalem that will be a delight (65:17–18). "Past troubles will be forgotten" (65:16), and "the sound of weeping and of crying will be heard in it no more" (65:19). The apostle John also spoke of the absence of crying and pain in the New Jerusalem: "He will wipe every tear from their eyes" (Rev. 21:4). This allusion to Isaiah 25:8 is repeated in Revelation 7:17, a passage that also mentions the removal of hunger or thirst or any scorching heat (v. 16, cf. Isa. 49:10). The Lamb will be the great Shepherd who will lead His people to springs of living water.

E. Longevity and the Elimination of Death

The ultimate cause of weeping and sorrow is death, the last enemy to be defeated. Surprisingly, Isaiah did not directly emphasize the elimination of death in his description of the new heaven and new earth. Instead he described life as it was in the early chapters of Genesis when the life-spans of men approached a thousand years. A person "who dies at a hundred will be thought a mere youth" (65:20), and this implies that once again men will live for hundreds of years. Longevity will be a sign of God's blessing on mankind.

Even Methuselah died, however, so it is much more comforting to read that God "will swallow up death forever" (25:8). Paul quoted this verse in 1 Corinthians 15:54 as part of his discussion of the resurrection body. Victory over death has been won through Christ, who died for our sins and then rose from the grave in triumph. Isaiah himself referred to the rising of dead bodies (26:19), though either the resurrection of the physical body or the restoration of the nation could be intended (cf. Dan. 12:2; Ezek. 37:11–12). According to Revelation 21:4, death will have no place in John's New Jerusalem.

The difference between long life-spans and unending life is

not an easy one to reconcile. Increased longevity could be viewed as a kind of transition between the average life span and eternal life, and it clearly moves in the direction of conditions not long after the Garden of Eden. Perhaps this transition will come during the Millennium, a period when there will be a "general housecleaning" in preparation for the eternal state.[4] Those who enter the Millennium in their natural bodies, along with their children, will be the ones who will enjoy increased longevity.

F. The Absence of Light From the Sun and Moon

In an earlier section on the Day of the Lord, I commented on the wonders that will take place in the skies. The sun and moon will be darkened, and the stars and their constellations will not give light. We are told that in the new age when the Lord is king, He "will be your everlasting light," and the sun and moon will not "shine on you" (60:19–20). Since creation, the sun and the moon have governed the day and the night (Gen. 1:16–18), but when the Lord reigns in glory, "the moon will be abashed, the sun ashamed" (Isa. 24:23). A somewhat opposite picture is presented in Isaiah 30:26, which mentions the intensification of the light of the sun and moon on the day of healing and abundant provision. This brilliant light may be a figurative description of the glory of God.

The apostle John twice asserted that the New Jerusalem will not need the light of the sun, "for the glory of God gives it light, and the Lamb is its lamp" (Rev. 21:23; 22:5). God's glory never grows dim, and hence there will be no night in the Holy City (Rev. 21:25; 22:5).

IV. ETERNAL PUNISHMENT

In contrast to those passages that depict a time of unending joy and prosperity for the righteous are the verses that describe the terrible fate of the wicked. Although not as numerous as the

---

[4]Alan F. Johnson, "Revelation," in *The Expositor's Bible Commentary*, ed. Frank E. Gaebelein (Grand Rapids: Zondervan, 1981), 12:581.

verses about joy and prosperity, the verses about the terrible fate of the wicked sound a solemn warning to any who rebel against a holy and righteous God. Sin must be punished, and those who pay no heed to God's call to repentance must face the judgment of a wrathful God.

A. Everlasting Burning

Isaiah often emphasized the use of fire as a means of judgment, referring to unquenchable fire in the first and last chapters of the book (cf. 1:31; 66:24). The very last verse in the prophecy describes what happens to the dead bodies of those who rebel against God: "Their worm will not die, nor will their fire be quenched." These lines were quoted by Christ in Mark 9:48, just after He urged individuals to cut off a hand or foot or to pluck out an eye that causes them to sin, rather than to be thrown into Hell with healthy bodies. The Greek word for hell, *geenna* (Gehenna), is derived from the Valley of Hinnom, *gē' hinnōm* in Hebrew. This valley, located south of Jerusalem, was probably in Isaiah's mind as he wrote about unquenchable fire. In 30:33 Isaiah mentioned the fires in Topheth, a shrine located in that valley (cf. Jer. 7:31–33).[5] It is possible that the symbolism of the "lake of fire" also comes from Isaiah 30:33, because the breath of the Lord, "like a stream of burning sulfur," sets ablaze the wood in Topheth. The "lake of fire" in Revelation is called either "the fiery lake of burning sulfur" (19:20; 21:8) or "the lake of burning sulfur" (20:10). Certainly the concept of burning sulfur goes back to the destruction of Sodom and Gomorrah (Gen. 19:24), but the idea of "lake" seems closer to the "stream" of Isaiah 30:33. In another passage that mentions eternal burning (Isa. 34:9), Isaiah stated that "Edom's streams will be turned into pitch, her dust into burning sulfur." The fire "will not be quenched night and day; its smoke will rise forever" (34:10; cf. Rev. 14:10–11). The smoke from Babylon (which, like Edom, symbolizes a world opposed to God) will rise for ever and ever (Rev. 19:3).

[5] R. Laird Harris, ed., *Theological Wordbook of the Old Testament,* 2 vols. (Chicago: Moody Press, 1980), 2:978–79.

The power of God's judgment is also seen in the phrase "consuming fire," which is applied to God three times in Isaiah (30:27, 30; 33:14) and is parallel to "everlasting burning" in 33:14. Mankind should rightly "worship God acceptably with reverence and awe, for our God is a consuming fire" (Heb. 12:28–29).

B. Everlasting Torment

The last twenty-seven chapters of Isaiah are divided into nine-chapter segments by the refrain "There is no peace . . . for the wicked" (48:22; 57:21). In life "the wicked are like the tossing sea, which cannot rest" (57:20), and in death the situation only grows worse. The fires of judgment are never quenched and there seems to be no end to the suffering. Those who refuse to trust in the Lord and His Word "will lie down in torment" (50:11). The torment takes a psychological twist in 66:24 where Isaiah described the dead, whose worm will not die, as those who "will be loathsome to all mankind." The word translated "loathsome," *dērā'ôn,* occurs elsewhere only in Daniel 12:2 where it is used of the "everlasting contempt" that is in store for the wicked after the resurrection. What a contrast to the "everlasting life" that awaits those who participate in the first resurrection!

The Book of Revelation refers to the everlasting torment of those who worship the beast and his image (14:10–11). The Devil, along with the Beast and the False Prophet, will likewise "be tormented day and night for ever and ever" in the lake of burning sulfur (20:10). The assurance that Satan will ultimately be defeated is a message of hope and encouragement, but the suffering in store for lost men and women should motivate believers to share the Good News of Christ with ever-increasing zeal so that many will be transferred from the kingdom of darkness to the kingdom of light and eternal life.

BIBLIOGRAPHY

BOOKS

Alexander, Joseph A. *Commentary on the Prophecies of Isaiah*. Rev. ed. 1875. Reprint. Grand Rapids: Zondervan, 1953.

Allis, Oswald T. *The Unity of Isaiah*. Philadelphia: Presbyterian and Reformed, 1950.

Archer, Gleason L., Jr. *A Survey of Old Testament Introduction*. Rev. ed. Chicago: Moody Press, 1974.

————. *Encyclopedia of Bible Difficulties*. Grand Rapids: Zondervan, 1982.

Aston, Frederick A. *The Challenge of the Ages: New Light on Isaiah 53*, rev. ed. Scarsdale, N.Y.: Research Press, 1969.

Barnes, Albert. *Notes, Explanatory and Practical on the Prophet Isaiah*. 1855. Reprint. Grand Rapids: Baker Book House, 1979.

Baron, David. *The Servant of Jehovah*. New York: George H. Doran, 1921.

Blank, Sheldon H. *Prophetic Faith in Isaiah*. New York: Harper & Row, 1958.

Blocher, Henri. *Songs of the Servant*. London: InterVarsity, 1975.

de Boer, P. A. H. *Second Isaiah's Message*. Leiden: E. J. Brill, 1956.

Brownlee, William. *The Meaning of the Qumran Scrolls for the Bible*. New York: Oxford University Press, 1964.

Buksbazen, V. *The Prophet Isaiah. New Translation and Commentary (Ch. 1–39)*. Collingswood, N.J.: Collingswood, 1971.

Bullinger, E. W. *Figures of Speech Used in the Bible: Explained and Illustrated*. Grand Rapids: Baker, 1968.

Bultema, Harry. *Commentary on Isaiah*. Trans. Cornelius Lambregtse. Grand Rapids: Kregel, 1981.

Calvin, John. *Commentary on the Book of the Prophet Isaiah*. Trans. Wm. Pringle. 4 vols. Edinburgh: Calvin Translation Society, 1850.

Childs, Brevard S. *Isaiah and the Assyrian Crisis*. Naperville, Ill.: A. R. Allenson, 1967.

————. *Introduction to the Old Testament as Scripture*. Philadelphia: Fortress, 1979.

BIBLIOGRAPHY

Clements, Ronald E. *The New Century Bible Commentary: Isaiah 1–39*. Grand Rapids: Eerdmans, 1980.

Criswell, W. A. *Isaiah*. Grand Rapids: Zondervan, 1977.

Culver, Robert D. *The Sufferings and the Glory of the Lord's Righteous Servant*. Moline, Ill.: Christian Service Foundation, 1958.

Delitzsch, Franz J. *Biblical Commentary on the Prophecies of Isaiah*. Trans. James Denney. 2 vols. 1877. Reprint. Grand Rapids: Eerdmans, 1949.

Drechsler, Moritz. *Der Prophet Jesaja*. 3 vols. Berlin: Gustav Schlawitz, 1865.

Driver, Samuel R. *Isaiah: His Life and Times*. New York: Randolph, n.d.

_____ & Neubauer, A. *The 53rd Chapter of Isaiah according to the Jewish Interpreters*. Vol. I *Texts* by AN (1876); Vol. II *Translations* by SRD and AN (1877). New York: Ktav, 1969.

Eissfeldt, Otto. *The Old Testament: an Introduction*. Trans. Peter R. Ackroyd. New York: Harper & Row, 1965.

Erlandsson, S. *The Burden of Babylon. A Study of Isaiah 13:2–14:23*. Lund: Gleerup, 1970.

Fichtner, J. *Isaiah among the Wise: Studies in Ancient Israel Wisdom*. New York: Ktav, 1976.

Fohrer, Georg, ed. *Introduction to the Old Testament,* initiated by Ernst Sellin. Nashville: Abingdon, 1968.

Freehof, S. B. *The Book of Isaiah*. New York: Union of American Congregations, 1972.

Garland, D. D. *Isaiah—A Study Guide*. Grand Rapids: Zondervan, 1968.

Ginsberg, H. L., and Werner, A. *Isaiah: A New Translation*. Philadelphia: Jewish Publication Society of America, 1973.

Goppelt, Leonhard. *Typos: The Typological Interpretation of the Old Testament in the New,* trans. by Donald H. Madvig. Grand Rapids: Eerdmans, 1982.

Goshen-Gottstein, M. H., ed. *The Hebrew University Bible: The Book of Isaiah,* parts 1–2. Jerusalem: Magnes, 1975.

Gray, George B., and Peake, Arthur. *A Critical and Exegetical Commentary of the Book of Isaiah*. New York: Charles Scribner's Sons, 1912.

Grindel, J. A. *The Gospel's Use of Isaiah 40:3 and Qumran*. New York: St. John's University Press, 1973.

Gutzke, Manford G. *Plain Talk on Isaiah*. Grand Rapids: Zondervan, 1977.

Harrison, R. K. *Introduction to the Old Testament*. Grand Rapids: Eerdmans, 1969.

Hasel, Gerhard F. *The Remnant: The History and Theology of the Remnant Idea from Genesis to Isaiah*. Andrews University Monographs, no. 5. Berrien Springs, Mich.: Andrews University Press, 1972.

Hengstenberg, E. W. *Christology of the Old Testament and a Commentary on the Messianic Predictions*. 2 vols. 1861. Reprint. Grand Rapids: Kregel, 1956.

Herbert, A. S. *The Book of the Prophet Isaiah*. The Cambridge Bible Commentary on the New English Bible. 2 vols. New York: Cambridge University Press, 1973, 1975.

Holmgren, F. *With Wings of Eagles: Isaiah 40–55. An Interpretation*. Choppaqua, N.Y.: Biblical Scholars Press, 1973.

Hooker, Morna K. *Jesus and the Servant*. London: S.P.C.K., 1959.

Horton, Stanley L. *Isaiah's Greatest Years*. Springfield, Mo.: Gospel Publishing House, 1959.

Ironside, Henry A. *Expository Notes on the Prophet Isaiah*. New York: Loizeaux Bros., 1952.

Jennings, Frederick C. *Studies In Isaiah*. New York: Loizeaux Bros., n.d.

Jensen, I. L. *Studies in Isaiah and Jeremiah* (Bible Self-Study Series). Chicago: Moody Press, 1969.

Jensen, J. *The Use of Torah by Isaiah: His Debate with the Wisdom Tradition*. (CBQ Monograph Series 3). Washington: Catholic Biblical Association of America, 1973.

Jones, D. R. *Isaiah 56–66 and Joel*. Torch Bible Paperbacks. London: SCM, 1972.

Kaiser, Otto. *Isaiah 1–12*. Trans. R. A. Wilson. London: SCM, 1972.

_____. *Isaiah 13–39*. Trans. R. A. Wilson. London: SCM Press, 1974.

Kaiser, Walter C., Jr. *Toward an Old Testament Theology*. Grand Rapids: Zondervan, 1978.

Katz, Eliezer. *A Classified Concordance to the Late Prophets in Their Various Subjects*. New York: Bloch, 1970.

BIBLIOGRAPHY

Kaufmann, Yehezkel. *The Babylonian Captivity and Deutero-Isaiah.* Part 4 of *History of the Religion of Israel.* Trans. C. W. Efroymson. New York: Union of American Hebrew Congregations, 1970.

Kelley, Page H. *Judgment and Redemption in Isaiah.* New York: Broadman, 1968.

Kellner, Max. *The Assyrian Monuments* (illustrating the Sermons of Isaiah). Boston: Damrell & Upham, 1900.

Knight, George A. F. *Deutero-Isaiah.* New York: Abingdon, 1965.

Kutscher, E. Y. *The Language and Linguistic Background of the Isaiah Scroll* (1QIsa). Leiden: E. J. Brill, 1974.

LaSor, W. S., Hubbard, David A, and Bush, Frederick W. *Old Testament Survey: the Message, Form and Background of the Old Testament.* Grand Rapids: Eerdmans, 1982.

Lawlor, George L. *Almah— Virgin or Young Woman?* Des Plaines, Ill.: Regular Baptist Press, 1973.

Leslie, Elmer A. *Isaiah.* New York: Abingdon, 1963.

Leupold, Herbert C. *Exposition of Isaiah.* 2 vols. Grand Rapids: Baker, 1968, 1971.

Lindblom, Johannes. *The Servant Songs in Deutero-Isaiah.* Lund: C. W. K. Gleerup, 1951.

_____. *A Study of the Immanuel Section in Isaiah.* Lund: C. W. K. Gleerup, 1958.

Lowth, Robert. *Isaiah: A New Translation.* London: T. Tegg & Son, 1835.

McKenzie, John L. *Second Isaiah* (Anchor Bible Series). Garden City, N.Y.: Doubleday, 1968.

Maclaren, Alexander. *Isaiah I to XLVIII* (Expositions of Holy Scripture). New York: George H. Doran, n.d.

MacRae, Allan A. *The Gospel of Isaiah.* Chicago: Moody Press, 1977.

Margalioth, Rachel. *The Indivisible Isaiah.* New York: Yeshiva University Press, 1964.

Marney, C. *The Suffering Servant.* Nashville: Abingdon, 1965.

Martin, Alfred & John. *Isaiah: The Glory of the Messiah.* Chicago: Moody Press, 1983.

Mauchline, John. *Isaiah 1–39.* Torch Bible Commentaries. New York: Macmillan, 1962.

Melugin, Roy F. *The Formation of Isaiah 40–55.* New York: Walter de Gruyter, 1976.

Meyer, F. B. *Christ in Isaiah.* London: Oliphants, 1970.

Morgan, Donn F. *Wisdom in the Old Testament Traditions.* Atlanta: John Knox, 1981.

Morgan, G. Campbell. *The Prophecy of Isaiah.* 2 vols. New York: Revell, 1910.

Morgenstern, Julian. *The Message of Deutero-Isaiah in its Sequential Unfolding.* Cincinnati: Hebrew Union College Press, 1961.

Muckle, J. Yeoman. *Isaiah 1–39.* London: Epworth, 1960.

Muilenburg, James. "The Book of Isaiah: Chapters 40–66." In *The Interpreter's Bible,* ed. George Arthur Buttrick. Vol. 5. New York: Abingdon, 1956.

North, Christopher R. *The Second Isaiah.* Oxford: Clarendon, 1964.

————. *The Suffering Servant in Deutero-Isaiah.* 2d ed. London: Oxford University Press, 1956.

Odendaal, D. H. *The Eschatological Expectation of Isaiah 40–66 with Special Reference to Israel and the Nations.* Nutley, N.J.: Presbyterian and Reformed, 1970.

Pieper, August. *Isaiah II: An Exposition of Isaiah 40–66.* Trans. Erwin E. Kowalke. Milwaukee: Northwestern Publishing House, 1979 (German edition 1919).

Rad, Gerhard von. *The Message of the Prophets.* New York: Harper & Row, 1968.

Radday, Yehuda T. *An Analytical Linguistic Concordance to The Book of Isaiah.* The Computer Bible 2. Wooster, Ohio: Biblical Research Associates, 1973.

————. *The Unity of Isaiah in the Light of Statistical Linguistics.* Collection Massorah, 2d ser., Etudes quantitatives et automatisées, 1. Hildesheim: Gerstenberg, 1973.

Rawlingson, George. *Isaiah.* 2 vols. *The Pulpit Commentary.* New York: Anson D. F. Randolph & Co., n.d.

Redpath, Alan. *Faith for the Times. Studies in the Prophecy of Isaiah Chapters 40–66.* Glasgow: Pickering, 1973.

Renckeus, H. *The Prophet of the Nearness of God—Isaiah.* Trans. J. M. Boumans; ed. L. McGaw. De Pere, Wis.: St. Norbert Abbey, 1969.

BIBLIOGRAPHY

Robinson, George L. *The Book of Isaiah*. New York: Y.M.C.A. Press, 1910.

Rosenbloom, Joseph R. *The Dead Sea Isaiah Scroll: A Literary Analysis. A Comparison with the Masoretic Text and the Biblia Hebraica*. Grand Rapids: Eerdmans, 1970.

Rowley, H. H. *The Servant of the Lord and Other Essays on the Old Testament*. 2d ed. rev. Oxford: Basil Blackwell, 1965.

Schiling, Sylvester P. *Isaiah Speaks*. New York: Crowell, 1959.

Schoors, A. *I Am God Your Saviour. A Form-critical Study of the Main Genres in Isaiah 40–55*. Supplement to *Vetus Testamentum* 24. Leiden: E. J. Brill, 1973.

Scott, R. B. Y. "The Book of Isaiah: Chapters 1–39," in *The Interpreter's Bible*, ed. by G. A. Buttrick. Vol. 5. New York: Abingdon Press, 1956.

Simon, Ulrich E. *A Theology of Salvation: A Commentary on Isaiah 40–55*. London: S.P.C.K., 1953.

Skilton, J. H., ed. *The Law and the Prophets: Old Testament Studies in Honor of O. T. Allis*. Wilmington, Del.: Presbyterian and Reformed, 1974.

Skinner, John. *The Book of the Prophet Isaiah. Chapters I-XXXIX*. Cambridge: Cambridge University Press, 1949.

_____. *The Book of the Prophet Isaiah. Chapters XL–LXVI*. Cambridge: Cambridge University Press, 1951.

Slotki, I. W. *Isaiah*. Boston: Soncino, 1949.

Smart, James D. *History and Theology in Second Isaiah*. Philadelphia: Westminster, 1965.

Smith, George Adam. *Book of Isaiah*. 2 vols. *The Expositor's Bible*. New York: Hodder & Stoughton, n.d.

Snaith, Norman H. *Notes on the Hebrew Text of Isaiah XXVIII–XXXII*. London: Epworth, 1945.

Stuhlmueller, Carroll. *Creative Redemption in Deutero-Isaiah*. Rome: Biblical Institute Press, 1970.

Todd, V. H. *Prophet without Portfolio. A Study and Interpretation of Second Isaiah*. North Quincy, Mass.: Christopher, 1972.

Wade, G. W. *The Book of the Prophet Isaiah*. Ed. Walter Lock. London: Methuen & Co., 1911.

Westermann, Claus. *Isaiah 40–66*. Philadelphia: Westminster, 1969.

Whedbee, J. W. *Isaiah and Wisdom*. New York: Abingdon, 1971.

Whybray, R. N. *The Heavenly Counsellor in Isaiah 40:13–14: A Study of the Sources of the Theology of Deutero-Isaiah*. New York: Cambridge University Press, 1971.

_____. *The New Century Bible Commentary: Isaiah 40–66*. Grand Rapids: Eerdmans, 1981.

Young, Edward J. *Isaiah Fifty-three*. Grand Rapids: Eerdmans, 1951.

_____. *Studies in Isaiah*. London: Tyndale, 1954.

_____. *Who Wrote Isaiah?* Grand Rapids: Eerdmans, 1957.

_____. *The Book of Isaiah*. 3 vols. Grand Rapids: Eerdmans, 1964, 1969, 1971.

ARTICLES & CHAPTERS

Achtemeier, Elizabeth R. "The Exodus and the Gospel in the Old Testament." *Theology and Life* 3 (1960): 188–97.

Albright, William F. "The Son of Tabael." *Bulletin of the American Schools of Oriental Research* 140 (1955): 34–35.

Anderson, Bernhard W. "Exodus Typology in Second Isaiah." In *Israel's Prophetic Heritage,* ed. Bernhard W. Anderson and Walter Harrelson, 177–95. New York: Harper & Brothers, 1962.

Archer, Gleason L., Jr. "Isaiah," in *The Wycliffe Bible Commentary,* ed. Charles F. Pfeiffer and Everett F. Harrison, 605–54. Chicago: Moody Press, 1962.

Aus, Roger. "God's Plan and God's Power: Isaiah 66 and the Restraining Factors of II Thess. 2:6–7." *Journal of Biblical Literature* 96 (1977): 537–53.

Baker, David L. "Typology and the Christian Use of the Old Testament." *Scottish Journal of Theology* 29 (1976): 137–57.

Beecher, W. J. "The Prophecy of the Virgin Mother." In *Classical Evangelical Essays in Old Testament Interpretation,* ed. Walter C. Kaiser, Jr., 179–85. Grand Rapids: Baker, 1972.

_____. "The Servant of the Lord." In *Classical Evangelical Essays in Old Testament Interpretation,* ed. Walter C. Kaiser, Jr., 187–204. Grand Rapids: Baker, 1972.

Beuken, W. A. M. "Mišpat: The First Servant Song and Its Context." *Vetus Testamentum* 22 (1972): 1–30.

BIBLIOGRAPHY

Birnbaum, S. A. "Date of the Incomplete Isaiah Scroll from Qumran." *Palestine Exploration Quarterly* 92 (1960): 19–26.

Blank, Sheldon H. "Studies in Deutero-Isaiah." *Hebrew Union College Annual* 15 (1940): 1–46.

Boadt, L. "Isaiah 41:8–13: Notes on Poetic Structure and Style." *Catholic Biblical Quarterly* 35 (1973): 20–34.

Cannanwurf, E. "Authenticity of Micah 4:1–4 (with reference to Isaiah 2:2–4)." *Vetus Testamentum* 13 (1963): 26–33.

Carlson, R. A. "The Anti-Assyrian Character of the Oracle in Isaiah 9:1–6." *Vetus Testamentum* 24 (1974): 130–35.

Culver, Robert D. "Isaiah 1:18—Declaration, Exclamation or Interrogation?" *Journal of the Evangelical Theological Society* 12 (1969): 133–41.

Dahood, M. J. "Textual Problems in Isaiah." *Catholic Biblical Quarterly* 22 (1960): 400–409.

_____. "Phoenician Elements in Is. 52:13–53:12." In *Near Eastern Studies in Honor of William Foxwell Albright,* ed. Hans Goedicke, 63–73. Baltimore: Johns Hopkins Press, 1971.

_____. "Weaker than Water: Comparative Beth in Isaiah 1:22." *Biblica* 59 (1978): 91–92.

Dodson, J. M. "Was Isaiah's Foreign Policy Realistic?" *Andover Newton Quarterly* 12 (1971): 80–90.

Driver, G. R. "Isaiah 1–39; Textual and Linguistic Problems." *Journal of Semitic Studies* 13 (1968): 36–57.

_____. "Isaiah 52:13–53:12: The Servant of the Lord." *Beiheft, Zeitschrift für die alttestamentliche Wissenschaft* 103 (1968): 90–105.

_____. "Isaiah 6:1, 'His Train filled the Temple.'" In *Near Eastern Studies in Honor of William Foxwell Albright,* ed. Hans Goedicke, 87–96. Baltimore: Johns Hopkins Press, 1971.

Engnell, Ivan. "The Ebed Yahweh Songs and the Suffering Messiah in Deutero-Isaiah." *Bulletin of the John Rylands Library* 31 (1948): 54–93.

Everson, A. J. "Isaiah 61:1–6: To Give Them a Garland instead of Ashes." *Interpretation* 32 (1978): 69–73.

Fensham, F. C. "Common Trends in Curses of the Near Eastern Treaties and Kudurru Inscriptions Compared with Maledictions of Amos and Isaiah." *Zeitschrift für die alttestamentliche Wissenschaft* 75 (1963): 155–75.

Flamming, J. "The New Testament use of Isaiah." *Southwestern Journal of Theology* 11 (1968): 89–103.

Ginsberg, H. L. "Isaiah in the Light of History." *Conservative Judaism* 22 (1967): 1–78.

Gordis, R. "Isaiah—Prophet, Thinker, World Statesman." In *Poets, Prophets, and Sages*. 255–67. Bloomington: Indiana University Press, 1971.

Goshen-Gottstein, M. H. "Hebrew Syntax and the History of the Bible Text. A Pesher in the MT of Isaiah." *Textus* 8 (1973): 100–106.

Gunn, D. M. "Deutero-Isaiah and the Flood." *Journal of Biblical Literature* 94 (1975): 495–508.

Habel, N. C. "He who Stretches out the Heavens." *Catholic Biblical Quarterly* 34 (1972): 417–30.

Hammershaimb, E. "The Immanuel Sign." *Studia Theologica* 3 (1949): 124–42.

Harner, P. B. "Creation and Faith in Deutero-Isaiah." *Vetus Testamentum* 17 (1967): 298–306.

———. "The Salvation Oracle in Second Isaiah." *Journal of Biblical Literature* 88 (1969): 418–34.

Hasel, G. F. "Linguistic Considerations Regarding the Translation of Isaiah's *Shear-Jashub*: A Reassessment." *Andrews University Seminary Studies* 9 (1971): 36–46.

Hayes, J. H. "Tradition of Zion's Inviolability." *Journal of Biblical Literature* 82 (1963): 419–26.

Hillers, D. R. "Convention in Hebrew Literature; The Reaction to Bad News." *Zeitschrift für die alttestamentliche Wissenschaft* 77 (1965): 86–90.

———. "Berît 'am: 'Emancipation of the People.'" *Journal of Biblical Literature* 97 (1978): 175–82.

Holladay, W. L. "Isaiah 3:10–11: An Archaic Wisdom Passage." *Vetus Testamentum* 18 (1968): 481–87.

Hollenberg, D. E. "Nationalism and the Nations in Isaiah 40–55." *Vetus Testamentum* 19 (1969): 23–36.

Holmgren, F. "Chiastic Structure in Isaiah 51:1–11." *Vetus Testamentum* 19 (1969): 196–201.

Huey, F. B. "Great Themes in Isaiah 40–66." *Southwestern Journal of Theology* 11 (1968): 45–58.

BIBLIOGRAPHY

Huffmon, H. B. "The Covenant Lawsuit and the Prophets." *Journal of Biblical Literature* 78 (1958): 285–95.

Hurst, C. J. "Guidelines for Interpreting Old Testament Prophecy Applied to Isaiah 40–66." *Southwestern Journal of Theology* 11 (1968): 29–44.

Jackson, R. S. "Prophetic Vision; the Nature of the Utterance in Isaiah 40–55." *Interpretation* 16 (1962): 65–75.

Jenkins, A. K. "Hezekiah's Fourteenth Year. A New Interpretation of 2 Kings 18:13–19:37." *Vetus Testamentum* 26 (1976): 284–98.

Jones, H. G. "Abraham and Cyrus: Type and Antitype." *Vetus Testamentum* 22 (1972): 305–19.

Kapelrud, Arvid S. "The Identity of the Suffering Servant." In *Near Eastern Studies in Honor of William Foxwell Albright,* ed. Hans Goedicke, 307–14. Baltimore: Johns Hopkins Press, 1971.

_____. "The Main Concern of Second Isaiah." *Vetus Testamentum* 32 (1982): 50–58.

Klein, Ralph W. "Going Home—A Theology of Second Isaiah." *Currents in Theology and Mission* 5 (1978): 198–210.

Knierim, R. "The Vocation of Isaiah." *Vetus Testamentum* 18 (1968): 47–68.

Kruse, Colin G. "The Servant Songs: Interpretive Trends since C. R. North." *Studia Biblica et Theologica* 8 (1978): 3–27.

Leiser, B. M. "Trisagion of Isaiah's Vision." *New Testament Studies* 6 (1960): 261–63.

Lindsey, F. Duane. "The Call of the Servant in Isaiah 42:1–9." *Bibliotheca Sacra* 139 (1982): 12–31.

_____. "The Commission of the Servant in Isaiah 49:1–13." *Bibliotheca Sacra* 139 (1982): 129–45.

_____. "The Commitment of the Servant in Isaiah 50:4–11." *Bibliotheca Sacra* 139 (1982): 216–29.

_____. "The Career of the Servant in Isaiah 52:13–53:12." *Bibliotheca Sacra* 139 (1982): 312–29; 140 (1983): 21–39.

Ludwig, T. M. "The Tradition of the Establishing of the Earth in Deutero-Isaiah." *Journal of Biblical Literature* 92 (1973): 345–57.

MacRae, Allan A. "Servant of the Lord in Isaiah." *Bibliotheca Sacra* 121 (1964): 125–32, 218–27.

McGuire, E. M. "Yahweh and Leviathan: an Exegesis of Isaiah 27:1." *Restoration Quarterly* 13 (1970): 165–79.

McKane, William. "The Interpretation of Isaiah 7:14–25." *Vetus Testamentum* 17 (1967): 208–19.

Melugin, R.F. "Deutero-Isaiah and Form Criticism." *Vetus Testamentum* 21 (1971): 326–39.

———. "The Conventional and the Creative in Isaiah's Judgement Oracles." *Catholic Biblical Quarterly* 36 (1974): 301–11.

Milgrom, J. "Did Isaiah Prophesy during the Reign of Uzziah." *Vetus Testamentum* 14 (1964): 164–82.

Morgenstern, J. "Suffering Servant—A New Solution." *Vetus Testamentum* 11 (1961): 292–320, 406–31.

———. "Two Additional Notes to 'The Suffering Servant—A New Solution.' " *Vetus Testamentum* 13 (1963): 321–32.

Murray, John. "Appendix C—Isaiah 53:11." In *The Epistle to the Romans: The English Text with Introduction, Exposition and Notes.* 1:375–83. Grand Rapids: Eerdmans, 1959, 1965.

Orlinsky, Harry M. "The Treatment of Anthropomorphisms and Anthropopathisms in the Septuagint of Isaiah." *Hebrew Union College Annual* 27 (1956): 193–200.

———. "A Light to the Nations (Isaiah 49:6). A Problem in Biblical Theology." 75th Anniversary volume of the *Jewish Quarterly Review* (1967): 409–28.

———. "The So-Called 'Servant of the Lord' and " 'Suffering Servant' in Second Isaiah." In *Studies on the Second Part of the Book of Isaiah. Supplements to Vetus Testamentum XIV.* 3–133. Leiden: E. J. Brill, 1967.

Otzen, B. "Tradition and Structures of Isaiah 24–27." *Vetus Testamentum* 24 (1974): 196–206.

Pannenberg, Wolfhart. "Redemptive Event and History." Trans. Shirley Guthrie. In *Essays on Old Testament Hermeneutics,* ed. Claus Westermann, 314–35. Atlanta: John Knox, 1979.

Payne, D. F. "Characteristic Word-Play in 'Second Isaiah:' A Reappraisal." *Journal of Semitic Studies* 12 (1967): 267–69.

———. "The Servant of the Lord: Language and Interpretation." *Evangelical Quarterly* 43 (1971): 131–43.

Payne, J. Barton. "The Unity of Isaiah: Evidence from Chapters 36–39." *Bulletin of the Evangelical Theological Society* 6 (1963): 50–56.

317

_____. "Eighth Century Israelitish Background of Isaiah 40–66." *Westminster Theological Journal* 29 (1967): 179–90; 30 (1968): 50–58, 185–203.

_____. "The Effect of Sennacherib's Anticipated Destruction in Isaianic Prophecy." *Westminster Theological Journal* 34 (1971): 22–38.

Pope, Marvin. "Isaiah 34 in Relation to Isaiah 35, 40–66." *Journal of Biblical Literature* 71 (1952): 235–43.

Rad, Gerhard von. "The Origin of the Concept of the Day of Yahweh." *Journal of Semitic Studies* 4 (1959): 97–108.

_____. "Typological Interpretation of the Old Testament," trans. by John Bright. In *Essays on Old Testament Hermeneutics,* ed. Claus Westermann, 17–39. Atlanta: John Knox, 1979.

Radday, Y. T. "Two Computerized Statistical-Linguistical Texts Concerning the Unity of Isaiah." *Journal of Biblical Literature* 89 (1970): 319–24.

Rice, G. "Interpretation of Isaiah 7:15–17." *Journal of Biblical Literature* 96 (1977): 363–69.

_____. "Neglected Interpretation of the Immanuel Prophecy." *Zeitschrift für die alttestamentliche Wissenschaft* 90 (1978): 220–27.

Sanders, J. A. "Isaiah 55:1–9." *Interpretation* 32 (1978): 291–95.

Sasson, J. M. "Isaiah 66:3–4a." *Vetus Testamentum* 26 (1976): 199–207.

Scullion, J. J. "An Approach to the Understanding of Isaiah 7:10–17." *Journal of Biblical Literature* 87 (1968): 288–300.

Skehan, P. W. "Some Textual Problems in Isaiah." *Catholic Biblical Quarterly* 22 (1960): 47–55.

Smith, Mark S. "Berît 'am / Berît ' ôlām: A New Proposal for the Crux of Isa. 42:6." *Journal of Biblical Literature* 100 (1981): 241–43.

Snaith, Norman. "A Study of the Teaching of the Second Isaiah and its Consequences." *Supplements to Vetus Testamentum XIV* (1967; see under H. M. Orlinsky): 137–264.

Songer, H. S. "Isaiah and the New Testament." *Review and Expositor* 65 (1968): 459–70.

Stamm, Johann J. "La Prophétie d'Émmanuel." *Revue de Theologie et de Philosophie* 32 (1944): 97–123.

_____. "Neuere Arbeiten zum Immanuel-Problem." *Zeitschrift für die alttestamentliche Wissenschaft* 68 (1956): 46–53.

Stampfer, J. "On Translating Biblical Poetry: Isaiah 1–24." *Judaism* 14 (1965): 501–10.

Stuhlmueller, C. "First and Last and Yahweh—Creator in Deutero-Isaiah." *Catholic Biblical Quarterly* 29 (1967): 495–511.

Tate, M. E. "King and Messiah in Isaiah of Jerusalem." *Review and Expositor* 65 (1968): 409–21.

Thomas, J. H. "The Authorship of the Book of Isaiah." *Restoration Quarterly* 10 (1967): 46–55.

Treves, Marco. "Isaiah 53." *Vetus Testamentum* 24 (1974): 98–108.

Trudinger, L. P. "To Whom then will You Liken God? A Note on the Interpretation of Isaiah 40:18–20." *Vetus Testamentum* 17 (1967): 220–25.

Uffenheimer, B. "The Consecration of Isaiah in Rabbinic Exegesis." *Script Hieros* 22 (1971): 233–46.

Whitley, C. F. "Textual Notes on Deutero-Isaiah." *Vetus Testamentum* 11 (1961): 457–61.

———. "Language and Exegesis of Isaiah 8:16–23." *Zeitschrift für die alttestamentliche Wissenschaft* 90 (1978): 28–43.

Willis, John T. "Genre of Isaiah 5:1–7." *Journal of Biblical Literature* 96 (1977): 337–62.

———. "The Meaning of Isaiah 7:14 and Its Application in Matthew 1:23." *Restoration Quarterly* 21 (1978): 1–18.

Wolf, Herbert M. "A Solution to the Immanuel Prophecy in Isaiah 7:14–8:22." *Journal of Biblical Literature* 91 (1972): 449–56.

SCRIPTURE INDEX

346